HN DAVIDSON OF PRESTONPANS

JOHN DAVIDSON OF PRESTONPANS

Reformer, Preacher and Poet in the Generation after Knox

BY

R. MOFFAT GILLON,

M.A., Ph.D.Edin.

JAMES CLARKE & CO., LTD.
5 WARDROBE PLACE, LONDON, E.C.4

PRINTED IN GREAT BRITAIN BY HEADLEY BROTHERS
109 KINGSWAY, LONDON, W.C.2 ; AND ASHFORD, KENT

TO
MY FATHER AND MOTHER

CONTENTS

PREFACE

APART from "Lives" of Andrew Melville and Robert Bruce singularly little has been done to revive the memories of leaders of the early Reformed Church in Scotland. John Davidson of Prestonpans is one who deserves to be better known and it is surprising that before now, no effort has been made to give some adequate account of so eminent a man. With the exception of a very brief sketch by Rogers in his *Three Scottish Reformers*, and some scattered references elsewhere, there has been no attempt to give a detailed narrative of his labours and influence. That he has failed to receive due recognition is possibly owing to the outstanding brilliance of one or two of his contemporaries. Although far behind Knox or Melville as an ecclesiastical statesman, and probably inferior to Bruce as a preacher, yet he was no less truly a Reformer than any of them.

The object of this work is to rescue the man from comparative obscurity by communicating full and authentic details of his history, and in doing so it will be possible to show how important a part he played in the great controversies of his day, to describe the contents and consequences of his literary efforts in poetry and prose, and to exhibit his worth and greatness.

To the Rev. Professor Hugh Watt, D.D., New College, Edinburgh, who suggested the subject, I am deeply indebted for kindly interest and generous guidance. My sincere thanks are also due and cordially given to the Rev. Principal John Macleod, D.D., Free Church College, Edinburgh, for many helpful suggestions ; to Dr. H. W. Meikle, National Library of Scotland and Dr. W. R. Cunningham, Glasgow University, for making available to me important manuscripts ; and finally to the Rev. Dr. Hector Macpherson, for his kindness in reading the proofs.

R. MOFFAT GILLON.

September 1936.

CHAPTER I

THE PERIOD IN WHICH DAVIDSON LIVED AND WORKED

THE sixteenth century was a period of expansion. It witnessed a new flowering of the human spirit, and great personalities, destined to influence the whole world, were constantly appearing on the scene. Predominant in its history, however, is the greatest religious upheaval of all times. For it was then that Martin Luther nailed his thesis to the door of Wittenberg Church and became the great guiding spirit of the Reformation movement. Somewhat later Calvin published his *Institutes* and gave to the Reformed Church a basis and a banner. It was a time of revolution, political and religious—the birthday of light and freedom.

The second half of this century is one of the most interesting and epoch-making periods, as it is one of the stormiest, in the history of Europe. Everywhere men were sternly resisting the menace to their liberty both civil and religious, and their sincerity gave life to a movement in which they were prepared to struggle and suffer and, if need be, die for their convictions. The upheaval had different results in different countries according to the circumstances in each. In the Netherlands, for example, the period marked a crisis in the long struggle of the Protestants with their Spanish oppressors. Against the absolute government of Philip II was set the resistance of

William of Orange which resulted in securing the independence of the Dutch people and the triumph of Calvinism in the Church of Holland. Then the struggle of the Huguenots in France ran concurrently with less happy results, as the French monarchy was growing strong, and the Protestant tide rolled back in Germany owing to unhappy divisions between the Lutheran and Reformed churches. Elizabeth was on the throne of England, though with dubious title, and for a time there was much uncertainty as to the religious future of that country. During her reign, however, England became a great Protestant power, standing with Holland against Spain and the Pope, although Tudor despotism was growing. In England the Reformation was thus imposed by a strong Crown, whereas in Scotland it was quite different ; there it was brought about by " ministers of religion, not ministers of state ". By this time Scotland had sprung into significance in the religious life of Europe. Hitherto her contribution to that life had been of little or no account, but now, through the tangle of dynastic successions, most of the countries were looking on at her struggle and were concerned in her success or failure.

This was the period of what is known as the Counter-Reformation. Besides the drive for absolute monarchy, the Reformers had to contend also with the efforts of the Church of Rome to recover the ground lost to the Reformation and her challenge to the Reformed Faith wherever it supplanted mediæval dogmas and practices. Scotland had to face an intensive counter-propaganda. The greatest menace of the movement was Spain, where Philip II had political ambitions to annex Britain to his dominion and consequently bring her under that universal Romanism and absolutism which he so much desired. Many were the plots and intrigues toward that end and, although these constituted a real menace to the Reformed Faith through many years, yet the Reformers eventually triumphed. As a well-known Romanist writer has admitted, " Scottish Catholicism seemed hopelessly destroyed and in effect never rose again."[1]

As time passed the Reformers came to regard their Protestantism less as a revolutionary achievement than as a part of the nature of things. What mattered supremely to them was the sanction of the Spirit. In later years entrance to the ministry may have become more formal, but at this stage faith and a sense of vocation meant everything. The faith had spread until, in the Lowlands at least, it had gripped the minds of most thinking people. The earlier years up to the time of Morton had been years of distracting civil war in which Queen Mary and her foreign advisers had played a prominent part, and yet years, despite all, in which the Reformation had made wonderful progress. The ministers by their sturdy preaching were training their people to think sturdily and independently. The parish schools were growing in numbers and were spreading education and intelligence. The people came to know their rights and in consequence felt their strength. The middle classes were rising in importance. Public opinion had been born and had grown into power. The Church of Scotland, however, instead of being given freedom to

[1] Pollen, *Counter-Reformation*, p. 17.

do the work for which God had called her into being, was constantly on the defensive. She had to fight on two fronts, political and religious, resisting efforts to make her a mere department of the State, and attempts to rob her of the Presbyterian liberty which she had chosen to enjoy, and force upon her the Episcopal system.

This last persisted through almost the whole period, and at the beginning it seemed doubtful what exactly the new Church was to be like. It has sometimes been maintained that at the beginning the Reformed Church was really Episcopal but it is not difficult to see that this is an entirely mistaken view. Doubtless it is due partly to a misunderstanding of the office of superintendent as instituted by the first Reformers, and partly to an erroneous construction put upon a concordat settled at Leith in 1572. We must look at each of these in turn.

The people had gradually thrown off the Papal yoke in the first half of the century and the cause of Rome was lost, when in 1560, the Scottish Parliament adopted almost with unanimity a *Confession* framed on substantially the same lines as the later Westminster one and drawn up by six notable men, and proceeded to abolish the Papal jurisdiction, to forbid the celebration of the Mass and to rescind all the laws formerly made in favour of the Roman Catholic religion and against the Reformation. Much, however, had still to be done for extending and consolidating the work of the Reformed Church. A new ecclesiastical system had to be organized, and to that end a *Book of Discipline* was prepared at the request of the Privy Council by a committee of ministers, Knox being the controlling mind. Row[1] declares that its principles were not taken from the teaching of any Church but from the Word of God alone. While that may be, in the main, admitted, nevertheless it may be inferred that Knox must have brought to it some influences from his intercourse with the greatest English and Continental thinkers of his time. It is also obvious that some sort of guidance had to be sought elsewhere than at home. Within two years of the organization of the first Protestant congregations then, the Reformers had to draw up a constitution for a National Church at the request of the secular government. Their experience being very limited, they simply had to make use of the example of foreign Protestant Churches and their own experiences abroad, although these were not blindly followed. Dr. Janet Macgregor says : " The only originality, observable in the Scottish Church polity, lay in adapting to the peculiar and temporary needs of Scotland the two offices of superintendent and reader."[2] It is with the first of these we are concerned. Possibly the greatest necessity confronting Knox was the establishing of a reformed ministry in place of the old priesthood. His plan was to set up a temporary order of officials. The country was divided into ten or twelve districts and over these were placed superintendents. In the *First Book of Discipline* these are named as one of the four kinds of office-bearers in the Church, the others being ministers, elders and deacons. The duties expected of the superintendents are thus summarized by Cunningham—" to erect kirks, appoint pastors in

[1] *The History of the Kirk of Scotland*, p. 12.
[2] *The Scottish Presbyterian Polity*, p. 62.

places hitherto unprovided, and give occasional benefit of a learned ministry in localities which could not otherwise enjoy that privilege at all. Their labours were minutely chalked out. They must preach at least thrice every week ; they must not remain in the chief town of the diocese, where their own church and residence were, longer than twenty days ; they must not only preach but examine the life, diligence and behaviour of the ministers, the order of the churches and the manners of the people : they must see how the youth were instructed and the poor provided for ; and finally take cognisance of any crimes which called for the correction of the Kirk."[1]

It will be seen from this, that the superintendents were not simply special preachers. Joined to their office as preachers was the duty of government which the other parochial ministers did not have. They had *prima facie* a suspicious resemblance to bishops and undoubtedly there was something in their office which suggested Prelacy. The superintendent discharged many of the functions of a bishop but, despite a strong external resemblance between them, they were as far apart as a priestly and non-priestly church. The idea of consecration to holy orders was not covered by the office. The superintendent was subject both to the trial of the Assembly and censure of his own Synod ; he possessed no exclusive power of ordination ; he himself was ordained by ordinary ministers and was not necessarily a minister at all. That good old baron, Erskine of Dun, for example, was among the first who were appointed. The office arose out of a necessity which Knox greatly felt; the diffusion of

[1] *Church History of Scotland*, Vol. I, p. 282.

the new faith in districts where it was so far unknown, demanded something of the kind ; Scotland required to be evangelized. MacEwen says that such an office was in line with the ideas of Luther and Melanchthon and had been erected in some districts of Germany.[1] It was evidently never intended to be permanent, however, for the *Book of Discipline* describes it as " expedient for this time ", while careful regulations were made to prevent superintendents from claiming or gaining such powers as those of Roman bishops. There might have been a possibility of the office developing into a kind of Episcopacy, for the early Reformers did not hold the divine right of Presbytery advocated later by Melville. But they were strongly opposed to anything that suggested " Papistry " and were always on their guard against it.

Alongside the growing operations of the superintendents was the framework of the old Church from which Scotland had been delivered. The bishops were still enjoying two-thirds of the revenues as decided in 1561 and priests were still in possession of churches and manses where Protestant preachers should have been. While the *Confession* had been accepted without difficulty, it was different with the *Book of Discipline* which raised other issues—the patrimony of the Church particularly. It led to a break with the nobility on the part of the Church. As the dignitaries of the " old " days passed away, the Reformed Church laid claim to the rentals and teinds as their inheritance, much to the annoyance of the nobles who hoped to annex a considerable proportion for themselves. According to the law,

[1] *A History of the Church of Scotland*, Vol. II, p. 166.

episcopal revenues could be drawn only by bishops and rents of abbeys only by abbots. To destroy these orders would have meant the extinction of the Third Estate, and to the lay mind that seemed to disturb the balance of the Constitution and to annihilate the tenure by which much of the kingdom's property was held. The nobles, on the other hand, were not anxious for the erection of bishops because they were desirous of appropriating the revenues of the sees. The Reformation clergy disliked bishops, but, as has been said, " they disliked sacrilegious laymen still more ".[1] The feeling of both parties, as well as Morton's desire to have the matter amicably settled, led to the Convention of Leith which was held on February 1st, 1572, between six members of the Government and six leading churchmen. According to the Concordat then drawn up, archbishops and bishops, abbots and priors, were to be continued as parts of the Spiritual Estate, these last being eligible for seats both in Parliament and Courts of Session. Many were of opinion that several of the titles introduced were too like the form of Rome's corrupt hierarchy, but notwithstanding they were permitted. The Assembly in consenting may be regarded as confirming Episcopacy but the new episcopate had very restricted powers and was to be subject to the Assembly's jurisdiction. It was agreed to with cordiality by some of the clergy, probably because they were assured that the way was open for other changes and that the articles were received only " till farther and more perfect order might be obtained at the hands of the King's Majesty's Regent and the

[1] Mathieson, *Politics and Religion*, Vol. I, p. 288.

nobility". Morton saw the possibility of a union of Scotland and England under James, and its consummation, he believed, would be hastened if the Protestant countries had the same kind of church government. There was nothing in the mongrel scheme for the advancement of living religion or the well-being of the Church. Mere financial or political considerations brought it about and the General Assembly's reluctant consent was merely given " as an interim ". The arrangement was not even calculated to bring in prelates after the old fashion. It was simply a device for getting possession of ecclesiastical endowment. The " bishop " would obtain his see on promise to hand over the greater portion of the revenue to his patron. As is easily understood, only weak or ambitious men were willing to become instruments of so dishonest a policy. Men like Douglas and Montgomery and others who lent themselves to this system of "Tulchan"[1] bishops were a source of weakness to the Church and were held in the greatest derision. They had no ecclesiastical standing as the Assembly refused to recognize them. Yet there was in their acceptance of the office sufficient evidence of the idea of episcopacy to form a battle-centre for a whole century to come.

What was the view of Knox on all that—Knox who was so soon to quit the scene of his labours for ever ? He did not like it, but, as far from declaring against it, he assented to the change of polity, advised the Assembly to accept the bargain for the time being and expressed a hope that the bishoprics would be

[1] Tulchan was a calf's skin stuffed with straw, set up to make the cow give her milk.

filled with qualified persons according to the order
taken at Leith. He evidently desired that the Church
should make the most of the new situation. At this
stage he did not raise any objection on principle to
the office or title of bishop, finding warrant for both in
the New Testament Church. Yet he feared that the
bishops might become creatures of the State. Proud,
prelatical pretensions were obnoxious to him. In
A Brief Exhortation published in 1559, he had objected
to the " yearly coming of bishops to Parliament "
and had derided " the glorious titles of lords and the
devilish pomp of prelates ". In agreeing to the
Concordat of Leith he was, therefore, sacrificing no
principle though he had grave apprehensions about it.
He could not but be influenced by his old friend Beza,
who, in a letter reminded him (probably with the
Leith agreement in view) that " the papal supremacy
had arisen out of episcopacy " and strongly urged him
never to give way to its readmission, however specious
might be the arguments by which such a revolution
was supported. It was not long till the Reformer's
worst fears were realized and the long struggle
between Church and State began. Doubtless the
simony which followed the Leith Convention filled
Knox with disgust. He was opposed to the election of
Douglas, Morton's nominee, to the see of St. Andrews,
finding in it the first attack upon the *Book
of Discipline* of whose polity he was so jealous. The
choice of Douglas, he felt, would be " subservient to
that robbery "—as he usually called it—of the
church's patrimony, which he had uniformly repro-
bated. He preached at St. Andrews on February 10th
1572, but refused Morton's invitation to inaugurate

the new prelate. In open audience of many then present he denounced " anathema to the giver, anathema to the receiver ". It was not that he believed Episcopacy to be without Scriptural sanction, but he was so concerned about the purity of the Scottish Church that he would not concur in anything that might impair it. He declared that " it was for the discharge of his conscience that the Church of Scotland should not be subject to the order of bishops " that he publicly expressed his dissatisfaction with the election of a primate.

It was in the second generation of the Reformed Church when Divine Right was becoming a watchword that the Episcopal polity was swept away and the full pattern of kirk sessions, presbyteries, synods and assemblies was worked out. The Church was determined to take to herself the form of organization which she liked best, which she believed to be suited to her and which, she felt convinced, was founded on the Word of God. That form, it has been said, was a definite challenge to all civil government—a challenge inescapable because the new organization was closer to the whole body of the faithful than the government of the time could even attempt to be. To Andrew Melville belongs the honour of leading the Church at this momentous period, and through his influence it gradually departed from the fatal compromise of the Leith Convention. He believed that the Presbyterian system was the right thing not only for Scotland, but for the whole world. It had, he maintained, a *jus divinum*, because it was the only Church government with, in his judgment, an unmistakable warrant in Holy Scripture ; he could not find in the New Testament anything suggesting the office of a " Lord Bishop ". By his learned arguments almost all his brethren were won to his view ; he threw all his gifts and influence into the Presbyterian scale, and after several conflicts attained to success in 1580, when the Assembly declared the office of bishop unlawful. The following year it adopted the *Second Book of Discipline*, in the preparing of which he had a large share and which drew a well-marked distinction between the civil power and the Church's ecclesiastical jurisdiction received directly from her Lord, as well as affirming the principle of Spiritual Independence and the Church's adhesion to the doctrine of the Headship of Christ. Presbyteries were now fully developed and, with the completion of the hierarchy of her courts, great was the influence which the Church wielded throughout the country.

It was soon very evident that the King had already a strong antipathy to Presbyterianism. That was not to be wondered at, since he was obsessed by the doctrine of the Divine Right of Kings and believed Episcopacy to be essential to the promotion of absolute monarchy. The influence of his favourites also— Lennox and Arran—was all against the Presbyterian system. They hated the Reformed Church with its pure and strict discipline and they gave to the King a prejudice against it which he never lost. He was their ready pupil and was quick to see that a compliant Episcopacy would be more likely to advance his interests than an uncompromising Presbyterianism. It was natural for the crown to support bishops, for by them Church and State would be closely interwoven Church government by bishops whom he himself had chosen would be an immense help to the kind of kingship James believed in. If, on the other hand, the Church were successful in obtaining the liberty it claimed in spiritual matters, it would be a blow to his theory of absolute monarchy. Besides, he was anxious to conciliate his Roman Catholic subjects, and add to the strength of the crown. Above all he must be friendly with all parties in England, to whose throne he hoped one day to succeed. His feelings were deepened by the outspoken deliverances of the preachers and especially by the incident known as the Raid of Ruthven, when he was snatched from the influence of his base favourites by a faction of nobles. Believing that the raid had been inspired by the ministers, from this time he stiffened his resolution to weaken and destroy the Presbyterian system. If, in the years following he was sometimes diverted from his plan, yet he never lost sight of it but returned to it from time to time with increased vigour. He never forgot that his only barrier to autocracy was the Presbyterian Kirk and he was eager for revenge. An opportunity to weaken it soon presented itself to him and he seized it in a parliamentary way. In 1584 the " Black Acts " were passed by the Estates, declaring the King supreme in all causes and over all persons, and placing the chief ecclesiastical authority in the hands of bishops. Freedom of Assemblies, freedom of speech, freedom of spiritual jurisdiction were all destroyed, and Episcopacy stood revealed as the ally and tool of civil and religious despotism. This was a terrible blow to the Reformed Church. Many of the ministers had to leave the country and for the next eight years there was in Scotland a confused medley of Episcopacy and Presbyterianism, which caused some consternation and suffering. The Court party however, could make no impression against the loyalty of ministers and people to Presbyterianism. The Black Acts did nothing more than confirm the nation in its hatred of Episcopacy, and the opposition which had formerly been justified mainly on Scriptural grounds, had now good practical reasons.

It was just at this critical juncture in the fortunes of the Church that Parliament passed the Act of Annexation which attached the temporalities of all benefices to the crown. This first direct act of disendowment connected with the Reformation rendered a dignified episcopate for ever impossible in Scotland and so was less objectionable to Presbyterians than otherwise it would have been. News of invasion tended to bind together the Crown and the Church. With the defeat of the Armada the fortunes of Romanism had failed. James had recently been married and in the pleasure of the people's welcome to his bride, as well as by the wise guidance of Lord Thirlestane, he praised the Church as never before, calling it " the sincerest Kirk in the World ". The Church's prospects were again bright. Two years later, in 1592, an Act was passed which has come to be known as the Magna Charta of the Church, ratifying the liberty of the Church, recognizing a legal jurisdiction in its courts, repealing the Acts of 1584 in so far as they impinged upon ecclesiastical authority in matters of religion, and providing that presentations to benefices by patrons should henceforth be directed not by the bishops but to the Presbyteries within whose bounds the vacancies lay. The anxiety of Thirlestane to clear the Court of suspicion prompted him to the passing of the Act, and James was coming to move away from the Catholics and lean upon the Protestants. Thus, without naming the *Second Book of Discipline*, its principles were accepted and the Church established on a Presbyterian basis. Though it was not quite satisfactory to all parties and had certain obvious defects, yet it was the foundation on which the Church of Scotland built in later days.[1]

The Reformed Church from the beginning has gloried in and jealously guarded her spiritual independence. Kings and Parliaments have from time to time sought its overthrow but without success. It has been expressed as the Headship of Christ and the final jurisdiction of ecclesiastical courts in things sacred as distinct from things civil. Melville stated this clearly and emphatically to King James at Falkland in the well-known passage on " the two Kings and two Kingdoms in Scotland ". Unfortunately, so sound a principle was not easy of application, with, on the one hand, a King who had an inordinate notion of absolute monarchy and, on the other, a Church so fully persuaded in her own position. If the King's claims were high, so also were those of the Reformed ministry. Great and vital as the principle of Spiritual Independence is, possibly in the conflict of those days the Church made too great a claim. At any rate the Presbyterian victory of 1592 was soon enveloped in dark clouds and perhaps both parties were to blame. The Protestant ministers had always dreaded the plots of the Roman Catholics who were eager to win Scotland back to the

[1] Thomas Brown, *Church and State in Scotland*, pp. 81, 85.

old faith. Some of their fears were well founded, as the attempt of the Spanish Armada to conquer England and the incident of the "Spanish Blanks" had proved. If the Spaniards had landed in Scotland they would have found a party of Popish plotters (headed by Huntly and Errol) ready to take part with them. The situation was darkened by the belief that the King was not unconcerned in these nefarious practices. Some have blamed the preachers for utterances which, they say, wrecked the fair promise of 1592, but it may be said in reply that it was highly distasteful to the ministers to find that James was always on the side of toleration where the Popish nobles were concerned. The vain and vacillating character of Scotland's King was well known to those who were plotting in France and Spain and elsewhere for the restoration of the Papal supremacy. His failure to handle effectively a widespread conspiracy and rebellion of well-known Roman Catholic earls in the North brought forth some vehement denunciation from the preachers. The rising was suppressed, it is true, but James would do nothing to enforce the extreme penalty of the law against these plotting Papists. It became known also that he meant to recall certain of them, and that fanned the flame of discontent. The ministers were convinced that dangerous reactionaries should not be welcomed at Holyrood, and the refusal of the King to "extirpate popery and idolatry" goaded them into violent and unmeasured statements. The General Assembly "thundered its denunciations," and one minister, David Black of St. Andrews, was prosecuted before the Privy Council for a somewhat furious utterance. He declined the jurisdiction of the Council and so raised the whole question of jurisdiction between Crown and Kirk. The royal reply was the dissolution of the Commission of Assembly then sitting, a command to the leading ministers to leave the city, and the prohibition of all future gatherings of clergy by Presbyterial authority. The outcome of the agitation was a foolish " riot " at Edinburgh in 1596 on the rumour of a Popish plot. That alarmed the King, caused him to remove the Court for a time to Linlithgow and confirmed him in his hatred of Presbytery. He saw in it limits to his absolute rule and was determined to reintroduce an Episcopacy which would suit his purposes. His view was expressed at a later time when he said, " To have matters ruled as they have been in your General Assemblies, I will never agree ; for the bishops must rule the ministers and the King both, in things indifferent and not repugnant to the Word of God." The English succession, too, was always in his mind and he would leave no stone unturned to secure that end. With Queen Elizabeth's advancing years he saw it was wise to promote friendship with the English clergy, and that could be done best by introducing to Scotland something in the nature of Episcopacy even if it were but superimposed on the existing Presbyterianism.

It will be our business to relate how James gradually followed the advantage afforded by the " riot ", with what kingcraft he went about this new effort to advance his polity, and with what success he managed to browbeat the Church. He was careful not to push matters too hastily or to extremes, and ere he had

succeeded to the throne of England, victory seemed to
be within his grasp. Yet the leaders of the Church
delayed and limited a triumph which in later days was
to be turned into defeat.

One cannot but admire the devotion and courage
of the ministers of the early Scottish Reformed Church.
They played a valiant part in the struggle between a
people of intense conviction wishing to realize itself,
eager to be free to follow the dictates of conscience,
and a King with a party greedy of wealth and power,
whose only consideration was the promotion of their
own interests. They have been blamed for meddling
too much with political matters and failing to keep to
their own religious province. We find an effective
answer to that in the following words of a noble Duke :
" There were no affairs of politics at that time which
were not pre-eminently affairs of religion. If the
Assemblies and pulpits of Presbytery had been silent
on the factions of the time, they would have been
silent on the dearest interests of the Church. On their
vigilance, activity, and resolution depended the
religious and civil liberties of the people, exposed as
they were to the combined danger of Romish intrigue,
of senile Parliaments, and of an ambitious, deceitful
King."[1]

Though their statements were sometimes rash and
intemperate, yet the Reformers rendered a great
service to their fellow-men. They taught them to use
that democratic freedom which claims the right to
criticize the conduct even of a ruler. The courts of
the Church, set up in this period, afford us the earliest
example of constitutional opposition to the measures

[1] Duke of Argyll, *Presbytery Examined*, p. 94.

of arbitrary power. The men who resisted the policy of a self-seeking and foolish monarch, broke for ever that power in Scotland and won for the nation its birthright of glorious freedom. Among these John Davidson (1549 ?-1604) occupies an honoured place. At the time of the Reformation he was but a lad of ten and doubtless was familiar with the story of what led up to the overthrow of the Roman hierarchy. Well known to him would be the contributions of Patrick Hamilton, herald of Lutheran doctrine, and George Wishart—both martyred for their faith. We know that he was mightily impressed by the advent of Knox, whose praises he was afterwards to sing. He felt that, in the hour of Scotland's need, the strong man had providentially arrived. The interest of Davidson's life, however, is that it coincides with the momentous changes of the early Reformed Church and the beginning of the contest between the Crown and the Kirk, which was to last for over a hundred years. From about 1574 when he first came into public notice, to the end of his days in 1604, he played many parts in the affairs of the Church, but particularly in opposition to Prelacy and in defence of the liberties of Presbyterianism.

CHAPTER II

EARLY LIFE AND LITERARY EFFORTS

To Fife belongs the honour of counting among her illustrious sons John Davidson, Reformer, Preacher and Poet.[1] He was born at Dunfermline about the year 1549. Nothing is known of his parents except that they were in comfortable circumstances, owning houses and lands which came in due course into their son's possession, and were used by him in the interests of the Church.[2] There is nothing recorded of his boyhood, but it is supposed, with considerable reason, that he was early attracted to the ministry of the godly David Ferguson who held the charge of Dunfermline and was one of the earliest ministers of the Reformed Church. Through his influence young Davidson gave himself to religion and to serious study. As Wodrow says, he was singularly zealous, devoted to the perusal of the Scriptures and divinity, and a serious seeker of God from his youth.[3] He could never forget his old minister and those early days, and in later years when addressing the Synod of Fife he made this interesting reference to them—" I have seene from the beginning, when the Frenchemen keeped the Abbey, before the Road of St. Johnstoun and Cowper Moore, and saw the forces of the Papists ryding to

[1] He must not be confounded with John Davidson, Principal of the Glasgow College (1557-72)—the error of Charteris in his account of Scottish Divines and Wodrow in his MS. Life. There was a third John Davidson alive at the same time ; he was minister of Hamilton (Melville's *Diary*, p. 59).

[2] M'Crie's *Life of Melville*, Vol. II, p. 510.

[3] Wodrow MS., p. 1.

both against the Congregatioun ; but our brother and father there, David Fergusone, was an actor, when I was but a spectator."[1]   When he entered the University of St. Andrews in 1566[2] it was natural that he should attach himself to the College of St. Leonard's which, in contrast to St. Salvator's, had early accepted the principles of the reformed faith.[3]   " The well of St. Leonard's was the fountainhead of the Scottish Reformation " and those who sat at the feet of the Reformers receiving the new teaching, were said to have " drunk of St. Leonard's Well ".   From 1566 to 1570 this college had for its principal George Buchanan whose fame brought to it a large increase in numbers, at the expense of the rival colleges, although at the most those could not compare with the crowds then attending continental universities.

It is greatly to be regretted that we have no account of Davidson's undergraduate years, no note on the teaching of his distinguished principal, no hint even of any friendship he formed.   James Melville entered St. Leonard's in 1569[4] and probably there began then an association and intimacy which were to last through life.   Melville always refers to him in warm and generous terms.   In the University records the name of John Davidson occurs amongst the Bachelors

[1] Calderwood, Vol. V, p. 435.

[2] *Early Records of the University of St. Andrews, 1413-1579.*   The date of matriculation in these Records (published from MSS. in 1926) is 1566 and this is more probable than the traditional date 1567 appearing in earlier works. " The 1566 corresponds with 1565 Old Style. Apparently students were sometimes enrolled at any period during the session at which they happened to present themselves, but the position of Davidson's name on the list makes it seem likely that he came at the beginning of the session " (Note to writer from the Librarian, St. Andrews University).

[3] M'Crie's *Life of Melville*, Vol. II, p. 343.   *Life of Knox*, p. 19 and p. 331.

[4] *Early Records of University of St. Andrews.*   Melville's *Diary*, p. 24, where he curiously gives the wrong date.

of 1569 and amongst the Masters of Arts in 1570.[1] He seems to have been appointed a Regent or master of his college on the completion of his curriculum,[2] continuing to study privately in theology and philosophy.

Perhaps the greatest event in Davidson's life at St. Leonard's and one which mightily influenced his career, was the coming of John Knox to St. Andrews in 1571. Knox's last year of residence there coincided with a part of Davidson's period as a teacher. From July 1571 to August 1572 the venerable Reformer preached every Sunday and taught the prophecies of Daniel, " always applying his text according to the time and state of the people ".[3] James Melville vividly describes the man—" that maist notable profet and apostle of our nation ", to whom he and Davidson and Robert Bruce who was still a student, would be inevitably drawn. " He ludgit down in the Abbay besyde our Collage,"[4] we are told ; that was the Novum Hospitium, built for the reception of Mary of Guise, Queen of James V.[5] It was very near to St. Leonard's as the following striking passage from Melville shows : " Our regents Mr. Nicol Dalgleise, Mr. Wilyeam Colace and Mr. Johne Davidsone, went in ordinarilie to his grace (or devotional exercises) after denner and soupper. . . . Mr. Knox wald sum tymes com in and repose him in our Collage yeard and call us schollars unto him and bless us, and

---

[1] *Records of University of St. Andrews* (footnote : 1569 in MS.), i.e. Old Style, it being clear from an entry just above that the date is in February. (Note from Librarian, St. Andrews University.)

[2] It was certainly as early as 1572. *Votiva Tabella, St. Andrews*, p. 251.

[3] Richard Bannatyne, quoted in Laing's *Knox*, Vol. VI, p. 624.

[4] Melville's *Diary*, p. 26.

[5] Mary of Guise spent her honeymoon there in the summer of 1538— quoted by Mitchell, *The Scottish Reformation*, p. 192.

exhort us to knaw God and his wark in our contrey and stand be the guid cause, to use our tyme weill, and lern the guid instructiones, and follow the guid exemple of our maisters." We can well believe that Davidson would readily take to heart the aged Reformer's advice, and that he would be as eager and interested a hearer as Melville himself when Knox discoursed from the pulpit with that tremendous effect which the diarist thus describes : " I haid my pen and my little book, and tuk away sic things as I could comprehend. In the opening upe of his text he was moderat the space of an halff houre ; bot when he enterit to application, he maid me sa to grew and tremble, that I could nocht hald a pen to wryt."[1]

The General Assembly of March 6th, 1572, was held at St. Andrews, partly at least for the convenience of Knox. It was the last at which he was able to be present and probably the first attended by Davidson and James Melville. The latter records that " thair was motioned the making of bischopes to the quhilk Mr. Knox opponit himselff directlie and zealuslie "[2] —the first rumble of a coming battle, in which Davidson was to take a great part. It may be said of him what Dr. A. F. Mitchell remarks concerning Melville, that doubtless in that Assembly there were implanted in the youthful mind the germs of those Presbyterian principles which were retained by him to the last with heroic tenacity.[3]

Knox soon afterwards returned to Edinburgh where he died a few months later. Surely that last

[1] Melville's *Diary*, p. 26.
[2] Ibid., p. 31.
[3] *The Scottish Reformation*, p. 197.

year of his life spent among the students of St. Andrews was the most beautiful and the most fruitful of all. Upon young men like Davidson he had made an indelible impression. His salutary advice, his fervent prayers, his great sermons and his magnetic personality could never be forgotten. We are not surprised at Melville's words, " Our haill collage, maisters and schollars, war sound and zelus for the guid cause."[1] We ourselves can add that thence proceeded several of the men who were to uphold it most resolutely in the evil days that lay ahead.

Several literary efforts were made by Davidson while he was regent at St. Leonard's and it is interesting that his first production had an association with John Knox. For some time after the Reformation play-going was not uncommon and, according to M'Crie[2] the writing of plays seems to have been an exercise among the students at the University. Knox, so far from discouraging it, evidently condescended sometimes to witness performances in which the errors of the Church of Rome were exposed. When he was residing in the Novum Hospitium of the Abbey at St. Andrews he was present at the marriage of a minister named John Colvin[3] to one Janet Russel, where part of the entertainment was a play written by Davidson. On the margin of his *Diary*, James Melville had this note, " This yeir, in the monethe of July, Mr. Jhone Davidsone, an of our Regents, maid a play at the marriage of Mr. Jhone Colvin quhilk I saw playit in

---

[1] Melville's *Diary*, p. 26.
[2] *Life of Knox*, p. 468.
[3] He later abandoned the ministry and became politician and diplomatist. After a somewhat chequered career he entered the Church of Rome.—Lang's *History of Scotland*, Vol. II, p. 236. Melville's *Diary*, p. 65, where he is called " first apostat fra the ministrie . . . to foull Papistrie ".

Mr. Knox presence ; wherein, according to Mr. Knox
doctrin, the Castle of Edinbruche was beseiged, takin,
and the Captan, with an or twa with him, hanged in
effigie."[1] Unfortunately the play has not been
preserved. The Captain who is mentioned in it, was
Kirkcaldy of Grange[2] and the performance was an
illustration of Knox's prophecy that his erstwhile
friend and later enemy would be hanged—a prophecy
which was soon fulfilled.

With the Reformation there came a decline in
vernacular writing for causes pointed out by Dr. Hay
Fleming.[3] For one thing Latin had become the
language of conversation in the colleges, and students
were encouraged in the cultivation of Latin verse.
Then there was also the increasing intercourse with
England in the latter part of the sixteenth century,
which, with the prospective accession of James the
Sixth to the English throne, brought the Scots nearer
in language to their southern neighbours. Yet many
of the Reformers, though zealous for the revival of the
learned languages, were also anxious to preserve and,
if possible, refine their native tongue. David Ferguson
the Dunfermline minister, whose sermon preached
before the Regent and nobility at Leith and afterwards
published, is considered a good specimen of Scottish
composition,[4] earned for himself some distinction in
that direction. His success was celebrated by John
Davidson in some Latin lines which are prefixed to
the sermon.[5]

[1] Melville's *Diary*, p. 27.
[2] Kirkcaldy held Edinburgh Castle for Queen Mary.
[3] *Critical Reviews relating chiefly to Scotland*, p. 515.
[4] M'Crie's *Life of Knox*, p. 445.
[5] The lines will be found in Appendix A.

Davidson himself was skilled in the use of the vernacular. He started in early manhood to express himself in homely verse and the works we have now to consider, while not ranking as great poetry, yet possess considerable merit. Mr. T. F. Henderson[1] makes special mention of Davidson when dealing with the Protestant verse writers of the later sixteenth century, although he scathingly describes all the poetry of the period as mostly " political or ecclesiastical diatribes " whose style, wit, thought and argument were " without exception, hopelessly mediocre ".

Davidson's first poem appeared in 1573. It is in praise of John Knox and its full title runs thus—" Ane Breif Commendatioun of Uprichtnes, in respect of the surenes of the same, to all that walk in it, amplifyit chiefly be that notabill document of Goddis michtie protectioun, in preserving his maist upricht servand, and fervent Messinger of Christ's Evangell, Johne Knox. Set furth in Inglis meter be M. Johne Davidsone, Regent in S. Leonard's College. Quhairunto is addit in the end ane schort discurs of the Estaitis quha hes caus to deploir the deith of this Excellent servand of God. Psalm XXXVII. Mark the upricht man and behauld the just, for the end of that man is peace. Imprentit at Sanctandrois be Robert Lekprevik. Anno 1573."[2]

This poem is dedicated in words and sentiments of singular beauty to Sir John Wishart of Pittarrow,[3] a well-known Scottish judge who became a member of the Privy Council and held many public offices. He

---

[1] *Scottish Vernacular Literature*, p. 275. Henderson has made a slip in giving Davidson a ministerial connection with Dunfermline.

[2] A copy of Lekprevik's impression, believed to be unique, formerly in the Britwell Library, is now in the Huntingdon Library, U.S.A.—Information from National Library, Scotland.

[3] *Dictionary of National Biography*. Article on John Wishart.

was a loyal friend of the Reformation and he signed
the letter which several noblemen sent to Knox inviting him to return from Geneva to Scotland. The
Reformer, on coming as far as Dieppe, found his
progress stayed owing to news of the waning zeal of
many of his Scottish friends. He addressed to them
letters of exhortation and sent private epistles to
Wishart and Erskine of Dun, on receipt of which,
these two called together the leaders of the reforming
party and urged them to immediate action. Consequently the "godly band" or first covenant was
signed on 3rd December 1557, by which they pledged
themselves to the destruction of the Roman Catholic
Church in Scotland and the maintenance of " the
blessed Word of God and His Congregation ".[1]

Davidson states, in the dedication, his purpose in
composing the poem. Contrasting the insecurity of
all earthly things with the " sure fortress and safeguard
of uprightness ", he has been moved to write by the
miraculous and wonderful preservation of Knox in
the face of all his enemies, " conducted to ane maist
quyet, peaciabill and happy end, to the greit advancement of Goddis glorie, and singulare comfort of his
Kirk, and to the confusioun of Sathan and discofort
of all his wickit instrumetis." That such a deliverance may not be forgotten, he has endeavoured in
this poem to make a memorial so simple that both
learned and unlearned may possess it. He does not
regard himself as qualified for such a task but he has
undertaken it, first, out of the gratitude of his own
heart ; next, that others better able may be induced

[1] *Knox's History*, pp. 134-5. Hay Fleming, *The Story of the Scottish Covenants*, p. 7.

to take up the theme ; and, most of all, that readers may be inspired by the example of so zealous a servant of God as the great Reformer. This small fruit of his labours Davidson offers to his honourable friend Wishart, not that he regards it as a worthy perform- ance but because, first of all, it affords him an oppor- tunity of showing his gratitude for favours received. Besides he knows Sir John to be a man who, from his earliest years, has favoured such uprightness as the poem extols. Moreover, the noble Knight has for long been a friend and lover of Knox, seeing in him the virtues he would himself possess. Davidson con- cludes by expressing the hope that his Honour will stand fast to the end of his life in that uprightness which he has hitherto shown and which ever makes men pleasing to God and sure in this world. And so he commits him to the protection and blessing of the Almighty.

The poem is a rather curious one and is of interest chiefly as an excellent specimen of the Scottish language and versification of the period in which it appeared. It is also of value in delineating the leading features of Knox's character, and the principal events of his life are set forth in it by one personally acquainted with him. Many of the rhymes and expressions seem crude and sometimes even unintelligible, but one cannot fail to be impressed with the fine vein of piety to be found throughout all the verses. To show the style of writ- ing and the author's enthusiasm for his theme, the following lines may be quoted :

> For weill I wait that Scotland never bure,
> In Scottis leid ane man mair Eloquent,
> Into perswading also I am sure,
> Was nane in Europe that was mair potent.

In Greik and Hebrew he was excellent,
And als in Latine toung his propernes,
Was tryit trym quhen scollers wer present.
Bot thir wer nathing till his vprichtnes.
For fra the tyme that God anis did him call
To bring thay joyfull newis vnto this land,
Quilk hes illuminat baith greit and small
He maid na stop bot passit to fra hand,
Idolatrie maist stoutly to ganestand :
And chiefly that great Idoll of the Mes.
Howbeit maist michtie enemies he fand,
Zit schrinkit he na quhit from vprichtnes.

In this poem Davidson reveals his great knowledge of Scripture and history. While the majority of his illustrations of " uprichtness " are, of course, from Knox's life, yet he makes considerable use of incidents from the Bible[1] and also from Quintis Curtius and other classical writers. There is one feature of his Biblical references which is worthy of note before we leave the poem. It has been pointed out by Professor James Moffatt[2] that writers of the later sixteenth century were interested almost exclusively in the Old Testament with its pictures of national life, but Davidson, while for the most part following his contemporaries, here makes the following allusions to the Gospels and the Acts of the Apostles, not common in the literature of the day :—

Thay that walks vprichtly with the Lord,
In greitest troublis wantis not inwart rest,
As the Apostillis doung (persecuted) for Godds word
Reioysit that for Christ sa that were drest (treated)
Peter in prisone sleipit but molest (without disturbance),
Paull in the stocks and Sylas with glaidnes
Did sing ane Psalme at midnicht, sa the best
Sureness (security) that man can hare, is vprichtnes.

---

[1] The majority of the lines have footnotes consisting of Biblical references.
[2] *The Bible in Scots Literature*, p. 102.

" The Brief Commendation " is accompanied by a shorter poem on Knox's death as we have seen from its title—" Ane Schort Discurs of the Estaitis quha hes caus to deploir the deith of this Excellent servand of God." Here the author calls in turn upon " the Kirk of God in Scotland scatterit far abrod ", the General Assembly, the Kirk of Edinburgh, the Lords frequenting St. Giles, the town of St. Andrews, as well as the people of Kyle and Cunningham—" to quhome this darling was maist deir ", to lament the passing of one who has meant so much to them. He adds a message to those who have forsaken the good cause and assures them that Knox ever wished them well, prayed that they might turn from their folly, and was their friend even when thundering against the ship-wreck they were making. A few lines in Latin follow much in the same strain and urging all to stand in the straight path and not be ashamed to live after the manner of this great man.

The next literary venture made by Davidson belongs to the same year as the " Brief Commendation ". This time, however, his theme was a controversial one, which offended the Regent and in consequence brought a great deal of trouble to himself. For a proper appreciation of this poem, it is necessary to look at its historical background.

On the day of Knox's death, James Douglas, Earl of Morton, became Regent. Despite many defects of character, he proved himself in course of time a very able ruler, caring for the public weal and bringing peace to the land in a somewhat stormy period.[1] Friend and foe alike bore witness to his ability and

[1] Mackie, *A Short History of Scotland*, p. 257.

success,[1] and his elevation might have given satisfaction to the Kirk—for he was strongly Protestant—had it not been for other considerations which filled the minds of the ministers with fear and misgiving. The Regent was not favourably disposed to them ; he dreaded their moral censures on his loose way of living, and he had a strong antipathy to what he considered their interference in political affairs. A strong believer in the supremacy of the Crown over the Church, he was determined to keep the preachers within bounds, and his treatment of them was ruthless in the extreme. When they desired his presence and counsel, he had no time to give them[2] and when they became persistent, he suggested that it would be well if some of them were hanged. While decidedly anti-Papal, he was sympathetic to Episcopacy and sought to bring the Scottish Church into conformity with that of England.

Morton's chief sin, however, was avarice—equalled only by his ambition and love of power, and to secure money for himself or the government, he unscrupulously robbed rich and poor alike. The preachers probably suffered most from his rapacity, for it was their very livelihood which he took from them. In 1561 an arrangement had been made whereby the Crown and the Protestant ministers were to share equally in one-third of the ancient Church's property. The ministers, however, had found the agreement far from being honourably observed and many of them were often in sore straits. Morton pretended to find a remedy by collecting the thirds

[1] Hume Brown, *History of Scotland*, Vol. II, p. 160.
[2] Calderwood, Vol. III, p. 385.

himself and he promised that, in future, stipends would be promptly and regularly paid. No sooner was the plan agreed to than it was evident that the position was likely to be worse instead of better. The Regent, declaring that the Church's portion was inadequate to maintain a minister in every parish, obtained an order of the Privy Council for uniting two, three, or four churches under the care of one minister. That was done under the guise of law and fairness, while Morton appropriated the surplus stipends and even the overworked minister of four churches was not always certain of getting his due.[1]

It was not to be wondered at, that such an arrangement should cause resentment among the ministers, for pluralities had always been considered as one of the worse abuses in the Romish Church. What followed may be regarded as but a minor battle in those troubled times, but it had far-reaching effects not only for Davidson but even for Morton himself. In that connection the young reformer made his first appearance in the public affairs of the Kirk, and, as we shall see, not of his own seeking. In a metrical dialogue of considerable length he condemned in somewhat vigorous terms the evil of Morton's new order and the motives by which it evidently was inspired. The title is, " Ane Dialog or Mutuall talking betwix a Clerk and ane Courteour, Concerning foure Parische till ane Minister, Collectit out of thair mouthis, and put into verse by a young man quha did then foregather with theme in his Jornay, as efter followis."

[1] Spottiswood, Vol. II, pp. 195-6.

Davidson evidently had never intended this poem to become public property. He had meant to show it only to one or two friends, or, at most, present it to the next General Assembly. It was printed, however, without his knowledge and its appearance caused a great sensation. Morton was sore displeased and his wrath fell first upon Lekprevik, the printer, whom he at once imprisoned in Edinburgh Castle under the provisions of an act of 1551, " against blasphemous rymes or tragedies ".[1]

Davidson was summoned to a Justice-air[2] at Haddington to answer for his book, was warded in Clerkington and afterwards brought before the Regent and Council at Holyroodhouse.[3] In the hope that he might be persuaded to retract what he had written or that the University or Assembly might condemn it, he was permitted, meanwhile, to return to his work at St. Leonard's. The University, occupied at the time with internal troubles and also rather anxious to please the Court, decided to take no action. Mr. John Rutherford, the Principal of St. Salvator's College, however, wrote a metrical aswer to " The Dialogue ", of which we shall hear in due place.

The next stage of the proceedings finds Davidson again before the Regent and Council, with many of the nobility, at Holyroodhouse. There, in answer to the Justice Clerk, he admitted the authorship of the book and his sole responsibility for it, but he denied the Clerk's assertion that there was anything in it

---

[1] *Acts of Parliaments of Scotland*, Vol. II, p. 489.
[2] A court of itinerant judges who went on circuit.
[3] Calderwood, Vol. III, p. 301. There is a full and minute account of the proceedings against Davidson in Calderwood's MS. History of the Church of Scotland. It has been extracted and appended to Maidment's *Poetical Remains*, 1829.

" against the conclusion of princes ".[1] Morton was
incensed by the boldness of his words and called for
his punishment, but the hour was late and the meeting
adjourned without decision.[2]

On the advice of the Abbot of Dunfermline,
Davidson now decided to wait the verdict of the
Assembly. Therefore, in due course, he laid the
whole matter before his brethren, desiring them to
examine the book and if they found it " dissonant from
the Word of God, condemne it : if consonant to the
truthe, approve it." He urged a speedy decision as
he had pupils, noblemen's sons, waiting for him at
St. Andrews and who were defrauded by his absence.

It seems strange that, after the University of
St. Andrews having declined so recently to consider the
matter, its commissioners should now complain of the
trial being held before the Assembly, whereby they
declared the privilege of the University was prejudged.
A lively passage between their Bishop and Davidson,
however, left them in no doubt as to why he had
sought the judgment of the Kirk. " Mr. John,"
said the Bishop, " yeare in the wrong to the University
that seeks trial of your book here." " I have been,"
said Mr. John, " as well kent to keep the priviledge
of the University as any other support of the same,
and shall be loath to hurt the priviledges thereof as
any of you shall be." " Why, then," asked the
Bishop, " sute ye not before us a trial ? " " But here
I see God worketh well," answered Davidson, " that

---

[1] There is an amusing passage in Calderwood, Vol. III, p. 310. The
Justice-Clerk said, " *Ne sutor ultra crepidam.*" " My Lord," said Davidson,
" what will yee mak *crepidam* to a scholar ? " " Marie, Sir," sayeth the
Justice-Clerk, " yee sall get your owne *crepida.*"
[2] For this and following details, Calderwood, Vol. III, pp. 309-13.

which ye did for my hurt, God hath turned to be a defence for me this day : when I sought your judgement ye denied it, and when we sought the priviledge of replegiation of the University from the evill judgement, ye would not grant it to us. God be praised, that makes you to be trapped in your own devices." The Moderator enjoined silence and the Assembly thereafter ordered that Davidson should produce his book and that Rutherford should also produce the reply he had made to it. The Principal demurred and it was only by the serious threats of the Assembly that he complied with the deliverance. He acknowledged that he had written it in order to be revenged on Davidson, who had, in his poem, made a disrespectful allusion to him.[1] Davidson said that he had named no man in his book, and he drew an admission from Rutherford that never at any time had he written against him. Finally the Principal involved himself in contradiction of his own words by

---

[1] He said that Davidson had called him a *crused goose*, that he had little Latin in his book, and that was false. Mr. Alexander Arbuthnot said "You take that to you which no man speaks against you" (Calderwood's MSS., Vol. II, pp. 432, 439, quoted by M'Crie, *Life of Melville*, Vol. II, p. 389.) The offending passage in Davidson's poem was :—

> Thair is sum Colleges we ken
> Weill foundit to vphold leirnit men,
> To teiche the youth in letters gude,
> And vtheirs also that ar rude ;
> Amang the rest foundit we se
> The teiching of theologie,
> With Rentis sum studentis to sustene
> To that science to give thame dene.
> Lat anis the Counsell send and se
> Gif thir places weill gydit be,
> And not abusit with waist rudis
> That dois nathing bot spendis yai gudis
> That was maid for that haly vse
> And not to feid ane Crusit Guse.

Dr. John Lee says that Rutherford was a man of great learning, but violent temper, whom nobody liked.—*Lectures on the History of the Church of Scotland*, Vol. I, p. 253n.

45

declaring that it was the manner and not the matter of the poem, to which he was opposed. The majority of the Assembly were in agreement with Davidson but they so feared the resentment of Morton, they would " nather damne nor allow, but passed over with silence ". The proceedings gave great offence to some, especially of the more zealous sort and perhaps most of all, to Robert Campbell of Kingzeancleuch, " the most zealous professor of the Kirk of Scotland ", in whose honour, a little later, Davidson wrote another of his poems, which, however, was not published for more than twenty years.[1] Disgusted with the Assembly's trifling the good man said to Davidson, " Brother, looke for no answere heere : God hath taken away the hearts from men, that they darre not justifie the truthe, least they displease the world ; therefore, cast you for the nixt best." So Davidson went home with Campbell at his cordial invitation but not without first seeking earnestly the divine guidance as he was rather averse to flight lest thereby he might discourage any of his brethren. Rather than do that, as he said later, he would choose to suffer a hundred deaths if it were possible. Efforts were made, through Kingzeancleuch, by several leading persons, to persuade the Regent to drop the matter, but Morton was adamant. Campbell, dying shortly afterwards, urged the young reformer to seek safety abroad and assured him that his wife would find him convoy to England where a certain Mr. Gudman would help him to reach La Rochelle. He gave him this farewell message—" Gird up your

[1] " Memorial of the Life and Death of two worthye Christians, etc." See Chapter IX.

loins, and make to your journey, for ye have a battel to fight, and few to take your part but the Lord only who shall be sufficient to you "[1] ; and referring to the recent Assembly, he added, " A packe of traitours " (meaning some ministers) have sold Christ as manifestly as ever Judas did, and that to the Regent."[2]

Davidson, however, lingered and proceedings against him now advanced quickly. The Regent having failed to obtain the execution of his wishes through University and Assembly, summoned Davidson to " underly the law " on June 3rd. He was " put to the horn " on May 3rd and, after visiting St. Andrews and Edinburgh, he passed to Ayr where he learned that, at Lord Boyd's intercession, Morton had continued his date till June 17th. Evidently Boyd was desirous, however, that Davidson should simply comply with the Regent's conditions,[3] but that he declined to do. Seeing that there was no hope of any further concession though noblemen, ministers and sureties had made further solicitation ; on the advice of some of his friends and with consent of his sureties, Davidson fled and they willingly paid the fine.[4]

" The prosecution of Davidson," says Dr. Thomas M'Crie, " does little honour to the administration of Morton. There is nothing in the book which could give ground of offence or alarm to any good government. It is a temperate discussion of a measure

---

[1] Calderwood's MS. History. (Printed in Maidment's Edition of the *Dialogue*, Appendix, p. 24.)

[2] Calderwood, Vol. III, p. 312.

[3] To renounce the positions in the Dialogue against Episcopacy and pluralities. (Woodrow MS.)

[4] Calderwood, Vol. III, p. 313. Wodrow MS., p. 7. Davidson wrote an apology or defence for his not underlying the law. See Appendix B.

which was at least controvertible. The reasons urged in its support are candidly and fairly stated, and they are examined and refuted in a fair and dispassionate manner. The evils which the act of council was calculated to produce are indeed exposed with faithfulness and spirit ; but without any thing disrespectful to authority, or tending in the slightest degree to excite ' sedition and uproar.' "[1]

It is now time to consider the poem itself. To begin with it must not be regarded as a mere rhyme.[2] Professor Masson refers to it as " clever vernacular poetry ",[3] and M'Crie says, " It is superior to most of the fugitive pieces of the time. Without any pretensions to fine poetry, the versification is easy and smooth, and the conversation is carried on in a very natural and spirited manner."[4] As the title indicates, the poem is in the form of a dialogue between a Clerk and a Courtier ; the representative of the Kirk, however, has very much more to say than the representative of the Court, and the latter is somewhat easily overcome by the former. Their words are supposed to be reported by a young man who has become their travelling companion on a journey. The Courtier opens the conversation by venturing the opinion that the Regent's " new order " has given satisfaction to the Church. He says :

> Bot this new ordour that is tane
> Wes nocht maid be the Court allane :
> The Kirkis Commissionars wes thair,
> And did aggrie to les and mair.

[1] *Life of Melville*, Vol. II, pp. 390-1.
[2] Dr. Kirkwood Hewat does less than justice to Davidson in calling him merely a " rhymster ". *Makers of the Scottish Church at the Reformation*, p. 331.
[3] *Register of Privy Council of Scotland*, Vol. III, p. lxxvi.
[4] *Life of Melville*, Vol. II, p. 391.

The Clerk replies to this :

> have thay condescendit,
> I think our speiking can nocht mend it ;
> Bot ane thing I dar tak on me,
> Gif as ye say the mater be
> That they of Kirk thairto assentit
> Thay sal be first that sall repent it.

—a prophecy which was fulfilled, for in 1575 and following years the preachers regretted greatly the concessions which they had made to Morton.

The Clerk brings three arguments against the Regent's " order ", treating them with reason and spirit. These we shall now indicate.

(1) The " order " prescribes burdens which are more than any man can bear. It is impossible for a conscientious minister to take the oversight of four churches when he finds one heavy enough ; he cannot have any satisfactory knowledge of his people and will be unable, either to comfort them in trial or reprove them in evil doing. The Courtier sets up to this a feeble opposition, instancing how St. Paul did not remain permanently at any one Church, but the Clerk in reply shows conclusively that the circumstances in the Apostle's time were quite different from those under discussion now.

(2) The present age stands to be defrauded of the Word of Life. Many people accustomed to hear preaching every Lord's Day are now to enjoy it only once in four weeks. It may be said (as the Courtier points out) that some churches have been without any preaching for years, but that is no justification for reducing the spiritual food of others. It is a divine law, that once in seven days at least, the soul must

4

have such nourishment, and those who experience spiritual hunger, long for it.

(3) Posterity, too, will be deprived of the Word in public places, for there can be no lasting ministry where there is no secure living. If the " order " succeeds, the preachers will have no law to prove that they are entitled to any stipends whatsoever. The thirds ought to be theirs without deduction—their " awin just patrimony "—but in future they will be dependent upon the goodwill of those in authority for any pensions they may enjoy, and these may be withdrawn if their preaching offends. Further, there will be no likelihood of increasing the number of preachers under this new plan, for posterity will be told that they ought to be content with one minister to four churches, as were their fathers.

Besides these objections, there is stated in the poem a remedy for the weakness of the Church. That will come by finding more preachers—a matter which constitutes no difficulty if decent livings are provided. Let those, therefore, who divert the teinds from their rightful purpose into other channels, restore these to the Kirk and men will be forthcoming for the ministry, not only through the colleges but also from other lands.

Doubtless such plain speaking, especially with regard to the monetary question—which was really the crux of the whole matter—called forth Morton's strong resentment. Not altogether at his door, however, does Davidson set the blame. Toward the close of the Dialogue, he shows his displeasure with the conduct of the majority of the ministers also,[1] and

[1] He calls them court flatterers and blames them for self-seeking.

wishes that Knox had lived a little longer to denounce such shameful doings.

> Forsuith, Schir (said the Courteour)
> I am assurit had ilk Preichour
> Unto the mater bene als frak
> As ye have bene heir sen ye spak
> It had not cum to sic ane heid
> As this day we se it proceid.
> Bot I can se few men amang thame,
> Thocht all the warld suld clene ouirgang thame,
> That hes ane face to speik agane
> Sic as the Kirk of Christ prophane
> Had gude John Knox not yit bene deid,
> It had not cum unto this heid :
> Had thay myntit till sic ane steir,
> He had maid hevin and eirth to heir.

From 1574, when he had to flee for having written the Dialogue, Davidson was an exile from his native land for a period of at least three years. It is difficult to arrive at the exact time of his return, but the General Assembly in October 1577 made a strong plea to Morton on his behalf which probably led to his home-coming soon thereafter.[1] Wodrow and M'Crie, strangely enough, have both made the mistake of placing his return after the death of Morton[2] and of that we have ready proof. James Melville tells us that the fallen Regent before his execution was visited by Durie and Davidson from whom he craved pardon for his harsh treatment of them, " the an for his pretching, the other for his buik against the four Kirks ".[3] The affecting scene is also described by

[1] *Book of the Universal Kirk*, p. 166.

[2] Wodrow MS., p. 8. M'Crie's *Life of Melville*, Vol. II, p. 390. M'Crie has acknowledged the mistake in a note to his *Life of Knox*, p. 469. Professor Masson makes the same mistake, *Register of Privy Council of Scotland*, Vol. III, p. lxxvi.

[3] Melville's *Diary*, p. 117.

Hume of Godscroft, who adds that, at the interview the condemned man took Davidson in his arms and said : " Yee wrote a little booke indeid ; but truelie I meant never evill towards you in my pairt : forgive yee me and I forgive you."[1] Davidson, we are told, was moved to tears.

We are able to tell with some certainty how the young exile spent at least part of the period of his absence from home. From Argyle, where he remained for a time and where he wrote a letter of admonition and warning to the Regent,[2] he passed to England and later to the Continent. He visited Switzerland and studied, probably for one session only, at the University of Basle. His name appears on the list of those who matriculated there in 1575, but as he took no degree, it may be inferred that he did not remain very long.[3] In the " matricula " of the University, however, he is stated to have paid a fee of ten solidi and ten denarii, which is more than the ordinary fee of six solidi and seems to point to a more elevated station than that of the common student.[4]

A minor incident serves to show that wherever he went, Davidson attracted a certain amount of notice and that he was already in touch with the like-minded in England. When, in 1577, the English Merchant Adventurers at Antwerp expressed a desire to have a chaplain, William Davison, Queen Elizabeth's

---

[1] *History of the House of Douglas and Angus*, Vol. II, p. 279.

[2] Contents of this letter, etc., in Appendix C.

[3] University of Basle. *General Information for Foreign Students* (n.d.), pp. 42 ff.

[4] Private letter from Professor G. Biny, Chief Librarian of the University of Basle. Dr. Biny thinks that, since Johannes Davidsonius Scotus is mentioned along with Laurentius Bodleus Anglus (identified with L. Bodley, d. 1615, Canon of Exeter, brother of Sir Thomas Bodley) in *The University of Basle*, p. 44, and the names are together in the " matricula ", these two may have travelled to the Continent together.

ambassador in the Low Countries and a good friend
of the Reformed religion, applied for help to Laurence
Tomson, Walsingham's Puritan secretary. Tomson
in his letter of reply promised what assistance he could
to secure the services of one William Charke, whom
the merchants had already approached, but, failing
him, he was prepared, he said, to recommend a
Scottish preacher of the same name as the ambassador.
Quite evidently this was the exiled John Davidson.[1]
His name, however, is not mentioned in that connection again, although Charke was not appointed.
Probably such an English chaplaincy held no attraction
for so decided a Scot or he had returned to Scotland
ere the matter was finally settled. At any rate we
know that the ardent young reformer was destined for
higher and more important tasks.

[1] This story is told by Dr. Scott Pearson in his *Thomas Cartwright*, p. 171.
He cites as authorities Cal. S.P. For. 1577-8, No. 394, and S.P. Eliz. Holl.
and Fland. IV, No. 38.

CHAPTER III

DAVIDSON AT LIBERTON (1579-1584)

DAVIDSON, shortly after his return to Scotland, was appointed, in 1579, minister of Liberton, a place of " commanding and noble prospects " near Edinburgh. It is first mentioned in a charter to Holyrood Abbey by King David I in 1143 to 1147, but the precise date of the foundation of its church is not known. Evidently it had its beginnings as a chapel which, previous to 1143, belonged to the Parish of St. Cuthbert, from which it was disjoined in 1240 and constituted into a rectory under the Abbey of Holyrood.[1] Davidson seems to have been the third in a distinguished succession of post-Reformation ministers which included Andrew Cant, the " Apostle of the Covenant ", and the famous Principal Adamson.

Beyond the date, we have no information concerning Davidson's admission to the charge of Liberton, but early in his ministry there he was called to take a prominent part in the affairs of the Church of Scotland. An early mention of him in the Assembly records is under the year 1581, when he was appointed one of the commissioners to examine into accusations made against certain ministers said to be leading scandalous lives.[2] The following year he was presented to King James, who had now assumed the reins of government, and so we have the first of many interviews which the

[1] Good, *Liberton in Ancient and Modern Times*, p. 1.
[2] Calderwood, Vol. III, p. 524.

minister was to have with the monarch. What led
to this meeting has been recorded by Wodrow.[1] The
King was still largely at the mercy of whatever party
for the time being prevailed. Lennox and Arran[2] had
now been reconciled after a period of enmity and their
joint influence on James was bad both for him and the
cause of the Reformation. The country was in a very
unsettled state with the Guises and the Papists busy
for their own ends even at court, and with a design
on foot to get the young king to resign the crown to
his mother and have it back from her with her consent
and blessing. Had such a scheme matured, it would
have meant the nullifying of the parliamentary
ratification of the Reformation and the wiping out of
all that the Reformers had contended for and won.
A conversation between certain ministers, of whom
Davidson was one, and the Earl of Argyle and Lord
Ruthven, regarding the dangers of the time and the
folly of leaving the King at Dalkeith with no company
save a stranger suspect of Popery, evidently spurred
Mr. John to action. Perplexed over the awful national
confusion, he obtained access to his Majesty and
delivered his soul on the matter. In a speech singular
for its choice of language as well as its perfect frankness,
he entreated the monarch to deal decisively with the
troublers of the nation. There were three jewels, he
said, precious to all who feared God in the realm :
true religion, the common weal and the King's person
and estate. The first two were bound up in the third.
He warned his Majesty against two sorts of men :
first those who feared him now because, in his minority,
they had committed such offences as made it impossible

[1] Wodrow MS., pp. 9-10.   [2] Captain James Stewart, brother-in-law of Knox.

for them to " underly the law " ; and also those who
were " the conjured enemeis to religioun both at home
and a-field ". He concluded by offering to name
certain godly and loving subjects who would show his
Grace whom they thought to be of those two ranks,
that, knowing them, he might discharge them from
his company.[1] James had nothing to say in reply.
One of his ministers, John Duncanson, who was
present said " his counsell, Sir, is verie good."
" Indeed," answered the King, " his counsell is verie
good " ; and with that he started away, according to
his manner.[2]

In this same year there arose the most notable
controversy in which Davidson was concerned during
his Liberton ministry. Since the Convention of Leith
in 1572 there had existed in Scotland a rather weak
and very unpopular form of Episcopacy which the
court upheld, while the Church, established by law,
remained presbyterian. As has been already
indicated, Andrew Melville ever since his return from
the Continent in 1574 had used all his influence and
eloquence to overthrow the new hierarchy, and the
Assembly, after setting many restrictions upon the
epicopsal office, abolished it—as far as it could set
aside the statute law—in 1580.[3] The *Second Book of
Discipline* also expressed disapproval of the " fashion
of these new bishops ".

While matters thus stood, widespread indignation
was caused by a most glaring " Tulchan " appointment.

[1] He purposed to have named the Lairds of Dun, Lundie and Braid,
Mr. Robert Pont and Mr. James Lawson, if the King had acquiesced in his
counsel. Calderwood, Vol. VIII, p. 214.

[2] Calderwood, Vol. III, p. 595, Vol. VIII, p. 214.

[3] *Book of the Universal Kirk*, p. 194.

After the death of James Boyd, titular archbishop of Glasgow in 1581, the Earl of Lennox had obtained disposal of the see and from it he was resolved to enrich himself. He had considerable difficulty in finding a minister who would accept the office on his conditions, but at length Mr. Robert Montgomery of Stirling agreed to do so. It soon transpired that Montgomery was to hand over the revenues to the Duke on the promise of an annual pension equal to one-fourth of the whole. Spottiswood describes the arrangement as a " vile bargain "[1] and so it was both in respect of its simony and because it set Church and government in sharp opposition.

In October 1581, the matter was brought before the Assembly, which censured Montgomery for accepting the appointment and interdicted him from undertaking it. The King and Council took up his defence and James intimated to the Assembly that, while he had no objection to their proceeding against Montgomery for faults of life or doctrine, he could not permit them to prosecute him on account of the bishopric. Thereupon Melville submitted fifteen articles against the obnoxious bishop, some of them of a most singular nature and none of them having any connection with his chief offence.[2] Though proof was ordered it does not seem to have been led and the charges were referred to the Presbytery of Stirling whose decision was to be reported to the Synod of Lothian who were empowered to pronounce sentence if so justified. Meanwhile Montgomery was commanded to remain at Stirling, and not to aspire to the

[1] *History of the Church of Scotland*, Vol. II, p. 282.
[2] *Book of the Universal Kirk*, pp. 225-6. Calderwood, Vol. III, pp. 579-80. Spottiswood, Vol. II, pp. 282-3.

Bishopric of Glasgow under the pain of the highest censures of the Kirk.[1] This order he soon disobeyed, for, in the month of March following, he entered the Church of Glasgow with a band of the royal guard and ordered the officiating minister to come down from the pulpit. The minister, however, held his ground and it was only by the prompt intervention of the magistrates that a tumult was prevented.[2] Nobody seemed to want the Duke's nominee ; the ministers composing the chapter would not elect him and the students of the University were summoned before the Council for causing riots in opposition to him.[3]

The Presbytery of Stirling, whose jurisdiction he declined, now suspended Montgomery from the exercise of his pastoral functions, but he disregarded the sentence. The ministers, feeling that the existence of the Presbyterian polity was implicated in the contest, resolved on more decisive steps. The Synod of Lothian summoned the defaulter to hear the sentence pronounced against him, but was stayed from further procedure by the interposition of the King, who summoned the members before the Privy Council. They appeared and protested, as they had previously arranged, through Robert Pont, that they were ready to yield all lawful obedience to his Majesty, but declined the jurisdiction of his Council[4] in a matter so purely ecclesiastical. They were quite willing, however, that his Majesty and any of the Council he pleased, should hear the whole affair *extra judicium*.[5]

[1] *Book of the Universal Kirk*, p. 234. Calderwood, Vol. III, p. 581.
[2] Calderwood, Vol. III, p. 595.
[3] *Register of Privy Council of Scotland*, Vol. III, p. 490. The council decided that the bishopric had devolved into the hands of the King and could now be disposed of as he only pleased.—*Register P.C.*, Vol. III, p. 474.
[4] Lee, *History of Church of Scotland*, Vol. II, p. 66.
[5] Calderwood, Vol. III, p. 597.

The ministers fearing that their appearance before the Council might be taken as meaning submission to its judgment sent John Durie and Davidson in the afternoon to request of the clerk an extract of the verbal declinature which Pont had made. This was refused as not having been craved at the time. " Then," said Davidson, " we must declare our parts in time and place, where God hath appointed us to speak, and how we are handled."[1] This utterance was, doubtless, reported to the King, for, on the next day, when Davidson and some others got access to him, he quite readily granted the request as a reasonable one. Not quite so agreeable was he, however, when later in the same interview, the ministers informed him that godly people were grieved at the present procedure and at the declaration of the Council claiming power to " dispone bishopricks, spirituallie and temporallie, *pleno jure*, as they terme it, at their owne pleasure ". To Durie's bold statement that it behoved the Church to proceed to Montgomery's excommunication, his Majesty replied with vigour that he would not suffer them, to be met with that rejoinder so loved of the ministers of those days : " We must obey God rather than men." That declaration and the affectionate warning given him as to the evil company with which he was surrounded, moved him much, at least for the time being.[2]

The Kirk was now resolved to proceed with the severe sentence, unless Montgomery desisted from his purpose, and accordingly he was summoned to the General Assembly to be held at St. Andrews on

[1] Calderwood, Vol. III, p. 597.
[2] Wodrow MS., p. 12. Calderwood, Vol. III, p. 597.

April 24th. He appeared, protested that the proceedings were not legal, declined their jurisdiction and appealed to the Privy Council. The King, anxious to save him, sent a letter to the Assembly requesting them not to trouble him concerning the bishopric, and a little later a messenger-at-arms entered the reverend court and discharged the brethren from all further interference with the prelate, under pain of being proclaimed rebels. Unmoved by this threat, however, the Assembly, after sending a respectful letter to his Majesty vindicating the course they were taking, found Montgomery guilty of new and more serious charges and declared him to have incurred the censures of deposition and excommunication. They were about to pronounce sentence, when he appeared, yielded to the Assembly, confessed his faults and promised not only to relinquish the bishopric but to accept no office without the Assembly's permission.[1]

Davidson had laboured hard to bring Montgomery to this seemingly happy act of submission. When the Assembly had been on the point of proceeding to the sentence of excommunication it was he who moved for delay to allow of Galloway, himself and others dealing further with him. In a rather difficult interview Davidson spoke to him very affectingly and pressed him to submit absolutely to the Assembly. He also proposed seeking Divine guidance in prayer, and when the brethren accompanying him desired that he himself should lead them, Davidson did so with such liberty and fervency as to deeply move them all. Montgomery was " so melted down in tears and seeming seriousness " that he resolved there and then

[1] *Book of the Universal Kirk*, St. Andrews Assembly, April 24th, 1582.

to accompany them to the Assembly and make his entire submission. When approaching the place of meeting, however, he changed his mind again and after some further dealing by Davidson, the ministers left him and went in. When the Moderator asked for a report on the matter, Davidson would say no more than that there was some ground of hope. Later that hope was realized and Montgomery came in and, as we saw, made his submission to the great admiration and contentment of all.[1]

Several members of Assembly, notably Andrew Melville and David Ferguson, were displeased with Davidson for his lenity in this matter and complained that he was protecting a man who would only later reveal his unworthiness. Such disapproval on the part of his friends grieved Davidson much, but it disproves the groundless accusation of his harshness to Montgomery. Surely no one had done more than he to bring the man to a sense of his guilt and a confession of it. His conscience was clear on the matter, and before the Assembly he justified himself in these noble words : " I see sundrie of the brethrein offended with that which is done in this mater. Therefore, for my own part, I will protest, that I have done nothing in this case, but in the feare of God, and for the quietness of His Kirk, and salvatioun of yon ' dead ' man, if it be possible. And howsoever men judge of it, I am sure God will jutsifie my part of it at lenth. Ye have heard what I have said of him, now ye have heard your selves. If you see anie signes of repentance, cast him not off. But if your hearts beare you witnesse, that ye see no signes thereof (as

[1] Calderwood, Vol. III, pp. 602-4, Vol. VIII, pp. 215-16.

for my part I see them not), heree will I give my vote, that he be excommunicat within a quarter of an houre."[1]

Montgomery's submission lacked reality. While some ministers, formerly his strong opponents, were so convinced of his sincerity as to cordially embrace him, the majority were not so emotionally impressed. The Assembly, as a safeguard, passed an act to this effect : " The General Assembly ordains the brethren of the Presbytery of Glasgow to try and examine diligently if Mr. Robert Montgomerie any wise meddles with the Bishopric of Glasgow or proceeds further in using thereof, against his promise made openly in public Assembly, and if they find him to meddle therewith in any wise, to discern him to have contravened the Act of Assembly and his promise ; and to report their process and decree thereupon to the Eldership of Edinburgh to whom the Assembly giveth power in that case to nominate a brother to excommunicate the said Mr. Robert out of the Kirk of God and society of the faithful."[2] The precaution was not without justification, for soon after Montgomery violated his promise, doubtless under the influence of Lennox, who with an eye to the temporalities, urged him to insist that the King had granted him the archbishopric *pleno jure*. He taught in the Duke's house at Dalkeith and elsewhere in defiance of his suspension and when Davidson went to confer with him he found him " so drunken that he was chassing his servants with a drawin whinger ".[3] The Presbytery of Glasgow, in

---

[1] Calderwood, Vol. VIII, p. 217. Calderwood says he found this information in a manuscript of Mr. James Carmichaell.

[2] Calderwood, Vol. III, p. 606. *Book of the Universal Kirk*, pp. 245-8.

[3] Ibid., p. 619.

terms of the recent Act of Assembly, cited him to compear and he entered the house where they were meeting, accompanied by the Provost of Glasgow, the magistrates and an armed force, and commanded them to desist in the King's name. On their refusal some violence was shown, especially to the Moderator, John Howieson of Cambuslang, who was pulled from his chair and hustled off to prison. Nothing daunted by such disgraceful intrusion the Presbytery carried out the decree and sent it to the Presbytery of Edinburgh which duly excommunicated Montgomery on June 9th and unanimously appointed John Davidson to pronounce the sentence in his own church at Liberton.[1] This he did on the following Sabbath before a great congregation. It was intimated on Wednesday at Edinburgh, and on the Lord's Day thereafter at Glasgow, and in most kirks of the south, despite the threatening and storming of the Duke and the court.

In justice to Davidson it must be emphasized that he did not undertake such a solemn duty without the express command of his presbytery, nor did he do it with a light heart. Andrew Lang dismisses the event somewhat scornfully, saying that Davidson " did the curse "[2] as if the minister had been pleased to do it. The Editor of Satirical Poems of the Time of the Reformation "[3] states erroneously that he did it " with evident satisfaction ". Spottiswood, who takes every opportunity of setting the good man in an unfavourable light, affirms that he had pronounced the sentence " pretending a warrant from the church " and that

---

[1] Calderwood, Vol. III, p. 621. *Book of the Universal Kirk*, pp. 256-8.
[2] Lang, *History of Scotland*, Vol. II, p. 284.
[3] Dr. James Cranstoun, p. xlvii.

it was " done against all form ".[1] It is difficult to understand how anyone with the registers of the Kirk before him, as presumably the Archbishop had, could make such a statement. It is an evident case of gross misrepresentation and a proof of the writer's insincerity and unfairness. Not only did Davidson act according to ecclesiastical law, but, as we have seen, he had sought hard to avert the taking of such a serious step. With a heavy heart he obeyed his presbytery's instructions. Wodrow[2] tells us that he expressed to the people his great sorrow at having to do such a thing but he could do it, he said, " with as safe a conscience as any minister of the Kirk ", for he had laboured hard to stay the Assembly upon the slightest hope of amendment. He described an incident that took place in the course of the proceedings. Montgomery, on leaving the Assembly on one occasion had expressed to him his sorrow at troubling the Kirk so much and had declared that he would not repeat the anguish of recent days for all the fear in the world. Davidson had made answer : " if you continue in this way, you shall be a dear man to me, if not I shall be a sore witness against you ". The evidence is plain that Montgomery did not long continue in so excellent a state of mind.

Lennox was enraged when he saw that, despite his threatening, Davidson had carried out the excommunication and also preached at Liberton on the Sabbath subsequent, and he publicly exclaimed, " *C'est un petit diable!* "[3] The preacher was kept in fear of his life by the Duke and for ten successive

[1] Spottiswood, Vol. II, p. 289.
[2] Wodrow MS., p. 15.
[3] Calderwood, Vol. III, p. 622.

Sabbaths was accompanied to church by an armed escort of his friends.[1] The next move of Lennox was to secure the royal permission to hold and preside over an assize where all concerned in the excommunication would be brought to trial. Meantime the Privy Council declared the sentence null and void ; insults were heaped upon the ministers who had condemned the late measures of the court ; an interdict was laid on the Glasgow College for its opposition to the new bishop ; a decree of the Council confirmed him in all the emoluments of the Archbishopric, and payment of the episcopal rents to him was demanded under pain of imprisonment at Inverness[2] ; and John Durie for abusing the Duke in his sermons was ordered to leave Edinburgh and cease preaching.[3]

Montgomery's appointment had led to the first clash in a contest between King and Kirk which was to last through many long years, and the burning question was whether the civil power was to be allowed to interfere with ecclesiastical rights and the Church give up her spiritual freedom. Other matters, however, increased the excitement of the time. The conviction that Lennox, despite his avowal of Protestantism, was working on Rome's behalf, as well as rumours and fears of Popish plots, French intrigues, the advent of priest or Jesuit from abroad, led to great plainness of speech in the pulpits. Particularly outspoken was the utterance of Durie, who, in the High Church denounced Montgomery as " an apostate and man-sworn traitor to God and His Church " and spoke very strongly against the King for receiving a

[1] Calderwood, Vol. IV, pp. 399, 402.
[2] *Register of Privy Council of Scotland*, Vol. III, p. 496.
[3] Calderwood, Vol. III, p. 620.

gift of horses from the Duke of Guise, " that cruel murderer of the saints of God ".[1] His discourse caused a great stir, and he was summoned before the Council with the result already stated.

Durie sought guidance from the Assembly as to what he ought to do and it was thought fit that two of their number should be sent to the King both to lament the summoning of the brethren of the Glasgow Presbytery to compear at Perth for opposing the Bishop, and also to desire his Majesty to exculpate Durie from the charge.[2] Davidson thought that this last matter had not been examined as fully as it ought and when the deputation was on the point of leaving, he rose and, in a vigorous speech, dissented from their going. He said that another method of replacing the minister might have been found, instead of seeking it at the hands of one who had no power of displacing him, though his flock had foolishly and wickedly yielded.[3] " What flesh," he asked, " may or sould displace the Great King's ambassader, he keeping the bounds of his commissioun ? and who gave kings especially power to meddle in that matter ? and if they may not displace, should we in this Assembly give power to them to repone, which as little belongs to them ? "[4] Some of the brethren said that they must beware of thinking evil of the King, to which Davidson replied that he did not think evil of the King but of their own childish yielding, and he was sure that wrongs were committed not by his Majesty

[1] Tytler, *History of Scotland*, Vol. VIII, p. 97.
[2] Wodrow MS., p. 15.
[3] Calderwood, Vol. III, p. 623. At this point Wodrow says, Sir James Balfour, a courtier, rose up and stared Davidson in the face, which, however, " did not dash him ".
[4] Wodrow MS., p. 15.

but by the ungodly men about him. The Moderator, Mr. Andrew Melville, desired him to moderate his zeal. Davidson went on to say that he had no objection to the brethren compearing at Perth, but he would have them compear as became them there, meaning that so many of the faithful should accompany them to afford them protection from " cruell murtherers " that there might be no recurrence of what had happened in that town at the beginning of the Reformation.[1] Wodrow fittingly comments thus on Davidson's speech : " If in this Mr. Davidson exceeded, it flowed from his great concern lest the ministry should be gradually debarred from all reproving of vice from the pulpit ; which afterwards in a great measure was brought about."[2]

The Assembly bore the amplest testimony to Durie's upright character and sound doctrine, and he was authorized to preach the Gospel wherever he might be placed. After mature deliberation they advised him only to quit the City when forced, but if forced, to go peaceably.[3] The King had, however, returned an evasive answer to the commissioners and had not relinquished his purpose, so the magistrates were reluctantly compelled to insist upon Durie's departure.[4] The same evening about nine o'clock, in the company of Davidson, two notaries and some other friends, he proceeded along the High Street to the Cross of Edinburgh, where he made his protest and, according

[1] Calderwood, Vol. III, p. 623. Wodrow in his MS. says this is Calderwood's explanation—which he had from his MS. *History.*
[2] Wodrow MS., p. 16.
[3] *Book of the Universal Kirk*, pp. 252, 253. Calderwood, Vol. III, p. 624.
[4] The magistrates were members of Dury's congregation and were divided between allegiance to their minister and allegiance to the King.

to legal form, " took instruments ".[1] Davidson " desired likewise an instrument upon his protestatioun which was this : that as that was the most sorrowfull sight to Edinburgh that ever he saw, in that they had removed their pastor speeking the truthe, for pleasure of fleshe and blood, so the plague and fearefull judgements of God sould light upon the devisers, inventers and procurers, actors, authors, consenters and rejoicers at the banishment of Christ in that man's person, except they speedilie repented."[2]

The expulsion of Durie from the city was keenly resented by his brethren, particularly Andrew Melville and James Lawson as well as Davidson himself. They considered it exceedingly unfair and saw in it danger to the whole question of a minister's freedom in the pulpit. Davidson, preaching on three consecutive days, referred to it at some length and " moved the auditors mervelouslie ". He said that he doubted not but God would dash the devil in his own devices, meaning that he would " supplee John Durie his rowme " and make him an instrument to stir up others wherever he went.[3] The Ministers were specially incensed against the Provost and Magistrates for their part in the affair, and when the former, in an interview, sought to justify them, Davidson turned upon him with passionate words. " What brasen faces," he asked, " are these that ye have, to despise the threatenings of the servants of God, who are sent furth from his throne ? " He ventured to say, that if

---

[1] Calderwood, Vol. III, p. 625. Tytler's *History*, Vol. VIII, p. 102. The taking of instruments, by placing a piece of money in the hands of a notary, was once very common in Scotland. See interesting note in Cunningham, Vol. I, p. 368.
[2] Ibid., p. 625.
[3] Calderwood, Vol. VIII, p. 221.

they did not repent of their treatment of God's servant, the Lord would pull them out of their thrones with shame and confusion.[1]

The evil intentions of Lennox toward the Church were frustrated by the incident known in Scottish history as the Raid of Ruthven. Some of the nobles, exasperated by his conduct as well as by that of Arran, and determined to separate the King from these base favourites, decoyed James to Ruthven Castle, where they kept him a prisoner and compelled him to send the Duke out of the country. Protestantism was, through this event, rescued from a great danger and the Church triumphed over the State. A royal proclamation was soon issued declaring that it had never been his Majesty's intention to restrain the freedom of the pulpit or to curtail the jurisdiction and liberty of the Church courts.[2] The exiled Durie now returned to Edinburgh amid a great procession of people singing the 124th Psalm, which, when Lennox beheld from his window, he tore his beard, cursed John Durie, hastened out of the town and afterwards escaped to France.[3]

It was about this time that James Lawson and Davidson, with some other ministers, appeared, by request, before the Council at Stirling[4] where their advice was sought regarding the preservation of quietness in the country and they were also requested to prepare a list of the wrongs done to the Kirk by Lennox and Arran. Davidson, at the desire of the others, discoursed to the Lords with much fervency

---

[1] Calderwood, Vol. VIII, p. 223.
[2] Calderwood, Vol. III, pp. 649-51.
[3] Ibid., pp. 646-7. Melville's *Diary*, p. 143. Burton, Ch. LVIII.
[4] Calderwood, Vol. VIII, pp. 227-8.

upon the necessity of reforming themselves and their houses. He exhorted them to put a stop to banning, swearing, filthy talk, whoredom and oppression. Above all, he urged them to obey the Word of God, which in the past they had not done, by denuding their hands of the teinds and applying them to the maintenance of the Gospel as soon as peace and tranquillity would allow. If they would do so, God would bless them ; but otherwise He would not, while in another way He would provide for His own cause. Later the ministers indicated several enormities needing reformation in the Church, especially that every congregation should have a minister, which they promised to see to as soon as the times would permit. Further, a " Band " to maintain the King and true religion was appointed to be subscribed by the nobility, gentry and presbyteries, and the ministers were very active in securing signatures, so Wodrow[1] tells us ; especially Mr. Davidson, who prevailed upon many to append their names to it.[2]

For a while the Church breathed freely, but its peace was short-lived. Fresh anxiety arose with the arrival of Fenelon, the French ambassador, on New Year's Day 1583.[3] Bowes, the English ambassador, solicited the aid of Davidson to secure the silence of the preachers on this event till the Frenchman's purpose should be known, venturing the opinion that that gentleman would probably welcome a difference between the King and the ministers at the beginning

[1] Wodrow MS., p. 17.

[2] He and Durie were directed by the Presbytery of Edinburgh and the Synod of Lothian to wait upon the barons of Lothian and Teviotdale to procure their signatures. Calderwood, Vol. III, p. 675.

[3] Calderwood, Vol. III, p. 694.

of his visit.[1] The King himself, fearing the clergy's outspokenness in the pulpit, by a message to the Presbytery of Edinburgh, communicated his desire that they should say nothing with regard to the ambassador and the King of France. The members, marvelling that his Majesty should suspect their discretion, resented such a request and replied that it was their sacred duty to warn their flocks of all approaching dangers to religion, and this was the time of danger, as they gathered, " from the sender, the person sent, the time of his sending and the particular occasion ".[2] Davidson was appointed with one of his brethren to deliver this reply to the King and humbly admonish him to be on his guard with the ambassador[3]—a warning which events proved to have been well warranted.

That the French were ready to make every effort to recover the ground lost through the expulsion of Lennox was made clear when a second French ambassador, Meynville, landed at Leith only three weeks later.[4] His arrival gave such offence to the ministers that the Presbytery of Edinburgh appointed several of their brethren to wait upon James and speak with much plainness upon the evils to be apprehended from the continued residence of men sent by a King who was an idolater and a court which had so actively persecuted the Protestant religion. His Majesty said that ambassadors did not meddle

[1] Calderwood, Vol. III, p. 697.
[2] Wodrow MS., p. 17. Calderwood, Vol. VIII, p. 229.
[3] Ibid.
[4] Calderwood, Vol. III, p. 697. Manningville or Menainville had been concerned in the Massacre of St. Bartholomew's Day, and was one of the chief advisers of the league against Protestants in Picardy.

with religion, and if they did they should be soon answered. It was pointed out to him in reply that such visitors, though they pretended to be concerned only with matters civil and political, yet had the advancement of their religion in view ; and that they sought, though indirectly, the overthrow of the Protestant faith.[1] Davidson was included in this deputation also, but, according to Wodrow, " had no commission to reason ".[2] He could not, however, remain altogether silent. In the course of the conversation one of the ministers remarked that if *they* did not speak, the Chronicles would yet declare the truth. " Chronicles," said the King, " ye write not histories when ye preach." Davidson replied, " Preachers have more authority to declare the truth in preaching than any historian in the world."[3] When the ministers took their leave, he remained for a moment behind, and said privately to the King, " Sir, I thot it my duty to advertise your Grace in your ear and not before the rest, that you swore, and in your fervour took God's name too aft in vaine in your discourse."[4] The King received the reproof quite graciously and, with a little laughter, thanked Mr. Davidson for the prudent manner in which it had been given.

The next conference which the ministers had with the King was one in which Davidson had a large share. His Majesty having now parted with the lords and counsellors concerned in the Ruthven Raid, was

---

[1] Calderwood, Vol. III, p. 698.
[2] Wodrow, MS., p. 19.
[3] Ibid.
[4] Calderwood, Vol. III, p. 698. Wodrow MS., p. 20.

again under undesirable influences.[1] The Presbytery
of Edinburgh sent a strong deputation[2] to meet with
him at Falkland in the month of August.   They
began by warning him against innovations at court
and by beseeching him not to hold his good subjects in
suspicion but to test all reports before giving them
credence.   Complaint was made of the favour he had
shown to Holt[3] the English Jesuit. James did not
take kindly the straight words of the preachers, and
the aged and witty David Ferguson sought to mollify
him by pleasant and facetious conversation. Davidson
spoke at some length and his replies to the King show
a remarkable combination of courtesy and frankness.
He began with a tribute of affection to his Majesty's
person and an acknowledgment of the blessings of
his government.   These, he said, caused the ministers
to be the more careful of his Grace's welfare especially
when obvious dangers were around him and they
who companied with him were not all " our wife's
sons ", as the proverb had it. When the King
answered that he saw no danger and few of the
nobility to be preferred to others for godliness, he was
met with this rejoinder from Davidson : " True it is
and to be lamented that there is so little godlinesse in
anie of them as there is. But yitt, Sir, there is great
difference betuixt them that, with their infirmiteis,

[1] Arran was restored to favour and for the next two years was to dominate
Scotland.—See Hume Brown, Vol. II, p. 193. Law Mathieson, Vol. I,
p. 229.

[2] Pont, D. Lindsay and Davidson. They took David Ferguson with them
and James Lawson appears to have been present also. When they arrived
they were met with unfamiliar faces save for the Earl of Argyle. (Wodrow.)

[3] What exactly the favour was, it is difficult to say. Father Holt did not
succeed in getting an interview with James, as he had hoped. Yet he was
so well received by the nobility that he considered Scotland ripe for Roman
effort.—Elder, *Spanish Influences in Scottish History*, p. 89.

alwise have professed the truthe and defended your authoritie ; and betweene them that never loved the truthe and have fitted the feild to pull the crowne off your head."[1] At this point, Ferguson, fearing that his friend, with his fiery spirit, would go too far, made an interruption, but Davidson, asking liberty to proceed, continued with great boldness to utter the following stern and solemn warning. "It will appeare, if your deeds be agreeable to your words, if yee love not them that hate the Lord, as the prophet said to Jehosaphat : otherwise, we will looke no more to your words but to your deeds and behaviour ; and if they agree not, which God forbid, we must damne sinne in whatsoever person. Nather is that face upon flesh that we may, or will spaire, incace we find rebellioun to our God, whose message we carie. Nather ought your Grace to mak light accompt of our threatenings ; for there was never one yitt in this realme, in cheef authoritie, that ever prospered after the ministers began to threattin them."[2] At these words the King was observed to smile but he made no reply.

Davidson's freedom and boldness with the King is characteristic of the sixteenth century, when access to the royal presence was easy and the utmost plainness of speech was common among all who availed themselves of the privilege. It has been said of the ministers of the Reformed Church that " they saw no special virtue in a royal argument and never dreamt they were bound to yield to it ; they saw no particular apology for a royal sin but thought it their duty to

[1] Calderwood, Vol. III, p. 718.
[2] Ibid.

rebuik it on the spot."[1] A very striking example of this is afforded by one of Davidson's pulpit utterances. By the end of the year 1583 most of those who had been concerned in the Ruthven Raid were prosecuted and forced to fly the country. The King and Court falsely alleged that the ministers approved of this procedure. Davidson felt it to be his duty to undeceive the people and let them know that, on the contrary, the prosecution gave the preachers grave displeasure. Preaching in Edinburgh on December 14th[2] with the evil character of Manasseh[3] for his subject, he bore a very full testimony against what he regarded as evil in the King and the courtiers ; and, deducing all he had to say from the Scripture passage he was expounding, he maintained that the King, unless he repented and departed from his recent evil courses, would close his race. This was, probably, the first time that James had been publicly and directly threatened.[4] Hitherto it had been usual to blame his evil companions for the wrongs of which he was guilty, but Davidson considered that he was now of an age to assume responsibility for himself. The preacher, nevertheless, is said to have spoken in such a way that none, save an enemy, could have regarded his words other than for his Majesty's good. That his motive might be plain and that he might appear perfectly free from personal animus, he declared himself a loving friend and subject to the King, though his office and the Cause demanded him, from the Word, to publicly reprove his public faults. " For honey,"

[1] Cunningham, Vol. I, p. 412.
[2] Calderwood, Vol. III, p. 762.
[3] 2 Chronicles xxxiii.
[4] Wodrow MS., p. 21. Calderwood, Vol. VIII, p. 257.

said he, " is sweete ; and yitt, being layed to a sore, it byteth vehementlie."[1] It was feared that the bold preacher might get into trouble over so outspoken a sermon, and, on the advice of some of his friends, he lay low for a time at Liberton.[2] However, no untoward consequence followed.

The Liberton years were very busy ones for Davidson as he was engaged in many enterprises besides those just narrated. Though doubtless not so prominent in history they are not without importance or interest. The young minister, as we have seen, very quickly attained to a high place in the affairs of the Kirk and right from the beginning his name is absent from few committees of either Presbytery or Assembly. The high esteem in which he was held by his brethren finds evidence in his being recommended by the Assembly to the Commissioners of Perth on their request for a good minister after the death of the celebrated John Row.[3] We find him on a commission for collecting acts of Assembly[4] ; examining evidence regarding a charge against the Bishop of Aberdeen[5] ; consulting with the Moderator as one of his assessors on fit subjects to be considered in the Assembly[6] ; visiting and counselling the newly-formed Presbyteries in the South and West.[7] Later, he is again in company of Durie, protesting against certain

[1] Quoted from Plutarch's *De Amicitia*. Wodrow MS., p. 22. Calderwood, Vol. III, p. 762.
[2] Calderwood says that he went not abroad for ten or twelve days. Vol. VIII, p. 257.
[3] *Book of the Universal Kirk*, p. 203. The request was for " a singular good man both for doctrine and good discipline." Davidson was recommended with Andrew Symson and James Anderson.
[4] Calderwood, Vol. III, p. 712.
[5] Ibid., p. 709.
[6] Ibid., p. 731.
[7] Ibid., p. 734.

ministers being sent to Berwick to persuade those concerned in the Raid to return to Scotland and submit to the King[1] ; whereas the quieter occupation of examining a student on the doctrine of the Church engages his attention at another time.[2]

At the beginning of that fateful year for the Church, 1584, the Presbytery of Edinburgh had a conference with Robert Browne,[3] the founder of the sect of Brownists which took its rise a few years earlier. He alleged that the whole discipline of the Church of Scotland was wrong, that he and his company had justly withdrawn themselves and would no longer be subject to it. If censured they would appeal from the Church to the magistrate. Davidson and James Lawson were appointed to examine his writings, to find out his own and his followers' practice and such opinions as they perceived or suspected them to err in. This done, Browne was cited before the Presbytery, where he " boldly avowed his books and opinions ". The matter was referred to the King, who did not interfere, however, and who, it was suspected, favoured and entertained the man and his followers simply for annoyance of the Kirk.

It must not be thought that one so occupied in the Courts of the Church failed in diligence where his own parishioners were concerned. On the contrary, Davidson was most conscientious in his pastoral work and in his preaching. Wodrow sums up his estimate of the ministry at Liberton thus : " There he continued many years zealously and faithfully preaching the

---

[1] Calderwood, Vol. III, p. 752. *Register of Privy Council of Scotland*, Vol. III, p. 611n. Davidson feared that such procedure would be prejudicial to the Cause.
[2] Calderwood, Vol. IV, p. 2.
[3] Ibid., pp. 2-3. Browne's views are outlined on p. 1, Vol. IV.

Gospel ; a most constant zealous affecter of the doctrine and discipline of this Church and great enemy to all ungodliness, profaneness, corruptions and innovations ; a serious convincing preacher and a mighty wrestler in prayer."[1]

Nor was Davidson unmindful of the obligations of friendship amid those busy and exciting years. In September 1582, soon after the Ruthven enterprise, George Buchanan, that illustrious Scottish scholar, passed to his rest. As the end drew near, he was visited by Davidson who was anxious to strengthen the faith of his old Principal and confirm him in the doctrine of the Reformed Church. Buchanan gave him his assurance that he believed in salvation through the atoning sacrifice of Christ, and also pleased the sturdy reformer with a caustic humorous remark on the absurd Romish doctrine of the Mass.[2]

With the King's regaining of his liberty in the middle of 1583, the tide again turned against the Church. The Earl of Arran regained his old ascendancy over James ; the Earl of Gowrie was condemned to death and other nobles who had engaged in the " raid " were banished. Early in 1584 Melville was summoned before the Privy Council to answer for some treasonable expressions which he was said to have used in a sermon ; and being ordered to enter himself a prisoner in Blackness Castle, on the advice of his friends fled to Berwick. A cloud descended on the Church ; the passing of the infamous "Black Acts" followed. A second attempt to control the King's person had failed, and Davidson, though

[1] Wodrow MS., p. 9.
[2] Hume Brown's *Life of Buchanan*, p. 352.

not privy to it, now made common cause with the Protestant lords and along with several of his brethren who were aware of a design against them because of their defence of discipline and their zeal against dangerous courses, followed Melville into exile in England. Thus the Liberton ministry came to a somewhat sudden close.[1]

[1] Calderwood, Vol. IV, p. 38.

CHAPTER IV

ACTIVITIES FROM 1584 TO SETTLEMENT
AT CANONGATE IN 1590

THE only reason for the exile of Davidson and his
brethren in 1584 was that, with Gowrie's fate and the
rough handling of Melville in mind, they felt themselves to be no longer safe at home,[1] and recent
happenings had filled them with fears and misgivings.
A certain English Roman Catholic, Allen[2] by name,
had, however, a different version of the story.   In a
printed book he charged the whole Scottish ministry
with responsibility for what he called rebellion against
his Majesty's person, and he declared that those who
had passed to England had fled on account of their
treason.   It fell to Davidson to pen a short vindication
of the ministers[3] from this grave charge, and in forceful
language he exposed the falsehoods of the Romanist.
To begin with he denied that there was anything in
the nature of " rebellion " in an enterprise which
aimed at the deliverance of the church, the nation and
the King himself from " godless and pestilent Papists ".
Then he showed that Allen's statement to the effect
that Gowrie, before his death, had imputed its
inception to the ministers, was utterly without
foundation.   On the contrary, on the very scaffold

---

[1] Calderwood, Vol. IV, p. 38.
[2] Allen or Alanus, William, Cardinal Archbishop of Mechlin (1532-94)—
Hole, *Biographical Dictionary*, London, 1866. Also article in *D.N.B.*
[3] Calderwood, Vol. IV, p. 38f.

the Earl had freed them from all complicity in it. Besides, the majority of the ministers, he said, were eighteen or twenty miles away from Stirling when the enterprise took place and some of them, like Melville,[1] had even left Scotland before that. The cause of their flight, Davidson maintained, was entirely due to the cruel persecution meted out to those who were " the good instruments of advancing the gospel and the good cause in the land."[2]

Davidson soon found even more important work to do than the defence of his exiled brethren. The banished lords at Newcastle were evidently desirous of religious instruction, so they sent a message to James Melville, who was then at Berwick, inviting him to come south to be their pastor. While waiting his arrival, they applied to the exiled ministers for some one to impart to them spiritual guidance. Davidson was chosen to minister to them for the time being and he did so with a thoroughness becoming the man. We are indebted to Wodrow[3] for an account of that brief but efficient ministry, not recorded in any of the printed histories. Davidson entered at once into a beautiful pastoral relation with that " honourable company and little congregation ", and he preached

---

[1] Davidson says, in his reply to Allen, that several of the lords when requested to subscribe Melville's sentence as altered by Arran (i.e. from the Castle of Edinburgh to Blackness) refused, and said that, to please his Majesty, they had already yielded too far in agreeing to it in its original form.—Calderwood, Vol. II, p. 348.

[2] Calderwood bears out this view in his notes on the perilous courses of Arran and Stuart toward " the Wracke of true religioun ". They retired, he says, to avoid their fury, " to the most sure girth and place of refuge commoun to all the afflicted members of Christ through Europe." The names of Davidson and some others he placed opposite this statement, in the margin. Vol. IV, pp. 423-4.

Davidson is said to have made a similar reply to the calumnies of one Sutliffe in defence of Patrick Galloway.—Calderwood, Vol. IV, p. 45.

[3] Wodrow MS., p. 23.

to them every Wednesday and Friday as well as on the Lord's Day Afternoon, his sermons being of an hour's duration. Family devotions, too, were observed with regularity and care ; prayer and Psalms before dinner, prayer again and a chapter read before supper. Then after meals some notes on the Scriptures were given and a psalm was sung. Besides these daily devotions there was also maintained a strict discipline ; ruling elders were appointed who, with the minister, convened after sermon on Wednesdays, when trial was made of evil doers. Many of these were merely censured but some, on conviction, were remitted to their masters as civil magistrates. " Thus as near as they could, they kept to the practice of their Mother Church when forced out of her."[1]

James Melville was not at all eager to assume the responsibility of such a work as he was now called to, partly because he was not yet in the regular ministry and was wanting in experience, and partly because he was not quite convinced as to the righteousness of the noblemen's cause or even of their sincerity. His scruples over his own fitness, however, were completely removed by the persuasions of his old master,[2] who showed him that it was the will of God as well as the desire both of the lords themselves and the brethren who had gone farther south, that he should remain in Newcastle and minister to the exiles till the time came for their return home. So he consented to do so and quickly drew up an order of discipline to be used " in the Company of those Godly and Noble Men of

[1] Wodrow MS., p. 23.
[2] Davidson had been his teacher at St. Andrews. Calderwood, Vol. IV, p. 149. Melville's *Diary*, p. 172.

Scotland ". Probably it was based upon the directions of Davidson who, it is said, to encourage Mr. Melville, set down his own order in writing with an exhortation and faithful warning prefixed to it.[1]

Thus resigning the little flock to the younger man's care, Davidson proceeded to London, where he was already no stranger. There is reason to believe that in his earlier flight when persecuted by Morton, he had come in contact with some of the Puritan leaders in the south. From an unpublished letter of his— probably the only letter in his handwriting extant— to John Field[2] the famous English preacher and opponent of Episcopacy, we gather that he had several friends in London, and that he felt the necessity of concord and unity between England and Scotland as helpful to the cause of Christ.[3]

In the company of other exiled preachers Davidson visited the two English Universities[4]—Oxford and Cambridge—in 1584, conferring with the godly and the learned. He returned to London in July, where in the following October his friend Mr. James Lawson[5] died. Davidson was with him at the end and thereafter acted as one of his executors.[6]

[1] Wodrow, MS., p. 23.

[2] *Nat. Lib. Scot.*, MS. 6.1.13, fol. 83. Copy of letter will be found in Appendix D. John Field was minister of Wandsworth and St. Giles, Cripplegate in London, and a prominent Puritan.—*Athenae Oxonienses*, Vol. I, p. 535 (Anthony A. Wood, 1813).

[3] That was in 1582, but in 1579 Davidson had been dealt with by the English Privy Council for uttering " certain lewde and disordered speeches to her Majestie's discontentacion ! "—*Acts P.C.*, Vol. XI, p. 289.

[4] Wodrow MS., p. 23. Calderwood, Vol. IV, p. 201.

[5] Lawson was the successor of Knox at St. Giles. Archbishop Adamson forged his Testament in which Davidson and other ministers were denounced in a letter supposed to have been written by Lawson himself.—Calderwood, Vol. IV., p. 715.

[6] Calderwood, Vol. IV, p. 207.

From the beginning of November till January 5th, 1585, Mr. John preached on all the Holy Days at St. Olave in Old Jewry.[1] His theme was the Book of Job and his discourses made a very great impression, notes of them being discussed at Court and among the Bishops. By reason of his passionate oratory and vehemence, he was called " the thunderer ".[2] That ministry, however, was brought to a sudden conclusion by the Bishop of London who, appearing one day, interrupted the preacher and would not even allow him to dismiss the people in decency. His Lordship afterwards alleged to Balcanquhall that it was not he but the Council who had discharged Davidson, whereupon the congregation in their fondness for the preacher presented a supplication to the Council without, however, obtaining any satisfaction.[3] It is characteristic of Davidson that, as a parting message, he should have warned his hearers of " a great visitation, affliction and danger " approaching the Church of God in England, telling them that " Scotland was the place where the furnace was kindled by the enemies and conspirators of the Council of Trent against the whole Church and especially against England. " The last duty we find him doing in London is preaching on Ezekiel xi. 14, 15, to the banished noblemen who kept a fast in their lodging at Westminster just before their departure from England.[4]

[1] Wodrow MS., p. 23. St. Olave's in Old Jewry has disappeared, except for the tower, which forms part of a house built on its site. It was a " Wren " Church, built after the Great Fire of London. None of its records are known to exist.

[2] Calderwood, Vol. IV, p. 247.

[3] Wodrow MS., p. 23.

[4] Calderwood, Vol. IV, p. 366.

November 1585 saw the recall of the Protestant lords who, on their return, repaired to the King and were again admitted to his Council. In the same month a letter was sent by a number of leading ministers[1] then assembled at Stirling to " their loving brethren, Mr. James Carmichael, Mr. John Davidson, Mr. James Melvil and the rest of the Scottish sojourners " in England. It runs thus : " Breitheren, we salute you hairtilie in the Lord. It has pleasit our God in his gudnes to offer occasion of liberty to his Kirk at this present within this countrie, while of the multitude of his mercy we houp he shall forder advance, praying you with all diligence, as ye are zealouse of the common cause, to repair hierfor toward this countrie ; that be mutuall conference we may (as our God will give us the grace) concurre and mutually put our hands to the work concerning the glory of our God and the advancement of the Kingdom of his Son Jesus Christ, whose Spirit rest with you and conduct you."[2] In response to this appeal, Davidson and his fellow-exiles returned to Scotland. He did not settle down to any particular charge, however, doubtless preferring for a time to do " the work of an evangelist ". For two or three years there is little or nothing known of him except that the Assembly of 1586 appointed him with several others to deal with the character and conduct of certain bishops and commissioners should need arise in the interval between Assemblies.[3] Probably, as Wodrow suggests, a large portion of the

---

[1] Among the names are Pont, Andrew Melville, Craig, Balcanquhall and Bruce.

[2] Wodrow's *Collections upon the Lives of the Reformers and Most Eminent Ministers of the Church of Scotland*, Vol. I, p. 182.

[3] Calderwood, Vol. IV, p. 570. *Book of the Universal Kirk*, p. 303.

silent period would be devoted to study, Davidson being a great scholar. In 1588 he declined an invitation to return to his old congregation at Liberton[1] and on June 3rd, 1589, he was chosen for St. Giles, where he was ordered to continue " till he be provided as the Kirk and Council crave ".[2] Evidently there was a proposal made to have him settled at Dalkeith as this minute in the Records of the Synod of Lothian and Tweedale suggests : " The transporattion of Mr. Ard. Symsoun from Dalkeith till Cranstoun, and Mr. John Davidsoun's planting at Dalkeith are remitted to the Presbytery of Edinburgh " (September 17th, 1589). Nothing, however, came of that.

In 1590 the King returned from Denmark with his young bride. Although largely indebted to the ministers and especially to Robert Bruce for the peace and prosperity of the country during his absence, he soon gave them offence by insisting that the Queen's coronation should be held on a Sunday. Some of them, it is true, had no objection, arguing that it was quite lawful on that day, since it was similar to a marriage—a mutual solemn oath between the prince and his subjects with God's blessing over all. Yet the Church generally insisted upon strict Sabbath observance,[3] so obnoxious to the King, and on this

---

[1] Scott's *Fasti*, Vol. I, p. 170. *Records of the Presbytery of Edinburgh*, Nov. 5, 1588.

[2] Ibid., p. 53.

[3] They seem once to have departed from it, when inconsistently in 1574 they ordered Rutherford to produce his reply to Davidson's *Dialogue* upon " Sunday at 4 hours afternoon ".

Some modern writers, like Law Mathieson, declare the observance of the Sabbath to have been much freer than the facts indeed justify. The Reformers departed a little from their strictness because some regarded the strict observance of the day as a merit for salvation.

occasion the majority were prepared to resist his Majesty and his Danish friends. Calderwood tells us[1] that these ministers were despitefully reviled by the Provost and Magistrates of Edinburgh for the stand they took, and Davidson came in for special opprobrium, as he seems to have been their doughty champion and persistent leader.

Another objection was raised by some of the preachers to the anointing with oil at the coronation, as being Jewish and superstitious.[2] That, however, was easily overcome by James, who threatened to send for the Bishops if the ministers declined to do it. On all arrangements the King had his way, so on Sunday, May 17th, 1590, Anne of Denmark was crowned Queen by Robert Bruce in the Chapel of Holyroodhouse. Spottiswood wrongly attributes to Davidson leadership of the opposition to the anointing ceremony and, while doubtless he did not approve of it, it was rather with the sanctity of the Lord's Day that he was concerned. The Archbishop describes him most unfairly as " an idle and turbulent man " who was without a charge in the ministry and was popular only with foolish people who desired to make themselves out more holy and zealous than others.[3] " Turbulent " he may have been, if a sometimes excessive zeal for a good cause can be so termed ; " idle " he certainly was not, as his multifarious services to the Church are proof. That he had been without a ministerial charge for some time was, as we saw, entirely due to his own desire. He was deservedly popular, not with such foolish people as seemingly

[1] Calderwood, Vol. V, p. 95.
[2] Ibid. Spottiswood, Vol. II, p. 408. Cunningham, Vol. I, p. 386.
[3] Spottiswood, Vol. II, p. 407.

existed only in Spottiswood's imagination, but with the most earnest and worthy of his brethren and indeed with almost the whole Church, as is evident from the congregations who desired his services and the amount of highly responsible work he was asked to undertake.[1] Indeed, at this very time we find him appointed, with some of the most distinguished ministers of the Church—and as we know, not for the first time—an assessor to the moderator, " to advise him what things were needfull to be propouned and treatted in the Assemblie ".[2]

At this time Davidson was translated to the Second Charge of Canongate or Holyroodhouse[3] and he seems also to have continued to preach frequently in the East (or New) Kirk of Edinburgh as he had done in years past. It was in this same year, 1590, that he discharged a great service to the Church of Scotland in the penning of a short but most important tract, the cause and sequel of which must now be related.

About this time the Church of Scotland was enjoying a measure of internal peace and was also on amicable terms with the Church of England. Most of the English prelates were ready to recognize their northern neighbours as a Christian Church although they regarded the Scottish system as defective in its ritual, in the ordination of its ministers and in other points.[4] The Scottish ministers, strongly opposed as they were to anything in the nature of Episcopacy, avoided as carefully as they could any reflections on

---

[1] He was on most important Assembly Committees, was a frequent preacher on important occasions, etc.

[2] Calderwood, Vol. V, p. 104.

[3] Scott's *Fasti*, Vol. I, p. 27.

[4] Grub, *Ecclesiastical History of Scotland*, Vol. II, p. 282.

English ecclesiastical polity.[1] The dangers of Roman
Catholicism, realized by the Armada, brought England
and Scotland as well as King and Kirk closer together,
so that at the beginning of 1589 the relations between
the two countries were on the whole friendly. Nevertheless the Scottish preachers were independent
enough to make common cause with the persecuted
English Puritans with whom they had strong affinities
and for whom they felt the utmost sympathy. That
sympathy had been strengthened by recent intercourse. When the Kirk was sore troubled Andrew
Melville, John Davidson and others,[2] as we saw, had
sought refuge in England where they had become well
acquainted with the Puritan leaders ; while men like
John Penry[3] and his printer Waldegrave, fleeing from
their Episcopal persecutors, found harbourage in
Scotland, and John Udall, a true Presbyterian, on
coming to Edinburgh, was given the high honour of
preaching before the King during a session of the
General Assembly.[4]

Not without obvious misgiving could the great
Church in the south view this growing intimacy
between Scottish Reformers and English Puritans, at
one in their opposition to Episcopacy ; and besides
the Scottish ministers were resentful at the English
bishops for carrying on objectionable intrigues with
those in Scotland favouring an episcopate,[5] and so an

[1] M'Crie, *Life of Melville*, Vol. I, p. 305.
[2] 1584. Calderwood, Vol. IV, pp. 12-38.
[3] John Penry was a Welshman, a leading Puritan in England and said to
be one of the authors of the Marprelate Tracts against Episcopacy. He spent
several years in Scotland where he was favourably received and entertained
by the ministers.
[4] Calderwood, Vol. V, p. 58.
[5] See Patrick Adamson's confession of having conspired with the English
bishops. Calderwood, Vol. V, p. 121.

estrangement arose between the two churches and grew until suddenly and unexpectedly it passed into open hostility. The amity between England and Scotland was marred by a notable incident in February 1588-9. Dr. Richard Bancroft, Canon of Westminster, afterwards Archbishop of Canterbury, preached a notorious sermon at St. Paul's Cross, London, at the opening of Parliament, just seven months after the Armada.[1] Bancroft was probably the most useful henchman of Archbishop Whitgift, that bitter opponent and persecutor of the Puritans, and it has been said that he outdid his master in his intolerance of dissent.[2] He was engaged in tracking down the writers of the Marprelate Tracts in which the office of Bishop was strongly denounced in the spirit of Andrew Melville, and which had caused a great sensation in English Church life. The English Puritans naturally looked to the Scottish Kirk for sympathy; Bancroft naturally regarded it differently. It has been said that he "when placed in charge of the detective agency, like a good general surveying the field of campaign, kept his eye shrewdly upon Scotland as an exposed frontier. It was a source of sinister influence; in any case it set forth a dangerous example of the democratic and anti-Episcopal principles of Geneva, at work on a national scale."[3]

In this sermon on " trying the spirits "[4]—a defence of Bishops and the Prayer Book—Bancroft made a

---

[1] *A Sermon preached at Paul's Crosse the 9th of February; being the first Sunday in the Parliament Anno 1588 by Richard Bancroft, Chaplaine to the L. Chancellor of England.* Printed in 1588 and reprinted in 1636.

[2] Mackinnon, *A History of Modern Liberty*, Vol. III, p. 24.

[3] Pierce, *Life of John Penry*, p. 259.

[4] The text was 1 John iv. 1 : " Dearly beloved, believe not every Spirit but try the Spirits whether they be of God."

violent attack first on the English Puritans whom he charged with all sorts of evils.[1] Then he turned his masterly invective upon the Church of Scotland in which he found an example of the very thing he desired to crush out in England. He began by railing at John Knox, whom he described as " a man of contentious humour and perverse behaviour ". That was bad enough, but he went farther and held up to ridicule the worship and discipline of the Reformed Church in Scotland, and Presbyterianism, especially in its anti-monarchical character. The ministers, in their recent contentions with the court, were set in a most unfavourable light. They were charged with having altered the laws of the land in defiance of King and Estates, with having disclaimed his Majesty's authority, with having established an ecclesiastical tyranny producing faction, sedition, confusion and rebellion, besides introducing Anabaptism. On this account, he said, the King at one time had overthrown the presbyteries. Both the accusations and the sources from which his information was gathered, caused the greatest excitement and keenest resentment among Scottish Churchmen. " It is scarcely possible," says M'Crie,[2] " to conceive a more perfect specimen of the argument *ad invidiam* than this oration exhibits. All the topics of declamation calculated to excite prejudice are carefully collected and employed with no small art."

One of the " authorities " cited by Bancroft was Patrick Adamson, titular Archbishop of St. Andrews, whose friendly entertainment by Anglicans in London

[1] See M'Crie's *Life of Melville*, Vol. I, p. 306, for a summary of these evils.
[2] Ibid., pp. 305-6.

had been anything but pleasing to the Scottish ministers, and round whom centred much of the bitterness of the controversy between the upholders of Presbyterianism and the defenders of Episcopacy. Bancroft made extensive use of a document called *The King's Declaration*, ostensibly from the pen of James VI, but really written and forged by Adamson.[1] His second source of information he found in Robert Browne, the founder of English Independency, of whose works, as we saw, Davidson had occasion to judge some years earlier.[2] The Reformers liked Brownism as little as did the Puritans, and the embittered Browne, conscious of that, became a very willing witness against the Scottish Presbyterians. Bancroft eagerly used any information Browne supplied to him and did not scruple to elaborate it ; he was convinced that the English Puritans were fast imitating the Scottish Reformers, and he spared neither. The Prelate, however, was not content with these two witnesses. More useful still, though humbler than either of them, was John Norton, an Edinburgh bookseller, whom he employed to spy upon the ministers and report certain information to him. The ministers on this occasion, however, beating Bancroft at his own game, intercepted one of his letters from Norton, who on examination confessed that he had been " sette on worke by his uncle, old Norton, at the requiest of Doctor Bancroft upon some

[1] Bancroft regarded Adamson as an excellent medium for his inquiries in Scotland, instructed him how to play his part and promised him, when he came again to England, the favour and patronage of Whitgift. But, in the Assembly of April 1591, Adamson recanted, and admitted having forged the *Declaration*, traducing the Kirk. See Calderwood, Vol. V., pp. 119-21, and Pierce, *Life of Penry*, p. 260.

[2] Page 77.

comoditie in his trade ". Bancroft had forwarded a questionnaire on the organization of the Presbyterian Church, to which answers were being sent. The following samples of his questions serve to show the drift and scope of his inquiries.[1] " Considering the King's edict 1584, how came it to passe that the bishops were so soone overthrowne again?" Whether have they in their consistories anie sett jurisdictioun? Whether have they anie sett assemblies termed Conferences? Whether the King be exempted from their censures? And how manie presbyteries (Kirk Sessions) doe apperteane to everie suche Conference? Whether is Buchanan's treatise *De Jure Regni apud Scotos*, approved there by the consistorians? How have the ministers dealt with the King from tyme to tyme? "[2]

It was not to be expected that the Scottish ministers would allow such a wanton attack as this upon their Church to pass without effective reply. It is true that John Penry forestalled them with his *Brief Discoverie*, but it was written naturally from the English stand-point and did not deal exhaustively with the subject.[3] His work suggested rather than obviated a specific answer to Bancroft by the Scottish Church itself. The Edinburgh Presbytery was specially convened on April 29th, 1589, to deal with the matter and it was remitted to three of its most influential members, including Davidson,[4] to prepare a suitable reply. It

[1] Calderwood, Vol. V, p. 77.

[2] Ibid., pp. 77 f. The questions are also in the British Museum. The answers have recently been discovered in MS. by Dr. H. W. Meikle in the National Library of Scotland.

[3] Pierce, *Life of Penry*, p. 279.

[4] The others were Robert Pont and Robert Bruce—Records of the Presbytery of Edinburgh. *The Miscellany of the Wodrow Society*, Vol. I, p. 470.

was also decided that the King, who was then in Aberdeenshire quelling the Catholic Earls at the Brig o' Dee, should " be spoken heir anent at his returne ". On June 10th at a further meeting of the Presbytery the reply was brought before the brethren, approved, and ordered to be presented to the General Assembly. For politic reasons, however, this answer[1] was never sent, nor was a similar " prolixe but pithy letter " said to be " penned by Mr. John Davidson at the desire of some brethren ".[2] After further earnest consideration of the whole matter, the ministers felt that their purpose would be best served by a short publication from Davidson's pen. Evidently the brethren were satisfied as to Mr. John's ability and wisdom, to make fitting protest against thec alumniator on their behalf ; and it is a proof of their confidence that the matter was left with him. It was a piece of work after his own heart ; he loved the Church of Scotland, believed implicitly in the divine right of Presbyterianism, and was an uncompromising opponent of the Episcopacy for which Bancroft stood. His retaliation, brief but to the point, was published in Edinburgh by Waldegrave. Its title runs : " *D. Bancroft's Rashnes in rayling against the Church of Scotland, noted in Answere to a Letter of a worthy person of England, and some reasons rendred, why the answere thereunto hath not hitherto come forth. By J.D. a brother of the sayd Church of Scotland*. It concludes : " Farewell, from Edin. the 18 of September 1590. Yours in the Lord, J.D."[3] The tract opens with an

---

[1] *Miscellany of Wodrow Society*, Vol. I, pp. 489-96.
[2] Calderwood, Vol. V, p. 73. There is nothing of importance in this letter, not referred to in Davidson's pamphlet which we have now to consider.
[3] *Miscellany of Wodrow Society*, Vol. I, pp. 505-20.

expression of sympathy for " the godlie brethren of Englande who urge Reformation of that Churche, and chiefly, the remoouing of that heavie bondage of Antichristian government by loftie Lordes, wrongfully called Bishops (an hurtfull relicke of Romish confusion) and restoring in the place thereof the joynt administration of Christian discipline by the Ministers and Elders of the Churche, which is most clearly prooved by them and others, to be established by the Word of God." The author then goes on to show how Bancroft, not content with denouncing the views of the Puritans, set himself to have those innocent people brought under the hatred of the magistrate and branded as traitors and rebels, who sought the overthrow of the Queen's authority in the Church, and even endangered her very life. The learned Doctor, having no proof of these grave charges, found an illustration of them in Scotland and in so doing slandered the whole ministry and discipline of the Church there. This policy, Davidson maintains, is inimical to the friendly relations of the two countries, and plays into the hands of foreign enemies.

Davidson next proceeds to examine the " credentials " of the agents employed by Bancroft in his eagerness to justify his theme, and from whose " frivelous reports " he managed to " builde uppe an uglie heape of most slanderous accusations against our sayde Church." He deals first with Adamson, " Diotrephes, apostat of St. Andrewes " and the anonymous work called *The King's Declaration* which he had forged. This declaration, first published in Edinburgh in 1585, had been reprinted in several editions in London, and had found a place in

Holinshed's *Chronicles of England*, published in 1586-7.[1]
Taking the Declaration at its face value Bancroft had
no difficulty in showing from the provisions of the
" Black Acts " that the King had restored bishops in
1584. " All this," he said, " you may find more at
length set down by the King himself in his *Declaration*.
. . . It may heer be said," he continues (and this
was, of course, the sting), " that now the King is of
another mind, and that this *Declaration* was made
when he had conceived some displeasure against [the
ministers]." " The King," Bancroft declared boldly,
" he is not altered. *Ictus piscator sapit*. His crowne
and their soveraigntie will not agree together."
Davidson relates how James took an early opportunity
of contradicting Bancroft's insinuation that he
dissembled in his recent concession made in favour of
Presbytery, and how sending for the pamphlet he
wrote in the margin against these " impudent assertions ", the words : " My speaking, writing and actions
were and are ever one, without dissembling or bearing
up at any time, whatever I thought.

" Ergo casts out the libel, ne quid asperius [not
true, to use no rougher terms]. I.R."

The use Bancroft made of so unworthy an agent as
Adamson is vigorously denounced in Davidson's
pamphlet while the writer at the same time makes an
astute bid for the King's favour. His Majesty he
realizes, has now reached years of discretion and may
be counted upon to show a regard for the scriptural
authority of discipline which was not possible for him
in his earlier days. Kings, however, must not look

[1] *Miscellany of Wodrow Society*, Vol. I, pp. 475, 510. M'Crie, *Life of Melville*, Vol. I, p. 230. Calderwood, Vol. V, p. 6.

to men like Adamson to sacrifice their profits for the sake of the honour of their thrones. Bancroft himself Davidson pillories as " that poor Demas (if he be no worse), hunting appearandly for promotion to some prelacie ". He ought to have known his " horrible accusations " to have been incredible in a Church like the Church of Scotland where so long the truth had been sincerely preached and professed.

The second witness cited by Bancroft—Robert Browne—is just as easily discredited by Davidson. Bancroft had not been too confident about Browne himself and evidently used him for want of someone better. " This man's opinion ", he declared, " I knowe will be greatly contemned because I thinke hee hath bin of an other judgement &c."[1] Though he never would have rested his accusations on Browne's evidence alone, yet he made free use of two of his writings[2] in which he found the bitter autobiographical material suited to his purpose. Browne, smarting under his cold reception by the Scottish ministers,[3] was only too ready to say the worst of Scottish Presbyterianism. He declared that if that system were adopted in England, " then in stead of one Pope we should have a thousand, and of some Lord byshops in name, a thousand Lordly Tyrants in deed which now do disdaine the name."[4] He went further and said that " he had knowne the King to be in great danger and feare of his life by their Lordlie Discipline,

---

[1] *Miscellany of Wodrow Society*, Vol. I, p. 486.

[2] A treatise against Barrow, and a letter of Browne to his Uncle Flower, December 31st, 1588.

[3] He was put in ward a night or two till his works were examined.

[4] Letter edited under the title " A New Years Guift ", by C. Burrage (1904).

7

the nobles and people at great discord and much distracted, and yet all men made slaves to the preachers and their fellowe elders." Davidson simply pours scorn upon such a statement as utterly false and shows that so far as the King's person is concerned, the very opposite is the case, as could be vouched for by English ambassadors and other worthy persons long resident in Scotland. Besides, he points out, Bancroft is now at loggerheads with Browne, who refuses to help him any more in his literary polemics. Moreover, if there be any danger to the State, the Queen and her Council would be well advised to demand better proof than what Bancroft calls " the treasonable outlandish practises " of the Reformers. Appealing, as was his wont, to the Scriptures, Davidson goes on to say that in the letter written by those who sought to hinder the rebuilding of Jerusalem, there was a claim to authority from the " authentik bookes of the Chronicles " but Bancroft leans upon the evidence of known and confessed infamous persons and upon a forged document. On such worthless evidence he accuses of treason good brethren of England. " If the envy of the sect of the Nazarites, urged by prophane Tertullus," asks Davidson, " is not sufficient to beare downe Paule as a seditious mover of the people . . . why should the good brethren of England that seeke Reformatioun be charged with a mind hereafter of sedition, by means of Discipline, because the Church of Scotland, in respect of the same Discipline exercised in it, is unjustlie condemned of sedition, by the Hie Preists of our daies, two false witnesses being alleaged for that purpose by their Tertullus at Paul's Crosse? "[1]

[1] *Miscellany of Wodrow Society*, Vol. I, p. 514.

Davidson next deals with the Scottish Church's reasons for delay in sending an answer to the Doctor's calumnies. It was not for lack of competent men to deal with the matter, although some English Doctors of Divinity evidently thought so—and he must be a very learned man whose knowledge the Bishops will recognize if once he sets himself in opposition to them. In the first place, the reply was not made simply because it was not considered necessary in Scotland where all the facts were so well known. Besides it was feared that it might cause dissension between the two countries, and the ministers were satisfied, so long as the truth and their innocency were safe without it. In the second place, the answer was deferred, because it was confidently expected that redress would come from Queen Elizabeth herself, who long before had professed that the Scottish ministers were among her most loving and loyal friends. Lastly, and yet most important, those most intimately concerned with the matter felt that they were restrained from proceeding by some secret reason which they could explain only as the hand of God.

Davidson concludes with a hope that someone having access to her Majesty will acquaint her with the truth, so that the Bishops may be led to discountenance for all time the " rashness in rayling " of Dr. Bancroft against the King, the people and the Church of Scotland ; he also suggests that to avoid rancour, a friendly discussion might be held based upon the Word of God.

Davidson's little brochure—two small octavo sheets—was addressed, as we see from the title, to a correspondent in England and was intended for circulation south of the Tweed. Probably, as has been suggested, it was a compromise between the views of those who had desired full and detailed contradictions of Bancroft's charges, and of those who held that the best policy was to ignore the whole thing. From Davidson's unpublished letter to Elizabeth we know the kind of gossip that passed from English Puritans to their friends in the North. Scottish witnesses, it was said, were twitted with their nationality in the English courts and London stageplayers had turned into mockery and laughter the staid Presbyterian discipline and " most ridiculously flooted " that and " the whole ministry ".[1] Though *Rashnes in Rayling* was published with some degree of secrecy, Bowes, the English ambassador, soon learned of its existence, which he reported to Burghley in London ; but it was some weeks later before he could secure and dispatch a copy.[2] The King, notwithstanding the unstinted praise he received in it and despite his anger at Bancroft, yet " earnestlie travailed to suppress it ". With all his care, however, some copies escaped from the press and Waldegrave was bound in sureties to print nothing hereafter without the King's permission.[3] His attitude seems strange, but one or two considerations go far to explain it. At this time Queen Elizabeth was urging him to banish Penry, the Puritan guest of the ministers. Though anxious to keep on friendly terms with Elizabeth on account of past favours and hopes of

[1] Calderwood, Vol. V, pp. 73-7.

[2] *Calendar of State Papers of Scotland*, Vol. X, pp. 401, 409.

[3] " The King favoureth the Jesuit James Gordon, and in the meane tyme, is offended with Robert Waldegrave, printer, for printing Mr. Johne Davidsone's answere to Doctor Bancroft's calumneis."—Calderwood, Vol. V, p. 112.

those to come, he could not afford to alienate the Kirk in view of his troubles with the Catholic earls. This is also partly the explanation of his behaviour in the General Assembly of 1590, where he made many gracious promises and heaped upon the Church the most extravagant praise[1] ; yet at that very time he had signed the Act of Council banishing Penry. It is dated August 6th, 1590, and Bowes forwarded a copy to Burghley on the 14th. Again, if we allow our minds to go forward to the Hampton Court Conference of 1604 we shall find another clue to his Majesty's attitude, in his words to the Puritans : " If you aim at a Scottish Presbytery, it agreeth as well with monarchy as God with the devil."[2] That had always been his view, and it was now evident that he had no desire to see in England what had been so irksome to him in Scotland. " James detested the Kirk for both in theory and practice it conflicted with his ideas of kingship. It claimed a divine right independent of the King so that if James was ever to establish uniformity of religion it was more likely to be English than Scotch."[3]

There is every reason to believe that Bowes would inform Burghley of the strong feeling roused against Bancroft by Davidson's pamphlet. He would also explain to him how his own position as guardian of Elizabeth's interests, had been rendered most difficult

[1] Calderwood, Vol. V, pp. 105-6. According to Wodrow, Davidson alone expressed himself doubtful of the King's declarations. To some who were sitting by him, he said : " I know well, for all these professions the King makes, he will not prove sincere, but will bring in the English modes, and rob us of our privileges." MS., p. 40.

[2] Cunningham, Vol. II, p. 459. Barlow's *Summary of Hampton Court Conference*, p. 4.

[3] Gwatkin, *Church and State in England*, p. 272.

by the prelate's gratuitous, indiscreet and unwarranted attack on the Scottish Church. The situation was a delicate one and no one wanted to push matters to extremes. Besides there was enough truth about James's dissimulation to make him anxious for compromise. To Burghley belongs the credit of finding a way out. He placed the complaints of the King before Bancroft and secured from him an assurance of regret, the " humble words and submission " of which pleased his Majesty. Bancroft was also to write an apology to Burghley which on being forwarded to Bowes, would be shown only to the King and to Maitland, his Chancellor.

There has recently come to light in the National Library of Scotland a contemporary copy of Bancroft's secret letter.[1] It is a long and exceedingly well-written document and one is not surprised at its author attaining to the high office of Archbishop of Canterbury. The early portion of it is in apologetic vein except for this slighting reference to Davidson—" for mine owne parte I give small creditt to this Alphabeticall nameless person, J.D." He seeks to justify himself by recent happenings in Scotland and then proceeds to deny that he charged the King with dissimulation. How would the ministers, he said, like their words " metamorphosed " ? What about Mr. Knox and his sayings concerning the Prayer-book ? Look what the present ministers say about the Church of England : " They call the favourers of our Church a generation of Bishopists." The works of Knox and Buchanan, Bancroft regards as "nothinge in effect but trumpetts of rebellion to arme

[1] Bancroft's Letter, *Nat. Lib. Scot. MS.*, 6.1.13, f. 46.

his subjects against his highness." His second witness, Robert Browne, was justified, he maintains, partly by recent Acts of Parliament and partly by recent news from Scotland.

It is not surprising that the King was satisfied with the letter, though he " misliked the testimony grounded upon Browne ".[1] He thought it well that Bancroft should, in the place where he preached the sermon or elsewhere, explain his words, " to quit him from that blemish ". Once more Burghley intervened. His letter to Chancellor Maitland has not been traced but Bowes reported that the Chancellor thought that Burghley had showed his wisdom. The King and Maitland were not fully satisfied but they were ready to pass from a matter whose renewing they deemed likely to bring " greater contention than profit ".

Thus the incident closed. Yet it was more than an incident, for Bancroft had raised a controversial issue regarding church government—illustrated by invidious comparisons much resented by Davidson and his brethren—which was to influence the relations between the two countries for many a day to come, and whose repercussions were to be felt not only under James but also under Charles I and even later. Hitherto the Church of England had made no greater claim for itself than that set forth by Richard Hooker, whose *Ecclesiastical Polity* was written for the purpose of showing that Episcopal government could be defended not only as an apostolical institution but on grounds of general utility. An Episcopacy which could only be defended by the arguments of expedience

[1] Letter, Bowes to Burghley, *Calendar of State Papers of Scotland*, Vol. X, p. 428.

and antiquity, however, did not go far enough for Bancroft and his followers. They must meet their opponents by maintaining the divine obligation of Episcopacy, and it was this theory which the prelate brought forward for the first time in British History.[1] Henceforth there was a large section of the Church maintaining an " exaggerated conception of both monarch and bishop which was to find mature expression in Laud."[2] This new position, as Dr. Gwatkin points out, was not very consistent with the Articles, the Ordinal or practice of the Church of England, but when the shock of novelty was overcome, it gained ground as a short and easy way with the Puritans and it had far-reaching effects.[3] While Davidson had not joined issue with Bancroft on this particular theme, the uncompromising Presbyterian must have found the prelate's contention stiffen his defence of his own Church, of whose *ius divinum* he was never in any doubt.

It might have been thought that after Davidson's telling reply, Bancroft would have exercised some caution, but subsequent events show that he remained as domineering and vituperative as ever. Having succeeded to the primacy, he carried through Convocation a code of canons which declared the royal supremacy over the Church and which were aimed at the Puritans. The result of the demand for subscription meant the deprivation of three hundred ministers who refused to comply.[4] So far from abandoning his scornful and hostile attitude he continued to publish

[1] Gwatkin, *Church and State in England*, p. 264.
[2] Mackinnon, *A History of Modern Liberty*, Vol. III, p. 25.
[3] Gwatkin, *Church and State in England*, p. 264.
[4] Mackinnon, *A History of Modern Liberty*, Vol. III, p. 24.

works which by their abusive nature added to his earlier offence.[1] In one of these he complains of the Scottish ministers attempting to " cast some of their contentious and disloyal seeds into England " and the only proof he can offer of his statement is Davidson's pamphlet which was called forth by his own " virulent invective ".[2]

It has been said that, at a later period, the Archbishop became milder and turned from the persecution of the Puritans to administrative reform.[3] That day surely had not yet dawned, when Andrew Melville, on trial before the Privy Council in London, made most effective reply to his insolent accusation of treason. " My lords," exclaimed he, " Andrew Melville was never a traitor. But, my lords, there was one Richard Bancroft (let him be sought for) who, during the life of the late Queen, wrote a treatise against his Majesty's title to the Crown of England ; and *here* (pulling the *corpus delicti* from his pocket) *here* is the book which was answered by my brother John Davidson."[4] Proceeding to address the stunned and silenced Primate, Melville referred to the book in which he had attacked Presbyterianism. " If you are the author," he said, " of the book called *English Scottizing for Geneva Discipline*, then I regard you as the capital enemy of all the Reformed Churches in Europe, and as such

[1] Calderwood, Vol. IV, p. 175. Bancroft's other publications are (1) *A Survey of the Pretended Holy Discipline ;* (2) *Dangerous Positions or Scottish Genevating and English Scottizing for Discipline ;* printed in 1593 and reprinted in 1662.

[2] *Dangerous Positions*, p. 30.

[3] Gwatkin, *Church and State in England*, p. 276.

[4] McCrie, *Life of Melville*, Vol. II, p. 159. This interesting passage is difficult to understand. There is no reference to the King's title to the English throne either in Bancroft's sermon or Davidson's reply. Yet Row refers to the treatise and reply more than once (*Hist.*, pp. 220, 285). Bancroft's work is also referred to by John Forbes (*Hist. of Ref.*, p. 33.)

I will profess myself an enemy to you and to your proceedings to the effusion of the last drop of my blood."[1] The calumniator of the Scottish Church had produced an indelible impression of evil upon the mind of this, as of every, faithful Scottish Presbyterian.

[1] M'Crie, *Life of Melville*, Vol. II, p 159.

CHAPTER V

ACTIVITIES FROM 1591 TO THE CALL TO PRESTONPANS IN 1595

THERE is nothing to record of Davidson's activities after he resumed the work of the regular ministry at Canongate till he came again into conflict with King James. Preaching on Sunday, June 6th, 1591, in his Majesty's presence, he admonished him with pointed severity, upbraiding him with want of success in the execution of justice, and affirming that he and his council lacked the assistance of God because he had not sufficiently repented of his former sins.[1] Two days later Davidson was brought before the court with other members of his Presbytery when the King demanded that they should desist from using such public censures. His Majesty alleged that David Lindsay had promised him, in the name of the ministry " another sort of behaviour ", but since the promise had not been kept, he was determined to have a General Assembly held at Edinburgh where that and other matters would be discussed. The ministers, convened in the Little Kirk, agreed to make arrangements in accordance with the King's wishes, but also to express to him their regret that he had accused them before the Lords of Session, some of whom were not very friendly disposed to them.

When the brethren appointed to take the Presbytery's reply to his Majesty, received access,

[1] Calderwood, Vol. V, p. 130.

James took the initiative by declaring that they ought to affirm nothing in the pulpit concerning vice until men were actually convicted by the law. Davidson, who seems to have been the leader of the deputation, ignoring that statement, conveyed to him the ministers' answers, and thereafter discussion turned upon that ever-recurring question—the power of the King and the jurisdiction of the Kirk. James alleged that none could charge him with any personal faults and therefore he would use the power of his office and his authority over them because they did so often exceed their duty. Davidson answered that the office of the ministers consisted for the most part in words and warning, but that of his Majesty in deeds. He counselled the King to use his regal authority against malefactors rather than ministers and he maintained that there was great complaint among the people that justice was not at all executed and almost every criminal was spared.[1] The King was so angry at these words that he threatened to correct Davidson as he had done others before. However, the royal wrath was appeased by the preacher's assurance that he and his brethren loved his Majesty and just because of their love, used such freedom with him. And so they parted on friendly terms.

In this same year, in the month of December, Davidson was afforded another opportunity of proving his zeal in conversation with the King. The ministers of those days claimed spiritual authority not only over congregations but also over households, and in the different presbyteries prominent families had to undergo a somewhat rigorous examination. The

[1] Wodrow MS., p. 25. Calderwood, Vol. V, p. 131.

Presbytery of Edinburgh, after completing the visitation of the particular congregations under their care, resolved not to omit their duty to the Royal house. So Davidson with two of his brethren, went down to Holyrood Palace on the 8th " to try what negligence was in pastors, and abusses in the familie ". They went again on the 10th when the King himself was present. They urged him to have some part of the Scripture read at dinner and supper time, and willed that new elders should be chosen for the session of his family, advising that the Comptroller should be left out of the new nominations, because his life was not so exemplary as such an office required.[1]

Davidson's hearty concern for the King and his household did not rest there however. The following week he visited the Palace alone and obtained a private interview with his Majesty, telling him that he had come to speak about some matters which he had not felt inclined to mention publicly, at the visitation. James seemed to take that in good part and Davidson went on to admonish him of what, in the Church's opinion, was his present great neglect of justice, the appointment of incapable magistrates, the placing of unfit men in positions of trust, and his unjustifiable clemency to offenders. James gave plausible answers to most of these charges. He found, he said, no concurrence in inferior magistrates ; many diverse officers claimed their place by heritage ; and while he was as careful as possible over pardons granted, yet sometimes amid the multiplicity of his business, some would deceive him and secure stolen subscriptions—a matter most difficult to avoid. Time not

[1] Calderwood, Vol. V, p. 140.

permitting of further conversation, Davidson asked if he might come again and his request was granted.[1]

Supporters of the Reformation became perturbed anew in November 1592 by accounts of the restless practices of Papists and also by the restoration to favour of the King's evil advisers. The ministers of Edinburgh applied to his Majesty who agreed to the holding of a Convention of well-affected noblemen, barons and burgesses to consult upon measures for personal safety, and other ministers were invited to come to Edinburgh to give their advice.[2] The result was the appointing of a solemn fast to be kept on December 17th and 24th ; and a committee was chosen, Davidson being a member, to meet every week to watch and report upon any proceedings of Papists that might come to light, and *providere in omnibus ne quid ecelesia detrimenti capiat.*[3] Meanwhile Davidson preaching on December 3rd from Exodus on the constancy of Moses and Aaron, showed the duty of the servants of God to follow their example, especially when men were so loth to forsake their evil ways. He discoursed upon the obstinacy of the enemies of Christ in Scotland, including the Queen Regent, the Queen Mother, and others, and their abiding influence " which appeareth now in bringing backe Captan Stuart to continue the same course ". Using as illustrations the history of Absalom, Joab, David and the woman of Tekoa, Calderwood[4] tells us, he described the evil nature of Arran, and the manner of

[1] Calderwood, Vol. V, p 140.
[2] Ibid., p. 179.
[3] Ibid., p. 181.
[4] Ibid., p. 188.

his return which tended to preferment, contrary to the promise of the King.

The fast began with a service in the East or Little Kirk of Edinburgh on the morning of the 17th and Davidson was again the preacher. His sermon on that occasion was very vehement and many of its expressions were highly displeasing to the Court. Particularly objectionable was the statement that, since D'Aubigny's coming to Scotland the King had received infection, which if vomited not out, he would not escape severe judgment ; that the corpse (meaning the Earl of Moray's mangled body) cried to the Abbey for justice, but neither the living nor the dead could procure justice to be executed, howbeit great severity had been used against the servants of God. The King, when informed of these expressions—which possibly were exaggerated to him—swore that Davidson would no longer be suffered to teach in Edinburgh. The Duke was so angry that he desired to kill him. Upon the following Thursday, James complained of him to the magistrates and ministers of Edinburgh. " I marvel much of Mr. Davidson," said he, " for I heard once that he was one of the greatest theologues in Scotland and learned and well approved both at home and abroad, and sometimes I have had good proofs of him in privy conference. But now I cannot tell how he is become so phrenetick that he does little but make ballads and playbills, and all his teaching is turned to railing against me and the State." Then the King asked the Provost if he was their ordinary minister and on receiving a negative reply asked further " What did he there ? " The Provost said that the Kirk Session had a warrant to place any preacher they pleased at that hour. "If yee avow him to be yours," said the King, "yee sall answere for him ; if not, I will not suffer him to byde there."[1] The ministers asked James to leave the Kirk to deal with him.

Notwithstanding his Majesty's threats, Davidson preached the next Sabbath in the same place. Acting upon the advice of some of his friends who lamented his excessive zeal, he was on this occasion very apologetic, protesting that he loved the King and his welfare in body and soul and he repeated the similitude he had used a week before, that " honie slipped doun to the bottom of a sore, and did byte als much as any liquor, and yitt ceased not to be sweete."[2] The ministers were about to meet and advise what was fit to be done for warranting his calling to preach in the Little Kirk without irritating the King. The matter, however, was disposed of more easily by Davidson himself who proposed to desist, considering the season of the year and his growing age and infirmity. After preaching a few more Sabbaths and realizing that some of the ministers and magistrates were " miscontent with his rough applicatioun " he was as willing to remove from them, as they were to part with him.[3] He did not appear again therefore in the Little Kirk till March 18th, 1593, when he declared the cause of his long absence and suggested that Satan envied his ministry, that his calling to them was questioned by the Court, and the magistrates had denied him to be their minister, though he was called by the Synod, the

[1] Calderwood, Vol. V, p. 191.
[2] Ibid., p. 192.
[3] Ibid.

Presbytery and the Session.[1] He desired the godly
not to blame him if he came not there again and said
that they might get worse guests in his place. His
hearers were much moved and shed many tears, not
without reason, for he was " a faithful watchman,
forewarning dangers, a free rebuker of sin, a familiar
and sensible teacher."[2] Calderwood relates[3] that on
the same day Davidson conferred with Andrew
Melville upon the iniquity of the time. It was natural
that two such scholars should descant on the words
of the Apostle in Ephesians iv., κυβεια των ανθρωπων
and a phrase of Cyprian, *Anceps temporum palpator*.
Melville complained that the ministry was now
turned to a kind of political dealing and that he never
thought to have seen such a general desertion and
coldness in his days ; a sentiment with which Davidson
doubtless found himself in entire agreement.

At the beginning of 1593 the city of Edinburgh
was greatly excited by the news that a fresh Popish plot
had been discovered of startling importance. We
must briefly relate the facts, as it will be seen that
John Davidson had a keen interest in the event.

For almost a quarter of a century the Roman
Catholics in Scotland had been plotting and scheming
to recover the ground lost to them through the
Reformation. Their hopes which had centred largely
upon the help of France or Spain did not materialize,
and even the crushing defeat of the Armada did not
serve to convince them that their project was doomed
to failure.[4] When, in 1592, the Church of Scotland

---

[1] This must have been simply as an occasional preacher.
[2] Calderwood, Vol. V, p. 238.
[3] Ibid.
[4] Maclean, *The Counter-Reformation in Scotland*, p. 71.

8

secured what is known as her charter of liberties, the Act of Parliament, sanctioned rather unwillingly by the King, formally ratified all previous legislation in favour of Presbyterianism and confirmed all repressive measures against Roman Catholics.[1] It was therefore a case of " now or never " with the Catholic nobles ; they must strike quickly before Presbyterianism should attain to complete supremacy. Too weak however, to do anything of themselves they must again seek foreign aid. So the next two years saw their last and rather desperate effort to overthrow the Protestant settlement and win Scotland again for the Pope.

The story of that final attempt and its failure is the story of the " Spanish Blanks ".[2] George Ker, brother of Lord Newbattle, was to be sent to King Philip of Spain with letters from the earls Huntly, Errol and Angus, soliciting his help in an effort to seize James VI and convert Scotland to Romanism, as preliminary to a similar attempt on England. A Spanish army was to land either at Kirkcudbright or in the river Clyde and such forces as the Earls could raise would be ready to act in concert with it. Ker was entrusted also with certain blank letters subscribed and sealed by the earls, with a commission to William Creighton S.J. (with whom the idea had originated), to fill them up with the above details and use them as he thought fit. The plot was found out, probably by the sharp-eyed English ambassador Bowes, who is thought to have given warning to some of the ministers.

[1] *Acts of Parliament of Scotland*, Vol. III, p. 541. Calderwood, Vol. V, p. 162.
[2] Elder, *Spanish Influences in Scottish History*, pp. 181-231. Law, *Collected Essays*, pp. 244-76. Walsh, *The Jesuits in Great Britain*, pp. 182-4. Calderwood, Vol. V, pp. 224-6.

Ker was seized off the island of Cumbrae as he was about to set sail by Andrew Knox, minister at Paisley, and some Glasgow students, who found in his possession the incriminating papers. He was taken to Edinburgh and placed in the Tolbooth and his associate, the notorious Graham of Fintry, was soon after apprehended. The King, who was absent at the time, was summoned home and was met by loud demands on the part of the ministers, magistrates and others for the arrest and punishment of the plotters. He must, they said, " tak ordour with the unnatural subjects, betrayers of thair countrey to the crewall Spanyeard ".[1] James, however, showed his usual weakness, and exasperated an excited and fearing people with a series of trifling complaints instead of promptly dealing with the matter, despite a strong urge from Elizabeth, who had heard all about it. It is true that he announced the discovery of the plot in a royal proclamation in which he promised to take drastic measures against the Catholic nobles and the Jesuits. But Scotland was tired of his promises so often unfulfilled ; the nation wanted deeds, not words; and the ministers, the guardians of the people's rights, urged him to immediate justice lest an undying stain should rest on his name and "the chronicles keep in memory James the Sext to his shame".[2]

So far no details of the plot were known and people were left guessing till Ker was forced by torture to make a confession. Similar disclosures were made by Graham of Fintry, who was immediately tried, convicted and executed at the Mercat Cross of

[1] Melville's *Diary*, p. 307.
[2] Ibid.

Edinburgh.[1]   Ker was kept in prison, but, like Angus,
whom the citizens of Edinburgh had arrested, managed
to escape probably by bribing the guards.   The
depositions of Ker and Graham were set forth in a
black letter tract, published with royal authority by
the King's printer, Waldegrave, and it was reprinted
almost immediately in London.   It was entitled
*A Discoverie of the Unnatural and Traiterous Conspiracie
of the Scotisch Papists against God, His Kirke, their Native
Cuntrie, the Kinge's Majesties Person and Estate.* Set
doune, as it was Confessed and Subscrivit be
Mr. George Ker, yet remaining in Prisone, and David
Graham of Fentrie, justly executed for his Treason in
Edinburgh, the 15 of Februarie 1592.   Whereunto
are annexed certaine intercepted Letters, written by
sundrie of that factioun to the same purpose."[2]   It
seems quite evident that John Davidson was the editor
of that tract[3] and that he wrote for it a short preface,
giving the story of the plot as gathered from the
confessions of its principals, and describing the blanks
—" Quhilkes blankis hes no designation on the bak,
nor declaratioun of the causes for the quhilk thai wer
send, bot blank and quheit on baith sydes, except the
said subscriptiounis." His address to the reader is
very brief but states clearly the purpose of the short
publication. " Many and dangerous points of
unnatural and treasonable practises of Scottish
Papists," he says, against their country, King and God,

---

[1] Fintry had a chequered career. Davidson and others had opposed a
supplication in his favour made to the Assembly in 1590. Calderwood,
Vol. V, p. 86.

[2] The tract is reproduced in Pitcairn's *Criminal Trials*, Vol. I, pp. 317-35.
It was first printed and published at Edinburgh in 1593. Later editions
appeared in London, 1603, and in Edinburgh, 1626 or 1627.

[3] Law, *Collected Essays*, p. 257. *Cf.* Calderwood, Vol. V, p. 251.

having come to light by the mercy of providence and the confession of some of the evil-doers, it has been thought good that the most substantial points of their depositions should be taken out of the original confessions and for the help of the reader gathered into this form following. Some of the most remarkable intercepted letters he indicates had been deciphered, translated and printed for the use of the people, to the glory of God, the edification of the Kirk and the " perpetual detection and shame of the unnatural enemy". All these things are so faithfully done, he maintains, in the volume following that no one can accuse the writer or writers of any false statement. The reader is then invited to note carefully the following considerations : (1) The goodness of God in delivering His Kirk from " such deep and dangerous practices " so cunningly and craftily conceived by a deadly enemy. (2) The necessity of being wakeful and alert regarding the power of those who are so cruel and diligent ; they must not be regarded as sleeping, for they are still planning evil to Scotland and encouraging the Spaniard in his cruel enterprise. (3) All true Scotsmen ought to unite to overthrow an enemy whose wickedness is unsurpassed, whether one considers the barbarity of selling King and country to Spain, or the pretence of friendship to the true religion which they have professed and in which they have participated. (4) What evil would happen to the Kirk, the commonwealth and the Prince, and to the miserable wretches themselves if their woeful purpose were successful ! (5) All good men and lovers of their country should be brought speedily to a state of repentance to the Lord, and to a resolve to withstand, according to their station in life, these desperate attempts on the common weal 'ere it is too late. They ought also, he adds, to take a part in the execution of justice upon the detected traitors, that such evils may be prevented and so the Lord, having begun the work, will bring it to a happy end.[1]

The necessity for this appeal was now as apparent to everyone as it was to Davidson himself. The discovery of the " Blanks " had brought to an end a period of prolonged nervous tension, and the certain danger of which all were now aware, was, at any rate, preferable to the haunting dread which for long had perplexed the lovers of the Reformed Church. Yet grave suspicion was still entertained concerning the King, who undoubtedly was not free from negotiating with Spain himself, although certainly actuated by a different motive from that of the Catholic lords. It was very awkward for James that among the papers found upon Ker was a memorial of his own referring to a possible Spanish invasion of England. Whether it had been entrusted to Ker or had fallen accidentally into his hands, is not clear. Calderwood has a paragraph on it, entitled " The King privye to the Traffiquing " in which he writes : " Mr. Johne Davidsone in his Diarie,[2] recordeth on the 26th of May, that among the letters of the traffiquers intercepted were found one to the Prince of Parma which tuiched the King with knowledge and approbation of the traffiquing, and promise of assistance, etc., but that it was not thought expedient to publishe it. Mr. Johne was acquaint with the discoverie and all

---

[1] Pitcairn's *Criminal Trials*, II, pp. 317-19.
[2] Davidson's Diary unfortunately has not been preserved. Calderwood had the use of it when writing his *History*. See Vol. VIII, p. 129.

the intercepted letters, and made a preface to be prefixed to the printed discoverie, and a directorie for understanding the borrowed and counterfooted names."[1] The letter here referred to was separated from Ker's other papers—" withdrawn for the safety of His Majesty's honour ". It revealed that James in the summer of 1592 was at least prepared to consider the advantages to himself of a Spanish invasion of England but there does not seem to have been anything more in it than that. There is no evidence to be found of the King's " approbation " or " promise of assistance" said to be contained in it. Davidson, in the excitement and suspicion of the time evidently either misapprehended it or read more into it than was actually there.[2] It is remarkable that no reference was made to it either by Ker or Fintry at their trial. Perhaps they were unaware of its contents or, if they were, they may have felt that it would be unwise to challenge a King who probably would deny all and take speedy measures to secure the silence of his accusers. There seems to have been nothing more in it than another evidence of James's dominating passion to secure the throne of England, for which end he was prepared to seek Spanish aid, as he was prepared to do anything. Nevertheless the letter gave rise to fresh suspicions in the minds of the ministers and people that the conspirators " doubted not the King's consent to the enterprise " or " perceived him inclined that way ".[3] They could not help concluding that

[1] Calderwood, Vol. V, p. 251.

[2] T. G. Law, *Collected Essays and Reviews*, pp. 267-8. Dr. Law says the letter was printed in 1892 by the Commissioners of Historical Manuscripts in their report of the manuscripts preserved at Hatfield House.

[3] Elder, *Spanish Influences in Scottish History*, p. 205.

the King was playing them false. The chief offenders were still at large and it was thought that he was not anxious to bring them to justice. Ker's escape confirmed their fears and was the subject of great denunciation, and when the Papist earls escaped forfeiture in the Parliament of July 1593 indignation knew no bounds. On the Sunday following, Davidson preaching on 1 Thessalonians i:, denounced this as "a blacke parliament, becaus iniquitie was come in rowme of equitie in the high court of justice ". " Our arch-traitours," said he, "have not onlie escaped but in a manner are absolved, in that they have escaped as men against whom no probation could be gotten. The absolving of the wicked importeth the persecutioun of the righteous, except God restrained the adversareis." He prayed that " the Lord would compell the King by his sanctified plagues, to turne to Him rather er he perish ; otherwise that he should guide his governement to the weelefare of the Kirk, whether he would or not."[1]

The Provincial Synod of Fife, that stronghold of the Reformed Church, meeting at St. Andrews in September, championed the cause of the ardent Protestants and excommunicated the Popish earls, justifying the action on the grounds that these earls had been, sometime, students of the University of St. Andrews.[2] Davidson was evidently a correspondent from Lothian on that occasion as his name appears on some of the committees.[3] When the dangers of the time and ways of meeting them came

[1] Calderwood, Vol. V, pp. 255, 256.
[2] Ibid., pp. 261-2.
[3] Wodrow MS, p. 27.

up for discussion he was invited to give his judgment.
Beginning with what was now with him a deep-seated
conviction, he set down all the trouble first to the
coldness and negligence of the ministers themselves
and he expressed the fear that, unless that state of
affairs was remedied, greater evils would result both
to them and to the people. After an impertinent
interruption by Mr. Thomas Buchanan, lately
become a favourer of the Court, he continued, at the
request of the Moderator. He showed further that
the present danger was also in part due to the defection
of the King and his disposition presently alienated
from the good cause. There is little use, however, in
pointing out the causes of an evil if one has no remedy
for removing them, but Davidson had his remedy.
He proposed recourse to " the ordinary and lawful
armour of fasting and prayer ", and he suggested the
making arrangements for a universal fast and the
sending of a grave message on the situation to his
Majesty from all Synods. So great was his influence
and so weighty were his words that all his proposals
were cordially agreed to.[1] Next day he was by
appointment the Synod preacher in the Parish Church
of St. Andrews. Taking for his theme the parable of
the Good Steward, Luke xii., in the course of his
sermon he freely rebuked the ministers for their
negligence and profaneness, and declared that he
thought a great part of the ministry were " the
mirriest and carelesest men in Scotland" and that
their message was not faithfully discharged, to the
King in particular.[2]

[1] Calderwood, Vol. V, p. 262.
[2] Ibid.

The Synod, following the excommunication of the Popish earls, went on to make some important appointments affecting the situation. Certain brethren were to visit the King, the barons and the burgesses, craving their assistance in the face of the danger and in defence of Christ's Cause. Mr. Davidson, with two of his brethren, was directed to deal with the Earl of Morton and his wife, to rebuke them for receiving to their home and entertaining Papist enemies of the Kirk and country.[1]

The excommunicated lords, in refuge in the North, finding that their trial was delayed, gathered their forces together and resolved to proceed South. When this became known, the most zealous of the barons, gentlemen of Fife, Angus and Stirling, came to Edinburgh to consult with the ministers and others in Lothian loyal to the Reformed Faith, for the safety of king and country. The meeting was not a success from the point of view of the zealots, as nothing more was decided than to send commissioners on the subject to the King then at Linlithgow. They had hoped that an effort would have been made to resist the enemy, and some of them expressed themselves thus to Mr. Davidson : " It is not tyme to goe to reasoun with words, when the enemeis appeared with swords ; we will provide for ourselves if the mater goe this way. This course will overthrow us that are mett heere : we looked for another kind of dealing."[2]

Mr. David Lindsay, who was by this time showing great leanings to the Court side, was Moderator at this meeting. When it was about to terminate,

[1] Calderwood, Vol. V, p. 266.
[2] Ibid., p. 275.

Mr. Davidson craved a hearing, which having obtained with great difficulty, he delivered a " short harangue " in his usual bold, open and zealous manner. The matter of it did not differ much from his earlier deliverances on the same subject. They were considering, he said, the imminent danger they were in, the greatness of which could not be denied whether they considered its cause or the instruments of it. The cause of it he maintained, was the great sins in all estates. Ministers neglected their duty and became self-seekers and worldlings ; the Prince and nobility were become either enemies of God's truth or disobeyers of it. He asked, who among the nobility had cleansed his hands of sacrilege, notwithstanding the long crying of God's servants to that purpose ? Who had reformed his life or family ? Who had shown mercy to poor tenants ? As for towns and burgesses, great contempt for God's Word and the ministry was to be found in most towns throughout the country. The enemies were mighty and many, either openly professing punishment to the ministers or craftily dissembling the same to their greater danger. He concluded with the following words : " Now, we have to avert the caus [of the danger] by unfained repentance, and to meete the instruments as becometh. As for repentance, it is to be had by publict fasting and prayer, and quicke stirring up our dulnesse by choice men of the ministrie, which would be appointed heere presentlie, to continue heere, till we receave a confortable answere of the King to your commissioners ; and thereafter, take purpose, before we departed how to meete the enemies ; which thing if they did, for my owne part, I would take part with

them in death and life by God's assistance."[1] As he
was leaving, he addressed this message to the
Moderator : " I pray you, Mr. David, Moderator,
that yee give me not an answere to these things of
your owne head, untill yee receave it of your
brethrein." After some discussion a fast was agreed
on for the next Wednesday. Davidson urged that
there should be preaching on the morrow and as
long as they were to continue ; he offered to begin
himself if any would follow, " which Mr. David
Lindsay hearing, would not heare, but praised
God ".[2]

Several brethren came to Davidson to thank him
for his motion, saying that they had seen nothing in
the way of turning to God or savouring of godliness in
the gathering till he had spoken. No salutary result
followed the meeting, however, for, at Linlithgow in
a day or two measures were taken to protect the
excommunicated lords. The accounts of that caused
Davidson to use great plainness when he preached
from 2 Chronicles xxx., in the Little Kirk on November
1st, 1593. He said he feared it would fare with them
as it did with the Israelites, of whom 40,000 were slain
before they truly humbled themselves (Judges xx.).
He added : " we had als great right to mainteane the
possessioun of the truthe, whether the prince would or
not, as our forebeares had to bring it in, and putt us in

---

[1] Calderwood Vol. V, pp. 275-6.
[2] Ibid., p. 277. Lindsay and Davidson could not agree. The former was
" the minister whom the Court liked best ". A few weeks later than this an
amusing encounter took place between them. When Lindsay had hurried over
an evasive message from the King and " would have been at the prayer ",
Davidson said, " If this Assemblie did their duetie . . . ye should be putt
in the coale hous, for not urging our articles and returning such shifting and
trifling toys to us." Ibid., p. 283.

possessioun of it, whether the prince would or not, if need so required."[1]

The Assembly of May 1594 ratified the action of the Synod of Fife in excommunicating the earls, and when Parliament opened a little later, the King promised to take strong measures against them.[2] Not only were *they* attainted but " wilful hearers of the Mass " were ordained to be put to death and Papists who refused to satisfy the presbyteries were to be summoned before the Council. When the King and commissioners, however, intimated these decisions to the Presbytery of Edinburgh, bidding them praise God for his Majesty's proceedings and exhort all men to remove suspicion from him, Davidson was singularly unimpressed and was not slow to express his dissatisfaction. " One dead," he said with great daring, " if it were but to execute Mr. Walter Lindsay[3] for his idolatry would do more good than all the King's letters and the Commissioners both." He felt so strongly about it, that, in the Great Kirk, he preached one of his most vehement sermons from Ezekiel, Chapter xxii. He inveighed against the corruptions of ministers who, he maintained, winked at the profanation of the Sabbath, admitted all and sundry to the Holy Sacrament, stole the word from the people and failed to rebuke sin in Kirk and country. It was not that they preached false doctrine so much as that they delivered the truth so unfaithfully and so coldly

[1] Calderwood, Vol. V, p. 279.

[2] Ibid., p. 330.

[3] Ibid., p. 337. Sir Walter Lindsay became a Gentleman of the Bedchamber to James VI in 1580. He became soon afterwards a convert to Catholicism and, according to his own statement, the first whom Fathers Gordon and Crighton induced to recant and openly profess the old faith. *Register of Privy Council*, Vol. V, D.N.B.

as to leave their flocks consumed with hunger. They were also ambitious and wordly, thinking more about their stipends and the welfare of their wives than about theology. Going on to deal with the proceedings of Parliament and the commissioners' letter to the Presbytery commending the same, he said that he was prepared to excuse the writers if they went not too far in the matter afterwards. " For," he declared, " I take it to be the worke of God's almightie hand, hearing our prayers and making the King to doe what in the judgment of many, he inclined not to have done ; if he performe the mater it is weill. But I looke not for anie great good at his hand, till he repent him of his sinnes." He reminded his hearers of Charles IX of France who on the eve of the Massacre of St. Bartholomew had done more for the cause of Reformation than James and yet minded nothing but murder and massacre. He would not have the King to be prophesied such an one, although he regarded him as " rather vaunting himself than humbly craving for his sinnes on his knees with teares as he sould have done ; which if he doe not he must goe from evill to worse till he be destroyed."[1]

Davidson made it clear that he always spoke from a sense of duty and a real desire for amendment. In proof of that, his castigations fell alike upon all. The nobility were accused of oppression, sacrilege, blasphemy and even worse ; the common people, imitating them, were guilty of evil living and of holding the word and the ministry in contempt. A special charge was made against Edinburgh with his rebels against God and His Kirk, traffickers with

[1] Calderwood, Vol. V, pp. 337-8.

Spain, hinderers of the planting of parishes and those who had set up the Monday market, which would be chronicled to their shame.[1]

Such outspoken language and such biting criticism of all ranks have been strongly condemned by those living in quieter and milder times. As Wodrow points out, however, when such utterances as Davidson's are compared with Scripture precedents, when the necessity arising from the circumstances of the time is remembered as well as the obviously genuine love of the ministers for the King, it will be seen that there is not so much that calls for censure as at first appears.[2] Davidson, at any rate, was inspired by the purest motives and had no idea of having exceeded his rights as a preacher. So on the 29th of June, he followed the same line and reckoned up the judgments already begun in all ranks. The King, he declared, was given over to evil company and loved them so dearly that it was to be feared he was not sound at heart. Ere long that would be apparent to all, as it was now to those with greater foresight. The Queen, though not ill-disposed naturally was in danger of being corrupted by her associates. The nobility were either young or corrupt, plagues both to themselves and the land. Few among the earls and lords could be reckoned on the side of true religion, and the barons were almost gone. " As for Edinburgh," he said, " I feare more the multitude and bodie of Edinburgh to be persecutors of me and my brethrein, and their readinesse to concurre to take our lives from us, than I feare the court, except they repented."[3]

[1] Calderwood, Vol. V, p. 338.
[2] Wodrow MS., p. 29.
[3] Calderwood, Vol. V, p. 339.

It must not be thought that it cost Davidson nothing to preach so boldly or that he was never apprehensive as to the results of his daring words. Quite often he needed comfort and encouragement. At this time he became greatly affected by a seemingly trifling coincidence which happened at service one morning during the meetings of the General Assembly.[1] As he sat in Church he noticed the skipper of the ship in which he had left Scotland twenty years before, enter at one door, which brought to his thoughts the great deliverance which he then had from shipwreck. While musing on that, he saw enter by another door the skipper of the ship in which he had first set sail at Leith but which had been forced back by contrary winds. The sight of those two good men and the thoughts of the kind providence of God toward him in the days of suffering brought great comfort to his heart and he cared not whether he should be called to suffer for his speeches uttered so freely the week before, and all the reproofs of sin he had lately given. Yet he was not troubled for some time, notwithstanding the Chancellor's advice to King James that if he were removed out of Edinburgh and out of sight of the Castle, he would not make mention of them so often in his sermons.[2] His removal, however, was yet a whole year off. He continued to exercise his ministry quietly in his own parish, with an occasional excursion into the public affairs of the Church. The excitement caused by the Popish plots had not been forgotten and when the Earl of Angus applied to the Synod of Lothian for

[1] Wodrow MS., p. 30. Calderwood, Vol. V, p. 341.
[2] Davidson " would not lett the Castelians (that is these who keeped the castell in the last civil warres) alone." Calderwood, Vol. V, p. 358.

a " conference " in October 1595, Davidson set up a strong opposition. He blamed the King for the part which he had in the matter and for granting the Earl, an excommunicated person, permission to stay with a nobleman while the matter was pending. Concerning Angus he spoke on this wise, " It savoureth greatlie of defectioun in these dayes, that such a notorious rebell to God, his Kirk, and this realme, that hath so oft and in so high degree mocked the Kirk, should be heard, before farther tryell be had of his repentance. He has beene twise excommunicated, and ever deceaved the Kirk, and polluted the land with his messes. Therefore we ought to do nothing rashlie, in so grave and dangerous a mater, least a doore be opin to bring in the rest of God's enemeis, without better prooffe of their repentance and amendment, than we have yitt seene."[1] After some argument about procedure with his old opponent David Lindsay, he finally consented that the Earl "sould be tryed to the quicke, by some sound and judicious men, but without authoritie or warrant from the Synod ". The following day he desired the brethren to request the King to execute justice on so manifest a traitor.[2]

Though Davidson's brethren had nothing but admiration for his personal piety and his unflagging zeal as a minister, yet they were somewhat embarrassed by his outspoken denunciations. A section of them whose ardour was never great felt themselves condemned by his enthusiasm, while those most sympathetic to his views were not sure that his zeal was

[1] Calderwood, Vol. V, p. 383.
[2] Ibid., p. 384.

9

always accompanied by discretion. He was advised
to accept a country charge, as his presence in
Edinburgh seemed to be attended with difficulties.
In the spring of 1595 an attempt was made to have
him settled in the second charge of Haddington[1] but
negotiations seem to have been suddenly broken off.
Later in the year he received and accepted a " call "
to Prestonpans and on December 9th preached a
valedictory sermon in Edinburgh. As a fine apologetic
for his recent ministry in the city and an indication of
the Christian motive behind all his preaching, we set
down the conclusion verbatim : " I came not hither
by haphazard, but sent of God more than sevin yeeres
since. So long as I had place to teache, I dealt
faithfullie according to the meane measure of knowledge bestowed on me, after a rude and familiar way,
of verie purpose for edificatioun's sake ; whereas I
could have done otherwise if my conscience would have
suffered me. It was compted rude and rough by
manie ; but I thanke God I wist what I spake. So
that I have uttered nothing against preacher, or
people, which I have not my warrant for, and by the
helpe of God will stand to the defence of it, in the
face of man or angell. So that my first preaching
and last are one, without differing, to witt, that the
princes of the land, the King, the chiefe prince, with
the rest of the rebellious nobilitie, the profane ministrie
are negligent for the most part to winne soules, and
the rebellious multitude sall be severlie punished except
they repent. I have sought to be away, but could
not till now that it has pleased the Lord to ryppin
my departure. It was nather a drinke of the Muse

[1] Scott's *Fasti*, Vol. I, p. 27.

Well, nor anie other benifite in Edinburgh that drew me to it like an adament stone, as some speeke, or that keeped me heere ; but the mightie hand of God sent me hither for causes known to Him. And so having cleered my ministrie hitherto, I take my leave of you in Christ."[1]

[1] Calderwood, Vol. V, p. 387.

CHAPTER VI

MINISTRY AT PRESTONPANS (1596-1604)

THE ecclesiastical history of Prestonpans goes back several centuries before the Reformation, and as early as 1320 it was a vicarage belonging to the Abbey of Holyrood.[1] The manorial chapel, ruins of which remained as late as the beginning of the seventeenth century, in common with many other church buildings, was burned down in the devastating expedition of the Earl of Hertford in 1544—a destruction, like others, wrongly attributed to Knox and his fellow reformers. For fully half a century thereafter the people of Preston and Salt Preston had no church, and little or nothing seems to have been done to provide them with religious ordinances. Those who desired to enjoy Protestant worship had either to avail themselves of the occasional ministrations of the minister of Musselburgh, or attend the Church of Tranent with which they considered themselves to have some parochial connection but which was three miles away. The circumstances were very unsatisfactory and few seem to have been interested enough to do either. In course of time Presbytery and Synod alike felt the growing need of a separate charge for the " populous tounes of Preston, the Grange and the Pans ", but for lack of means nothing was done. At length, however, Hamilton, Laird of Preston, offered a site as well as monetary contributions, for the erection of a Church and the finding of a stipend. The Presbytery,

[1] Scott's *Fasti*, Vol. I, p. 387.

encouraged by this generosity and influenced by the spiritual needs of the district, set about to induce Mr. John Davidson to become minister of the evangel within the bounds of " South Preston and ye Panns, east and west, and ye haill bounds yairabout, belonging, alsweill to my Lord Newbottle, as to ye laird of Prestoun ".[1] The Presbytery of Edinburgh was approached and consent was given, provided that Davidson was agreeable and sufficient provision was made for his maintenance.[2] We have no hint as to why the Presbytery of Haddington should have been so anxious to secure Davidson for such a charge. Remembering, doubtless, the ancient zeal of the Preston branch of the house of Hamilton for the Reformed doctrines, they probably felt that a man of such perfervid enthusiasm would fit splendidly into the situation. They may also have been influenced by the consideration that, since he was a man of private means, the matter of stipend would not be so pressing, at least at the beginning. Whatever their motives, Davidson at any rate acceded to their request without waiting for any guarantee as to what provision might be made for him. More important considertions weighed with him. He desired, for one thing, a "lawful call" and for that end preached at Salt Preston on November 19th 1595, and again on December 17th.[3] The impression he produced on these occasions was more than favourable. One wonders, however, *where* he preached ; was it on the sea-shore, the public street or in some hired house, since there was no

[1] It seems that the original parish church would be located at Preston. McNeill, *Prestonpans*, p. 29.
[2] Records of Presbytery of Edinburgh.
[3] Struthers' MSS.

Church ?   On that point there is no reliable information.   We are more fortunate, however, concerning
the theme of the discourses, at least on the first
Sabbath.   In the preface to his Catechism,[1] Davidson
reminds his flock that on his first appearance in their
midst he took for his text " the people which sat in
darkness saw great light " (Matthew iv. 16), while
his subject in the afternoon was Revelation iii. 20 :
" Behold I stand at the door and knock."   Referring
to the former sermon, he says, " I made choice of this
place of Scripture, to bee as a ground of that doctrine
whilk thereafter I minded to builde thereupon, during
our continuance together at God's pleasure."   Then
he goes on to show how he treated the subject.   After
speaking to them of God's mercy in offering to them
again the light of His Gospel, he gathered " some
general grounds of Christian religion " from the text
after this manner.   First, the miserable blind estate
of man by nature.   Secondly, the most comfortable
light of salvation in Christ.   Thirdly, that men receive
Christ's light by faith wrought by the Holy Spirit in
the preaching of the Gospel.   Fourthly, the end that
walking in that light of Christ, we may glorify him who
has translated us out of darkness into his wonderful
light.[2]

    After that first Sabbath—the Presbytery's record
runs—" ane gritt multitude of ye honest men of the
both tounes aforesaids came and shew yair guid
lyking of ye said Mr. John and his doctrine, to us of
ye Presbytery, disyring us maist earnestly with ane
voyce yat we wald hald hand to the work for bringing

---

[1] Discussed in Chapter IX.
[2] Bonar, *Catechisms of the Scottish Reformation*, p. 326.

and planting ye said Mr. Johne to be minister among yame with all diligence." The brethren readily responded to such an earnest petition and instructed their Moderator, James Gibson, to write "maist affectionately" to Davidson on the matter.

The second visit evidently did more than confirm the earlier impression and the greatest enthusiasm prevailed. When the preacher appeared at the Presbytery of Haddington a day or two later, the brethren praised God for his coming. A number of parishioners were also present and on being asked if they liked Mr. Davidson, answered "with ane voyce as of before, that they were wiell contented with him and feirit nathing to separate him fra them but yair awin unworthynes." They besought the Presbytery "to travell for his provision and settling among yame."[1]

Everything pointed to a very happy settlement—a competent faithful minister and an enthusiastic expectant people—even if it had to begin without church, manse or stipend. The prospect, however, was indeed brighter than had at first appeared, for, at Mr. Davidson's request, the Presbytery had secured the goodwill and assistance of Lord Newbottle,[2] and Mr. George Hamilton, laird of Preston, was always ready to help. So the Presbytery, praising God for the great success and the consent of all the chief persons interested, served the edict at Tranent and "Ye panis," and Mr. Davidson was inducted on January 5th 1596. James Gibson presided and

---

[1] Records of Presbytery of Haddington. Struthers' MSS.

[2] Lord Newbottle was not on the most friendly terms with the laird of Preston, the party mainly interesting himself in the appointment.

preached[1] and there was " ane verie frequent convention of ye parochiners and chief persones yairof".
At the close of his discourse Gibson called upon the
new minister to declare publicly whether he
acknowledged the proceedings thereof to be of God
and sufficient warrant for his conscience. Davidson
then delivered an earnest and moving address.[2] He
declared that besides the outward calling of the Kirk
and the people, he had also the effectual inward
calling of God. Since his work was quite evidently
finished in Edinburgh—where also he had been sure
of the Divine warrant—he was prepared to accept the
charge of that flock with certain stipulations. These
he proceeded to state, as follows : (1) so long as God
and His Kirk would think good and as infirmity would
serve, (2) so long as there was provision for his maintenance either by himself or from any other lawful
source, (3) so long as the people would be obedient
to the voice of God in his ministry, " wherein he would
crave no obedience of them bot according to the
reveilit will of God and His word", (4) So long as
they were willing to defend him against the persecution of such as would pursue him for the true and
lawful execution of his office. Evidently he anticipated
something in the nature of " Church Extension " for
he concluded by accepting " so great ane multitude
not to be a perpetual pastor but for ane tyme till
convenient occasion could be offerit that they would
be distribut in competent flocks."[3]

[1] The subject was Acts xvii. 10, 11, 12. " Bereans . . . searched the
Scriptures . . . therefore many believed." Struthers' MSS.
[2] Ibid.
[3] Ibid.

When the speech was ended, the congregation, on being asked if they were content to " allow and accept " of Mr. Davidson on the conditions he had set before them and if they would promise all due obedience to him as their pastor, according to the Word of God, consented most willingly " be ane uniform voice and gesture of holding up of their hands ". The commissioners of the presbyteries being witnesses, declared their approbation of the same, praying God to give success to the work.

And so the courageous John set himself to the greatest task of his life. The necessity of providing a church and manse, and having to rely upon his own resources for his temporal support surely presented difficulties great enough. But these were not all that he had to contend with in the initial stages of his new ministry. From an entry in his diary or a private burial register which he kept, it seems that he found it almost impossible to secure a place of interment for his parishioners. The quaint memoranda may be quoted as revealing a terrible state of affairs in those days. " Thomas Sherila ye first yat deied after my coming to Prestoun. The lairde's boundes having nae buriall place and L. Setoun on ye east hand and L. Newbottle on ye west, refusing buriall to him in Tranent and ye west Kirke yarde ; I, Mr. John Davidsoun, new come to be minister at Salt-prestoun, wrote at ye desire of ye defunct's friendis west to Musselburgh Session for grant of buriall amang yame ; quhilk was granted on conditioun yat we sought not ye like again. Such was ye hardnes of ye entry of Godis word amang us. Hereupon ye Ladye Prestoun, Barbara Cockburne, dealt with ye Lairde,

George Hamiltoun, for grant of a piece of grounde at ye west syde of ye manse-houses and yarde, having James Pincartoun's yaird, where now our Kirke stands, on ye west syde thereof. This was a great ease provided of God in oure straite, for ye people were beginning to cry out and tumultuously to rage."[1]

The reference in the above record to the Kirk shows that Davidson had as soon as possible consulted the interests of the living by setting himself to secure a suitable place of worship. The Presbytery of Haddington, realizing the urgency of the matter, sought to assist the minister with the work. A Committee was appointed to confer with Lord Newbottle on the subject and also on the provision of a stipend. It looked at first as if his Lordship was to be most helpful, as he agreed to join in the undertaking with the Laird of Preston. He soon began to demur, however, to the Presbytery's proceedings, and so far from keeping his promise, is said to have become a hindrance " by lying out and causing his tenants also ly out."[2] Finally he excused himself on the grounds that he thought of repairing the Kirk (the ruined manorial chapel) on his own estate and providing a minister for it. Hamilton of Preston, however, without waiting for him, now volunteered the promised site for church and manse with three acres of land for a glebe, besides monetary assistance conjunctly with the rest of the people. Davidson then engaged to erect the Church at his own expense if need be. Through his influence in Edinburgh and surrounding

---

[1] Fraser : *Church and Manse*. Article by Struthers, p. 217.
[2] Struthers' MS. He became the subject of one of Davidson's prophecies. See Appendix H.

neighbourhood he was able to collect a considerable sum[1] but he gave lavishly of his own means. It is interesting to find that in material and personal service, people of all classes afforded him what assistance they could. Williamson of Mureston, the Laird's future son-in-law, provided the roof, and "like the ancient craftsmen of Jerusalem rebuilding portions of the city wall, the salters and sailors, and coal-hewers, and others, willingly co-operated to some small extent, but for the accomplishment of the whole, the gratitude of the district was specially tendered to Mr. John Davidson."[2] It must have been, however, a stupendous undertaking carried through with alternate hopes and fears and in the face of considerable opposition. Wodrow[3] gives some indication of that for he relates that Davidson, passing the building when in the course of erection, addressed a friend thus—" with difficulty did we get that Church brot that length, but those walls shall stand to the comming of the Lord, as witnesses against the hinderers of it, and God shall root them and theirs from this place."

Some interesting details of the Prestonpans ministry have been found in a charter[4] granted November 19, 1615, by John Hamilton of Preston the superior of the lands on which the Church was built.

[1] Fraser's *Church and Manse*, p. 217.
[2] Ibid.

No part of the ancient church remains. Over the principal or North door was a tablet with the inscription :
> Sedem dedit Prestouns :
> Aedificavit Davidsouns ;
> Texit Williamsonne.

Unfortunately, when the Church was partly pulled down in 1774 the tablet was destroyed.

[3] Wodrow MS., p. 41. Davidson said to a friend that he began the work with 50 merks and faith.

[4] Charter of Mortification, quoted by M'Crie, *Life of Melville*, Vol. II, p. 510.

Davidson is said to have deserved highly of the whole Church and commonwealth and particularly of Saltpreston. Reference is made not only to the Church which he built there but also to the fine clock with which it was furnished, to the Manse, the garden and the glebe. It is stated that he preached for many years without any fee or reward and that death alone had prevented him from carrying out his intention of selling his whole patrimonial inheritance, consisting of valuable houses and lands in Dunfermline, and devoting the proceeds to the support of the church and ministry of his parish.

Like many of his contemporaries, the minister of Prestonpans was deeply interested in education.[1] He was one of the most learned men of his time and knew the value of his knowledge in the conflicts of the Kirk. He completed his great service to the community by building at his own expense a school in which instruction was to be given in Latin, Greek and Hebrew, and he also provided a dwelling-house for the master.[2] Nor was that all. By bequeathing his furniture, his clothes, his library, his bills and obligations for debts owing him, and all his money, with the exception of one or two legacies to friends, he secured its future. The endowment[3] was sufficient to attract as the first master, Mr. Alexander Hume, a noted scholar, who passed to it from the rectorship of the High School of Edinburgh in July 1606,[4] nearly two years

[1] The Melvilles did much for education. James Melville paid the salary of a schoolmaster out of his own stipend. Howieson endowed a school at Cambuslang.

[2] M'Crie, *Life of Andrew Melville*, Vol. II, p. 510.

[3] Said to be £1,400 Scots. (XIVc ji) Rogers, *Three Scottish Reformers*, p. 52. Scott's *Fasti*, (1866), p. 349.

[4] Steven, *History of High School of Edinburgh*, p. 42.

after Davidson's death. The minister's endowment remained the only provision for the educational wants of the district for nearly two centuries. When in 1803 it became compulsory by Act of Parliament to have parochial schools, the buildings erected by Davidson were restored and the master provided with statutory emoluments. That has been described as practically an appropriation of Mr. Davidson's endowment by the parochial landowners.[1]

Davidson's advent to the district of Prestonpans seems to have led to a quickening of spiritual life. A significant minute of Presbytery soon after his settlement runs as follows :—" The haill gentlemen being required to reform their houses and use prayers at morn and evening, with reading of the Scriptures after dinner and supper, promised to obey ; and for execution thereof every minister was ordered to visit their houses and see whether it was so or not ; and for behoof of the unlearned Mr. John Davidson was ordained to pen short morning and evening prayers, with graces before and after meat, to be communicated to each minister for behoof of his flock." These forms of prayer Davidson submitted to a later meeting of Presbytery where they were approved and ordered to be printed.[2]

Under such an earnest ministry the Church at Saltpreston made steady progress. On 27th December, 1597 " the lands and barony of Preston and the Pans " were dissolved from the vicarage of Tranent

---

[1] Rogers, *Three Scottish Reformers*, p. 52. According to Struthers the master was entitled to the additional emoluments provided by Davidson, yielding annually five per cent. of the original endowment.

[2] *Miscellany of Wodrow Society*, Vol. I, pp. 538-9. The Prayers will be found in Appendix E.

and erected into a distinct vicarage by James VI, " to be callit the Vicarage of Preston ".[1] Davidson was formally presented to it by his Majesty and was installed by the Presbytery on 12th January, following.[2] It was not till some considerable time after his death, however,—11th July, 1606—that, through increasing numbers, it was erected again into a parish by Parliament.[3]

So well did Davidson by the Church and people of Prestonpans that his name has become inseparably associated with the place. Surely we may dispute the verdict of a modern writer who ventures to say that had he remained at Holyrood instead of going to " this sea-coaste village " his name and fame as a reformer would have been much higher.[4] It is difficult to assess the value of the Prestonpans' ministry. That Davidson was held in the highest esteem by his people is obvious. He laboured among them untiringly, and for the instruction of youth, whose spiritual interests he had at heart, he prepared the Catechism already referred to and which we shall consider later. There also he is said to have penned a special version of the twenty-third psalm.[5] In 1598, on the 15th of July, a visitation of the parish was held by the Presbytery when, the minister being removed, the people were asked if they found anything in their pastor's life and conversation to find fault with. They answered they had nothing. Being demanded if he taught sensibly and plainly, " they all with ane voice

[1] Scott's *Fasti*, Vol. I, p. 387.
[2] Records of Presbytery of Haddington, Struthers' MS.
[3] *Acts of Parliament of Scotland*, Vol. IV, p. 302.
[4] McNeill, *Prestonpans and Vicinity*, p. 54.
[5] See Appendix F.

thanked God for him ". At this visitation, Davidson conveyed to his people the Manse on condition that they would refund the cost of erection save for " four hundred merks " which he bestowed as " a free gift ".[1]

There are one or two interesting incidents which happened in the period of the Prestonpans ministry, in which Davidson had a large share and these fall to be related ere this chapter closes.

It has been felt by students of this period that the Kirk sometimes exceeded its rights and dealt with matters which seemed to be outwith its province. The ministers, for example, constituted themselves a kind of moral police and no one, from the King and Queen down to the humblest subject was free from their censures. Davidson was one of a small but influential deputation, Melville and Bruce being the others, who were sent to the Palace of Holyrood to deal with the Queen concerning her religion, her favouring of the enemies of truth, and her light contemptuous criticism of the ministry. They were also to charge her with spending her time in frivolity with her maids and they were to offer to teach her the doctrine of the Church and the better way of life. Anne of Denmark, however, would not grant the ministers access ; she was busy at a dance and desired them to come at some more convenient time.[2] Whether the interview ever took place or not, we cannot tell. At this time there began those rumours which persisted through the rest of her life, that the Queen had embraced the Roman Catholic faith.[3]

---

[1] McNeill writing of Prestonpans in 1902 says : " The Parish still reaps the benefit of this sum as ' Davidson's Mortification.' " (p. 44.)

[2] Calderwood, Vol. V, p. 460.

[3] *Calendar of Domestic State Papers*, Vol. cclii, pp. 36, 391, quoted by Walsh, *The Jesuits in Great Britain*, p. 205.

One wonders if the ministers had any suspicion of that kind.

On January 17th, 1598, Davidson made his last visit to the Palace of Holyrood, where he was admitted to a private interview with the King.[1] To appreciate the matters referred to in this interview, it is necessary to recall the fanatical outbreak or " riot " of December 17th, 1596, when the King became alarmed for his personal safety. Although the ministers had little or nothing to do with it, they were held largely responsible and in consequence had to flee. James, turning the affair to the securing of his own ends with the Church, forbade assemblies to be held in Edinburgh and forbade the ministers to live together as they had done " in the circuit of the close ".[2] He was vested with power to make ministers preach or desist at his will and he was to have a voice in the filling of vacant churches.[3]

Davidson was resolved to speak frankly to his Majesty on certain of these subjects. He began, therefore, with the necessity of restoring the ministers' houses, but to that he received little reply. Then he touched on the choosing of the new ministers, in which he maintained the people had not had their privilege and the χειροτονια spoken of in Scripture, preserved to them. When the King declared that nothing had been done against their interests and that the Kirk and Council were satisfied save " five or six caprician heads and some foolish weomen ", Davidson replied that his Majesty was misinformed as he knew the whole

[1] Calderwood, Vol. V, pp. 677-80.
[2] Lang, *History of Scotland*, Vol. II, p. 422.
[3] *Register of the Privy Council*, Vol. V, p. 357. *Act. Parl. Scot.*, Vol. IV, p. 107. Calderwood, Vol. V, pp. 536-7.

multitude to be of a different mind, since the people's consent had not been obtained. He quoted Julian the Apostate as having said, " *Nescit recte imperare equis bobus, etc., qui nihil concedat eorum voluntati.*" " That is a good sentence," said the King. "Mr. Johne, take that sentence to yourself, for yee will give me none of my will." " Yes, Sir," answered Davidson, " so farre as may be, and may doe you good."

The next matter discussed at this interview was the relation between the King and the preachers. Davidson urged his Majesty to send for the clergy from time to time and confer with them familiarly, as he believed that would tend to promote mutual understanding and goodwill. While agreeing that the advice was good, James nevertheless said he would not send for them, but, if they came, as Davidson had done himself, he would make them welcome. Mr. John stated in reply that most of the ministers were not bold enough to make advances of their own accord but it would be a matter of great encouragement to them if they were sent for by their monarch.

The parties to the interview evidently agreeing " verie weill ", as his Majesty indicated—at least for the time being, Davidson intimated that he had some weightier matters to deal with but he desired not to irritate the King. He was encouraged to proceed since he had come in so friendly a manner. He then demanded that the right of publicly rebuking obnoxious persons might be restored to the ministers. The King, however, was not prepared to concede so much and warned the preacher not to meddle with Assembly decisions. A lively piece of dialogue followed. " I trust," said Davidson, "your Majestie will not deny us the priviledges granted to us by long custome and the lawes of the realme." " Yee may raise schisme that way," said the King. " Not we," said Mr. John, " yitt, *oportet haereses esse, ut qui probati sint, manifesti fiant.*" " O then, yee approve schismes and heresies ? " said James. " It followeth not, Sir," answered Davidson ; " Woe be to them by whom offences come. They are good as they are of God, but evill as occasioned by men." The King, becoming a little impatient and possibly feeling that he was having the worst of the argument, was about to retire with the angry retort, " Weill, doe as yee will " when Davidson " pulled upon his gowne sleeve " and held him fast till he had concluded his words of counsel. To his request that he should be dismissed with favour, his Majesty graciously complied, and clapping him on the shoulder said, " Mr. Johne, yee sall be welcomer with me because yee are plaine."

During the years spent at Prestonpans Davidson continued, as long as strength and opportunity permitted, to take a prominent part in the public affairs of the Church of Scotland. Not long after his settlement in 1596 he was called to be leader in a great movement of spiritual awakening which affected almost the entire Church and especially his ministerial brethren. In the ensuing years he was engaged in the early stages of the prolonged conflict with the King over his Majesty's fresh attempt to establish Prelacy. These matters were of such importance that they have been considered deserving of separate treatment in the two following chapters.

CHAPTER VII

THE REVIVAL[1] OF 1596

FROM his utterances, especially at the Synod of Fife in 1593 and at the Assembly in 1594 we have seen how grieved Davidson was over the growing apostasy of the people from true religion, and especially the carelessness and indifference of so many in the ministry. He was convinced that such slackness in life and conduct had much to do with the fears and difficulties from which the Church and Nation suffered. A generation had passed since the Reformation had brought to Scotland new life and enthusiasm, and many who had taken part in it were now no more. A revival of religious devotion was greatly needed. Again and again he had spoken out boldly on the subject and so had earned a good deal of ill-will for himself. At length, feeling very deeply that the prevailing corruptions were likely to lead to disastrous consequences, he sought the guidance of his own Presbytery of Haddington on the subject. There it was resolved to make a proposal to the Assembly that the " grosse sins " of all estates should be inquired into, and a memorial was accordingly drawn up.[2] This was probably from the pen of Davidson himself and if so, proves him very different from the firebrand

---

[1] The word " revival " was not used to describe a reawakening of religion in a community till 1702, according to the *Oxford English Dictionary*. It is, however, a convenient and appropriate word to use here.

[2] Calderwood, Vol. V, pp. 394 ff.

some have made him out to be.[1] It would be difficult
to find a more earnest, and yet restrained, statement of
so crying a necessity, suggesting minds wide awake to
the spiritual peril of the nation. It was described as
the advice of the Presbytery " tuiching the two heeds
propouned by the Commissioners of the General
Assemblie to their brethrein, to advise upon against
this Assemblie, viz., of Universall Repentance and
earnest turning to God ; and of order taiking for
resisting the enemeis and maintenance of the libertie
of religion and countrie." A few lines, however,
sufficed to deal with the second part, although at the
time a fresh attack upon the people's liberty was
expected from Spain and the Privy Council was seeking the Church's approval of the levying of a tax to
enable them to co-operate with England in preparing
for resistance. The conviction of the Presbytery
apparently was that little good would result from considering means of resisting the enemy, till reformation
of morals and manners had been brought about and
men were right with God. The overture dealt first
and specially with the sins of the ministers—" we
acknowledge our publict transgressions in our persons
and office particularly wherof the catalogue is in readinesse to be seen . . . least it be found, according to the
saying of the apostle, that we that teache others teache
not ourselves and so be found reprobats " (Joel. ii. 17 ;
Romans ii. 21). Next the sins of princes, magistrates, nobility and people were to be dealt with duti-
fully, faithfully and without flattery, " for their
true amendment " and for the " provocatioun

[1] Spottiswood and Law Mathieson write of him as if he had always been
hot and unreasonable.

of the whole bodie of the realme to earnest repentance ".

The Assembly met at St. Giles Cathedral, Edinburgh, on 24th March, 1596. It was the sixtieth held since the Reformation and Robert Pont, minister of St. Cuthbert's, a worthy and learned divine, was Moderator.[1] There were also present, among others, ministers whose fame as leaders of the Reformation Church is well known and whose names are held in honour to this day—the two Melvilles, Robert Bruce, Principal Rollock and Patrick Simson. When Davidson presented his overture, it gave rise to some discussion as to what had really brought the brethren together. Pont maintained that their first and chief purpose was to consult about resistance to the Spaniards. Though many agreed with him, yet the great majority on hearing the Commissioners' letter, felt that Davidson was right and that the communication from the Presbytery of Haddington on the state of religion and morals should be their main consideration. Quite evidently the Assembly was more concerned about righteousness than anything else ; piety was after all more than policy. Here was no body of mere, cold ecclesiastics bent upon some petty victory of their own, but a company moved by more serious considerations. Their present danger they considered to be the manifestation of God's wrath against them for their sins. More important meantime than how the enemy might be resisted, was the necessity for universal repentance and earnest turning to God— the best preparation against national disaster.

[1] *Book of the Universal Kirk*, p. 423. Calderwood, Vol. V, p. 394.

A resolution was agreed to that Davidson be asked
to " give up the particular catalogue of the cheefe
offences and corruptions in all estats ".[1] This proposal brought consternation to the King who feared
that it might have reference to himself. The following day he entered the Assembly and entreated for
sanction of the tax requested by the Privy Council and
was firmly informed that " the purging of offences "
must be dealt with first. With the approval of his
brethren Davidson insisted to his Majesty that the
estates of the exiled Popish lords which their families
still retained, should be confiscated and the proceeds
applied to the needs of the nation. To this James
gave an evasive reply but he expressed his willingness
to undergo ecclesiastical discipline if it were adminis-
tered privately and not during public worship.
Davidson thereupon exhorted the Assembly to do
their duty in dealing with his Majesty, and his freedom at this Assembly and in the King's presence was
so highly commended by the godly that they desired
it to be recorded for a testimony to posterity.[2] Next
day he presented the catalogue of offences in ministers,
which evidently met with unanimous approval, the
only emendation being suggested by Andrew Melville,
that there should be added in each case the censure
answerable to the offence. That was agreed to and a
committee was appointed for the purpose, consisting
of nine ministers " of scharpest and best insight "[3]—
Dalgleish, Blackburn, Balcanquhall, Macquherne,

[1] Calderwood, Vol. V, p. 396.
[2] Ibid., pp. 398, 399.
[3] Melville's *Diary*, p. 347.

Adam Johnston, Knox (nephew of the famous John), Law, John Johnston and Davidson himself.[1]

Terrible was the indictment which was made before the Assembly. No one was spared, from the King on the throne down to the meanest of his subjects.[2] It may be urged that it was rather a gratuitous and presumptuous thing to do, but the times and the circumstances warranted it. Besides, the earnestness of the compilers was obvious and their sincerity well proven by the strictures which they made upon their own order. More space was devoted to the abuses of the ministry than to the evils of the other estates put together. To-day it is difficult to believe—even making allowance for possible exaggeration—that such corruptions existed in the most sacred of all callings and in what, with an ignorance of history some have called " the good old days ". Mentioning first the sins of omission, the Assembly deplored such culpable negligence of ministers " as sall be found not givin to their booke and studie of Scriptures, not carefull to have bookes, not givin to sanctificatioun and prayer, that studie not to be powerfull and spirituall, not applying the doctrine to his corruptions, which is the pastoral gift, obscure, and too scholastick before the people, cold and wanting zeale, negligent in visiting the sicke, cairing for the poore, or indiscreit in choosing parts of the Word not meetest for the flocke, flatterers and dissembling at publict sinnes, and speciallie of great personages in their congregatiouns for flatterie or for feare." Then followed others equally culpable—" sleuthfull in the ministratioun of

[1] Calderwood, Vol. V, p. 396.
[2] *Book of the Universal Kirk*, Assembly 1596. Cunningham, *Church History of Scotland*, Vol. I, p. 430.

the sacraments and irreverent, as profaners, receaving cleane and uncleane, ignorants and senseless, profane and making no conscience of their professioun in their callings and famileis." But that was not all, although it would have been enough to justify the taking of some drastic action. The list of positive sins which follows is simply amazing, and if only the merest fraction were true, one can appreciate the anxiety of good men like Davidson to see something in the nature of amendment and revival. The Reformed Church at this period was evidently in a bad way, possibly due to the inevitable reaction after the enthusiasm of the early Reformation days. It is almost incredible that at any time it could be possible for an Assembly of the Kirk to give a deliberate judgment on its ministers, like this—" That suche as are light and wantoun in behaviour, as in gorgeous and light apparrell, in speeche, in using light and profane companie, unlaw-full gaiming, as dancing, cairding, dycing and siche like, not beseeming the gravitie of a pastor, be sharpelie and gravelie reproved by the presbyterie according to the degree therof ; and continuing after due admoni-tioun, that he be deprived as slanderous to the Gospell. That ministers being found swearers or banners, pro-fainers of the Sabboth, drunkards, fighters, guiltie of all these, or anie of them, to be deposed *simpliciter ;* and siclyke, leers, detracters, flatterers, breakers of promises, brawlers and querrellers, after admonitioun continuing therein, incurre the same punishment."[1]

After such a terrible list, it seems an anti-climax in evil to go on to speak of " unlawful trades and occupa-tions for filthie gains ", the keeping of taverns and the

[1] Calderwood, Vol. V, pp. 401-6.

exacting of excessive usury. These seem mild after the earlier accusations.

What was the Assembly to do in the face of an indictment which was known to be unanswerable? When the matter came before them two days later, they had no difficulty in reaching a speedy conclusion " that there should be a humiliation among the ministry before their departure". The choice of a man to lead them on such a solemn occasion was a matter requiring careful deliberation. Some of the best men in the house were nominated. Master Robert Bruce, the saintly Edinburgh minister, Robert Rollock, the learned Principal of the University in the same city, Andrew Melville, scholar and churchman, Patrick Simson, the historian, James Nicolson, a former Moderator, and John Davidson, the originator of the fast. Principal Rollock was chosen by the majority of votes " to make the exhortation " but for some reason which we do not know, he declined to act. His reluctance, however, must not be taken, as it has sometimes been, to mean that he was unsympathetic. It must be remembered that he was younger than most of his brethren and, although a very learned man, was no ecclesiastic and was of a timid and retiring disposition.[1] On his declinature, the Assembly turned to Davidson, and although he too was diffident about assuming such a responsibility, the brethren would hear of no excuse. He pleaded want of time for preparation ; it was now Friday and the act was fixed for Tuesday and he had to ride home to Saltpreston for Sunday duty among his own people. The Assembly felt, however, that the man with whom

[1] Calderwood, Vol. V, p. 732.

the proposal had really originated and who was so intimate with the whole matter, was best fitted to lead them in their confession. So the following ordinance was passed at next session :—" Concerning the defectiouns in the ministrie, the same being at length read out, reasoned and considered, the brethrein concluded the same, agreing therewith. And in respect that, by God's grace, they intend reformatioun, and to see the kirk and ministrie purged, to the effect the work may have the better successe, they think it necessar that this Assemblie be humbled for wanting suche care as became, in suche points as are sett doun, and some zealous and godlie brother in doctrine to lay them out for their better humiliatioun ; and that they make solemne promise before the Majestie of God, and make new covenant with him, for a more carefull and reverent discharge of their ministrie. To the which effect was chosin Mr. Johne Davidsone, and Tuisday nixt, at nyne houres in the morning, appointed in the New Kirk for that effect, wherunto none is to resort but the ministrie. The forme to be advised the morne in privie conference."[1]

According to this ordinance the form of procedure was agreed upon at a private conference on the Saturday and the following Tuesday the great day dawned. The meeting place was the same as that in which the Assembly had gathered during the past few days. It was known by different names, as the " New ", " East " or " Little " Kirk and was the eastern portion of St. Giles, partitioned off to serve as a parish church. Robert Bruce had become

[1] Calderwood, Vol. V, p. 401.

its minister in succession to Knox and had brought to it distinction, while in later days and through the baser uses to which it was put it was irreverently referred to as " Haddo's Hole ".[1] It was a most uncomfortable building with an earthen floor and could not be said to lend itself to the creating of a devotional atmosphere. The Reformers had thus to rise above their surroundings and could count on no external aids. The meeting began at nine o'clock and continued till after one. None but those entitled to be present were admitted, " the one Kirk doore being shutt, and the other sett opin for a certain space ", and so the company consisted of " foure hundred persons, all ministers or choice professors ".[2] We can well believe that it was a very solemn company, for all were gathered together after due deliberation, to acknowledge before God their individual sins and the sins of their order. Davidson was a leader who had won their respect by his fine Christian character, purity of motive, and zeal for the cause of righteousness. Besides, he was " an expert in deepening the sense of defection and shortcoming ". Beginning with prayer, he thereafter caused the Reader[3] to recite the thirteenth and thirty-fourth Chapters of Ezekiel, most appropriate passages that must have impressed everyone, for they dealt with the lying prophets and the shepherds who

[1] Melville's *Diary*, p. 352n.

[2] Calderwood, Vol. V, p. 406.

[3] In 1580 the General Assembly passed a resolution that the office of the Reader " is no ordinary office within the Kirk of God ", and in 1581 made an act that no one was to be admitted to the office " by any having power within the Kirk ". Readers, however, evidently continued without hindrance. McMillan, *The Worship of the Scottish Reformed Church*, pp. 112-13. Calderwood, Vol. III, pp. 471, 526.

feed not their flock. One wishes that the sermon which
followed had been preserved. Calderwood gives
us the merest outline of it.[1] While the preacher
disclaimed any qualification for the task with which
he was confronted, yet since God had chosen him
" the least worthie and unmeetest in the number "
to occupy the place of teacher that day, he came not
to be censured of them but to speak to them with the
authority of a teacher to his disciples. He granted
to them, nevertheless, the liberty to try the spirits
whether they were of God or not. He went on to
show that the purpose of their meeting was confession
of their own sins and promise of amendment for the
future. They were all to enter into a new covenant
with God that, being sanctified by repentance, they
might be the better able to provoke others to the same.
The preacher pressed home his message by urging
his hearers to examine themselves and compare their
advantages with those of the prophets mentioned in
their Scripture lessons, and see if there were not now
as many false and as few true and sincere prophets
as in the ancient days. Although avoiding anything
rhetorical, Davidson's preaching must have been
most impressive. " He was verie moving," says
the historian, " in application to the present times
so that within an hour after they entered the Kirk,
they looked with another countenance than that
wherewith they entered."[2] Evidently perceiving the
effect of his discourse and, like a real master of
assemblies, realizing his opportunity, he then exhorted
the brethren to enter into private meditation and

[1] Calderwood, Vol. V, p. 406.
[2] Ibid., p. 407.

confession, with promise and purpose of amendment.
Then it was that the ancient Cathedral Church saw
a strange sight. A sudden emotion took possession
of the gathering as they humbled themselves, and for
a quarter of an hour the building resounded with
the sobbing of strong men. " There were suche
sighes and sobbs, with shedding of teares among the
most part of all estats that were present, everie one
provoking another by their example, that the Kirk
resounded, so that the place might worthilie have
been called Bochim ; for the like of that day was
never seene in Scotland since the Reformatioun, as
everie man confessed. There have been manie
dayes of humiliatioun for present or immanent
dangers, but the like for sinne and defectioun was
there never seen."[1]

The solemn assembly, however, was not to end
in that way. Following public confession and more
prayer, Mr. Davidson proceeded to a second discourse, this time mostly for the " building up " as
the earlier one had been more for " casting down ".
The theme was the twelfth of Luke, the parable of the
faithful and wise steward, and the words must have
been most comforting, as they were delivered " with
rare assistance of God's spirit ". The preacher's
practical turn of mind and his evident knowledge
that the object of preaching is not simply to stir
emotions but to lead men to some practical decision
caused him to secure a definite pledge from his hearers

---

[1] Calderwood, Vol. V, p. 407. Scot, *Apologetical Narration*, p. 66. It is
regrettable that Lang should belittle such a solemn event. He says : " These
impressive scenes displayed the sincere belief of the Assembly that they
represented the people of Israel. Scotland was their promised land, to
extirpate Amalekites was their bound duty. . . ." *History of Scotland,*
Vol. II, p. 406.

ere they retired. At his earnest call, they held up
their hands " to testifie their entering in a new league
with God ". We are told that many were moved
at the sight of so many hands being so readily raised
in an act of consecration. Only one was out of
sympathy with the whole affair, Thomas Buchanan,
nephew of the famous George. This was the man
who, as we saw, rudely interrupted Davidson in the
General Assembly some time before.[1] That he was
either " not moved " or " despised that exercise " is
not to be wondered at, as for some time his heart had
been cold to the good cause which he ultimately
forsook, and later as Calderwood remarks he came
to a violent end. One can hardly blame the ultra-
zealous for associating his untimely death with his
scorn of the revival of 1596.

As a great many of the ministers were not present
on that memorable occasion, and as the Assembly
naturally desired the blessing of that day to be passed
on to the absentees, the afternoon session enjoined
" the brethrein of the synodall assembleis to make
the like solemne humiliatioun and protestatioun as
was observed by the Generall, at their nixt conveen-
ing ; and so manie as be not at their synod, to doe
it at their presbytereis ".[2] Seemingly, it did not
stop at presbyteries but was observed in some congregations as well.

It is impossible to say just how far the Assembly's
injunction was honoured but the matter seems to
have been taken up with a considerable measure of
enthusiasm. Wodrow says that it was " much

[1] Calderwood, Vol. V, p. 261.
[2] Ibid., p. 408.

countenanced of the Lord ".[1] M'Crie, however, has perhaps allowed himself to exaggerate somewhat when he says " this ordinance was obeyed with an alacrity and ardour which spread from synod to synod, from presbytery to presbytery and from parish to parish the inhabitants of one city saying to another, ' Come, and let us join ourselves to the Lord in a perpetuall covenant that shall not be forgotten,' until all Scotland, like Judah of old ' rejoiced at the oath.' "[2] Nevertheless it is true that synods, presbyteries and congregations did respond, though not universally.[3] We know that the Covenant was renewed by the Synod of Fife on May 13th, by the Presbytery of St. Andrews in July and by the Congregations of Kilrenny and Anstruther in September. At the last-named place it was conjoined with the celebration of the Sacrament. " We thought meet to enter in tryell of ourselfes for the better preparation to the Covenant and Lordes Supper " so the session records say. James Melville laments that the ministers of Edinburgh omitted the exercise in their congregations. " I dar nocht bot mark it," he writes in his Diary, " whowbeit against my will, that the Ministers of Edinbruche and Kirk thairof neglected and omitted this actioun of the Covenant, with the effect of a feirfull desolatioun, gif we dar judge ! "[4] No blame for that, however, can be imputed to the Presbytery, for this instruction had been issued : " It is concluditt, according to the act of the General Assemblie, a covenant salbe renewitt in all the bounds

---

[1] Wodrow MS., p. 31.
[2] The Story of the Scottish Church, p. 37.
[3] Scot, Apologetical Narration, p. 66.
[4] Melville's Diary, p. 368.

of this presbitrie and that upon the VII. of October next." [1]

The most notable observance of the Assembly's order was that of the Synod of Fife, then the stronghold of Presbyterianism in Scotland. We are indebted to James Melville for a rather full account of it, and from his narrative we are able to arrive at some idea as to how the inferior courts took it up. [2] (He describes also the manner of its observance at St. Andrews and in his own congregation at Kilrenny.) He was himself moderator when the Synod was constituted on May 12th in John Davidson's native city of Dunfermline and he proved himself as worthy a leader there as his old master had been in the General Assembly. He went about the business in a methodical way, first causing to be read the Articles of Reformation set down by the last Assembly, which were ordered to be inserted in the Synod records and of which every Presbytery was to have a copy. Next, for the preparation of hearts, a service was arranged, with the aged David Ferguson, minister of Dunfermline, as preacher. The following day the solemn meeting began with a sermon from David Black on Ezekiel xiii. and last verse of Psalm v. (" For thou Lord wilt bless the righteous : with favour wilt thou compass him as with a shield "), which was said to be " copius, powerfull, percing and pertinent ". Then Melville took the gathering in hand. With singular fitness he read the last chapter of the book of Judges, the story of the covenant made by Israel under Joshua's leadership, and his comments

[1] Records of the Presbytery of Edinburgh.
[2] Melville's *Diary*, pp. 353-60.

thereon were most appropriate to the occasion. He pointed out the benefits which God had bestowed on the Church of Scotland, especially in preserving her from notable enemies, particularly the Spaniards and from the conspiracy of the Popish Earls. That was followed by a word or two on their own ingratitude and their lack of earnestness in caring for the flocks over which God had placed them. The effect of his words was similar to that produced by Davidson in the Little Kirk. He himself tells us that "The Lord steirit upe sic a motioun of hart, that all war forcit to fall down befor the Lord, with sobbes and teares in aboundance, everie man mightelie commovit with the affectionnes of thair conscience in the presence of thair God, in privat meditatioun, rypping out thair wayes, confessing and acknawlaging thair unworthines and craving earnestlie grace for amendiment, and that a lang space." For some time longer, Melville continued to deal with points of doctrine, admonitions and exhortations. Thereafter "be lifting upe of the hand, everie an testified befor God, and mutualie an to an uther, the sinceare and ernest purpose of the hart to studie till amend and serve God better in tyme to come, bathe in their privat persones and in the office of that grait Ministerie of God's honour and salvatioun of the peiple concredit to thame." [1]

The Synod was then addressed by several of its own leaders—Ferguson, Black and Andrew Melville ; and also by Patrick Simson and John Davidson who attended by appointment of the Assembly. Davidson, the diarist tells us, was "a zealous grave father", who spoke very movingly and profitably. He said

[1] Melville's *Diary*, pp. 355, 356.

11

that he was as deeply moved as were the Jews at the
building of the second temple, only in another way.
He was greatly pleased with the effort at amendment,
but it grieved him to compare the Kirk as it had come
to be with its beginning which he had seen, and to
mark how far he and his brethren had wandered
from the godliness, zeal, gravity, love and other
virtues of early Reformation days. He lamented
also such a lack of learning in the ministry, where
time and opportunities for acquiring knowledge were
so great ; he could scarcely find any one who could
talk reasonably and learnedly on difficult passages
of Scripture or controversial questions, or who could
show evidence of having read the ancient Doctors
or the History of the Kirk. He therefore urged upon
them all, the Apostle's injunction, " *Attendite lectioni
etc.*" [1]

When the speeches were ended and some small
matters of business attended to, the Moderator
concluded the meeting with earnest prayer for the
" getting of grace to remember, practise and pey
the vowes thair maid, and efter hartlie thanksgiffing
for that memorable benefit of God " and the Assembly
was dismissed. The brethren had come to the gathering fasting and now they felt themselves amply
rewarded, for they went away " als full of spirituall
joy in the saull as emptie of corporall fuid ; everie
brother, with exceiding grait gladnes, glorifeing God
for that actioun above all uther that ever they haid
been partakers of."

The same procedure evidently was followed in
the Presbytery of St. Andrews, under the same

[1] Melville's *Diary*, pp. 357-8.

Moderator in July when gentlemen and burgesses as well as ministers took the same vows " testefeing of a true conversioun and change of mynd ". In congregations a somewhat different line was followed. To take an instance, the people of Kilrenny received a whole month's instruction. The Covenant was carefully explained to them as the obligation whereby God binds Himself to be the loving Father of His people in Christ, and the people in turn promise to be His servants and children. To be within the covenant was to be a child of God ; to be outwith it meant that " maist miserable esteat of Nature, without God, without Chryst, a chylde of wrathe, alian from the comoun-weill of his peiple, under slaverie of the devill and sinne, and finalie, a faggot of helles-fyre ".[1] Instead of holding up of hands as in the courts of the Church, the congregation, like the brethren at Anstruther, signified their assent by partaking of the Sacrament of the Lord's Supper.[2]

What exactly was this Covenant, it may be asked, which figured so largely in the revival of 1596 ? It is remarkable that more than one eminent historian[3] has made the mistake of regarding it as a renewal of the National Covenant of 1580-1 or of that part of it described as the " King's Confession ", the " Second Confession of Faith " or the " Negative Confession ". That is not so. Unfortunately, we do not have the full text of it—perhaps it was never

---

[1] Melville's *Diary*, pp. 360, 362.

[2] Ibid., p. 367. " Thus was our people catechised the haille monethe of August, and upon the first Sabbathe of September, the Covenant, with the Holie Communion, celebrat, to thair grait comfort."

[3] Row, *History*, p. 78. M'Crie, *The Story of the Scottish Church*, p. 86. King Hewison, *The Convenanters*, Vol. I, p. 138. Also Hill Burton and Andrew Lang.

fully committed to writing—but its nature and intention are clear. We know that the vows taken referred for the most part to religious duties, private, domestic and public, including " the resisting of all enemies of relligioun without fear or favour of anie persone ". It was thus a covenant of a purely religious nature made by people more concerned with the removal of their personal transgressions than with any political or national consideration. Spottiswood, here at least quite impartial, brings that out clearly when he says, " This is the covenant that by some is so often objected and said to be violated by those that gave obedience to the canons of the Church ; albeit in it there is not a word or syllable that sounds either to the confirming of the Church government then in use, or to the rejecting of that which since has been established. . . . By this covenant ", he continues, " all did bind themselves to abide in the profession of Truth and to walk according to the same as God should enable them. But for the rules of policy or ceremonies serving to good order or decency, let inspection be taken of the Register which is extant and it shall clearly appear that at the time there was not so much as mention thereof made."[1] James Melville, himself a participant, describes it as " a entring of new againe in covenant with thair God in Jesus Chryst, the grait Pastor of the saulles and Mediator of the Covenant "[2] while the Assembly itself says that its members " entered into a new covenant with God, protesting to walke more warilie in their wayes and more diligentlie in their charges."[3]

[1] *History of the Church of Scotland*, Vol. III, p. 6.
[2] Melville's *Diary*, p. 352.
[3] Calderwood, Vol. V, p. 408.

One regrets that there are no records to tell of the effects of this movement in the lives of individuals. Yet we believe that these must have been many, and we know how impossible it is to tabulate spiritual results, even if such a thing had been attempted. Calderwood doubtless had in mind this great spiritual awakening and its influence on the Church, when he wrote that 1596 was " a remarkable yeere to the Kirk of Scotland ", she " was now come to her perfection and the greatest puritie that she ever atteaned unto, both in doctrine and discipline, so that her beautie was admirable to forraigne Kirks. The assemblies of the sancts were never so glorious nor profitable to everie one of the true members thereof than in the beginning of this yeere."[1] James Melville pronounced the beginning of it as having " a schaw of profit " and the middle " verie comfortable for the exerceise of Reformatioun and renewing of the Covenant ", although ominous clouds were gathering and the end of it was "tragicall".[2] God had assuredly visited his people in a special fashion and at an opportune time, and doubtless the zealous Davidson felt the satisfaction of having been instrumental in the Divine hand, in bringing about such a quickening and deepening of the Church's life, as was to be mightily helpful in the difficult days that were looming ahead. So great a work of grace must have had an incalculable potency for good. From time to time such revivals come, in which the careless are awakened and the faithful enriched. The method and the manner, however, may be different on different

[1] Calderwood, Vol. V, p. 387.
[2] Melville's *Diary*, p. 330.

occasions, but it is interesting to remember that a very similar result to that of the revival of 1596 came about in a very similar way, when in 1844 Dr. Charles J. Brown preached a remarkable sermon before the General Assembly of the Free Church of Scotland.[1] Had he, one wonders, any thought of John Davidson?

[1] Thomas Brown, *Annals of the Disruption*, pp. 628-30.
Jonathan Edwards, writing of the New England revivals of the eighteenth century, tells how his father had seen a letter from Scotland " that gave account of a sermon preached in the city of Edinburgh, in the time of the sitting of the General Assembly of divines in that Kingdom, that so affected the people that there was a great and loud cry made throughout the Assembly." Dr. W. J. Couper thinks this probably points to the proceedings of the Assembly of 1596.

CHAPTER VIII

THE KING'S NEW SCHEME FOR
ESTABLISHING PRELACY

FOLLOWING up the success which he had obtained
through the " riot " of 1596, the King now laid his
plans for a new attempt to establish prelacy in Scotland.
The time seemed most opportune. " Precisely at
this moment ", says Hume Brown,[1] " there was not
a single noble of ability and authority who took his
stand on the side of the Presbyterian party."
Edinburgh, with her ministers punished and her
dignity terribly hurt, was ready to accept almost
anything that would restore her to favour. His
Majesty saw his chance to strike at Presbyterian
domination. With the help of his Secretary, Lindsay,
he drew up a list of fifty-five questions relating to the
government and discipline of the Church.[2] Many
of these dealt with matters in which he knew the
ministers to be themselves divided, and all of which
were very disturbing to them. His design was,
doubtless, to throw discredit upon the existing practices of the Church. He inquired, among other
things :—Whether it belongs to the King by himself
or to the ministers by themselves, or to both conjunctly, to establish acts respecting the Government
of the Church ; whether it is lawful for the Church

[1] *History of Scotland*, Vol. II, p. 227.
[2] Melville's *Diary*, pp. 390-403, 523.

to call Assemblies without the consent of the magistrate and whether Acts of Assembly are valid without the King's sanction ; whether for anything but notorious vices previously rebuked in private, ministers may denounce men by name from the pulpit ; whether excommunication of Papists, who have never professed the Reformed Faith, is lawful ; whether a minister may use further application than is necessary for his own flock, or whether the whole world is the flock of every particular pastor.

The Reformers regarded such a questionnaire[1] with something like dismay. Had not the forms of their ecclesiastical polity been fixed by act of Parliament, founded on the Word of God, and in 1592 even praised by the King himself? Why should they be called in question now ? The ministers could not but feel, despite his Majesty's protests to the contrary, that here was a deeply laid scheme to discredit the Presbyterian system and introduce Episcopacy. Evidently this was the great purpose which now filled the royal mind and this the Church was ready to resist. Many private conferences were held to consider what ought to be done, and the Synod of Fife, meeting at St. Andrews, after " tossing of the King's questions for sundry days " drew up replies which disposed of all the royal claims and decided everything in favour of the Kirk.[2] It is unnecessary here to pursue these answers. From them, however, as well as from the true Presbyterian spirit shown in the southern presbyteries, James

[1] Lord Burghley had helped in preparing the questions. Cunningham, Vol. I, p. 440.
[2] Calderwood, Vol. V, pp. 579-99.

learned that his scheme was likely to meet with stern opposition.

Yet, he addressed himself to the situation with all his usual acuteness and dexterity. He summoned an Assembly to meet, concurrently with a Convention of Estates, at Perth on February 29th, 1597. James saw that his only hope of success lay in outnumbering the southern churchmen by their humbler brethren from the north. The place was thus chosen to suit those north-country ministers who could not afford to travel far. They were likely to be useful to the King as they were known to be rather lukewarm in their Presbyterianism. Indeed, at this stage " Presbytery had acquired no hold on the country north of the Firth of Tay."[1] To make absolutely sure of their support Sir Patrick Murray was sent north to interview as many of them as possible and he was most successful in his mission. When the Assembly met, it seemed to be in a most conciliatory mood. After some discussion, and despite some opposition from James Melville, it was decided by a majority that the meeting should be held to be a lawful General Assembly extraordinarily convened. The King's questions were then considered and a submissive answer given to nearly every one of them.[2] His Majesty, however, was not fully satisfied with the answers although they were to prove helpful to him in the carrying out of his future plans against the constitution of the Church. He had obtained a basis upon which his own system of ecclesiastical government could be built, free from all clerical intrusion. The principle

[1] R. S. Rait, *The Making of Scotland*, p. 150.
[2] *Book of the Universal Kirk*, Assembly, 1597. Calderwood, Vol. V, pp. 606-23.

was now recognized that the King, either by himself or commissioners, might propose to the General Assembly any alteration in the external government of the Church and that was all that James desired for the present. An Assembly had thus for the first time yielded to that secret and corrupt influence of the King, which was afterwards to render the General Assembly of the Church a mere organ of the court to register and issue royal edicts in Kirk affairs.[1] His Majesty appointed the next Assembly to meet at Dundee on May 10th, 1597.

The composition of the Dundee Assembly was as carefully regulated as had been that of Perth. Yet, with all his efforts to secure the return of members favourable to the court, James found it no easy matter to have his plans adopted. The ministers resented very strongly his encroachments on the laws and liberties both of the Church and Kingdom. It was to this Assembly that John Davidson, detained through sickness, sent an interesting letter stating his views on the situation, with his usual freedom and plainness,[2] yet coming, as he said, " of a loving minde to Christ's caus and weale of his Kirk ". Doubtless he had been alarmed at what happened at Perth, as he does not seem to have been present. It is clear that his object in writing was to advise the brethren against further discussion of the King's questions. He began by remarking that the unity and liberty of the Kirk in doctrine were maintained by the free execution of discipline and whenever freedom of that discipline is invaded, there is sure to arise danger to liberty

[1] M'Crie, *Life of Melville*, Vol. II, p. 17.
[2] Calderwood, Vol. V, pp. 630-2.

and unity in doctrine. Now discipline, he maintained, had been preserved by the avoidance of thorny questions. When these did arise, the fathers had usually kept them to the close of the Assembly, so that unnecessary heat would not interfere with its business. Then, the kind of questions considered were, for the most part, referred in orderly manner from the inferior courts of the Church, and if they were of weight they were remitted from one assembly to the next, so that by due consideration contentions and rash conclusions might be avoided. " Where questions gett over-great libertie," he said, " godlie edifeing is excluded . . . they breed strife as the apostle writteth." Let them leave off, he advised, ere contentions had begun. The subject most needing consideration in these days was not change in external things but rather that which concerned a substantial part of doctrine, viz. the rebuke of open and obstinate vice which had grown to such a height, it would free itself of the law and yet put in bondage the liberty of the truth. He urged that all passion for innovations—*libido novandi circa ecclesiam*—should be far from them, and as there were many more needful things in the Church than the questions proposed for discussion, they should resist these and stand fast in their Christian liberty and unity. The letter concluded with this bold announcement so characteristic of the writer—" if anie act sall passe, as God forbid, in contrare anie jote of our Christian libertie, agreeable to God's Word and the lawes of the realme, I, in my owne name and the rest of Christ's faithfull messingers within this realme, will stand by God's grace to the protestation made verballie by me in his Majestie's presence, at the last General Assemblie holdin at Edinburgh ; for it will not be the new cords of the Philistins that will keep Samsone bound."[1]

Davidson's attempt by this letter to have the Assembly resist the royal proposals and withstand the encroachments on the ecclesiastical province did not meet with any success. Nor was that to be wondered at, since by so many he was regarded simply as one of " the popes of Edinburgh " whose desires the men of the north were eager to thwart. Moreover, the King when he saw that he was not likely to gain his point openly, resorted to that craft of which he was a master. He appeared in person and gave an address in which he made a great pretence of promoting the Church's interests and took great care not to disclose prematurely the extent of his " reforms ". Well he knew the aversion of the Church to anything in the nature of a hierarchy. Proceeding with caution he referred sympathetically to the many matters which, owing to brevity of time, received inadequate or no consideration in an Assembly ; he stressed the necessity, and his own anxiety, that there should be a minister for every Kirk and a stipend for every minister. In face of these and other needed reforms, let them consider the advisability of appointing a Committee of their

[1] Besides the King's questions the Assembly had to consider whether the Popish lords recently professing conversion to Protestantism should be freed from excommunication. Davidson was evidently against relaxing the sentence, at least meantime. In a postscript to his letter he advised that, in the event of their being absolved " they gett *annum probationis* injoynned to them before they be admitted to court, or have accesse to sitt at the helme ". He quite clearly doubted the sincerity of the " coversion " and declared " though they have Jacob's voice, yitt I feare Esau's hands." Calderwood, Vol. V, p. 633.

ablest and wisest brethren to confer with him on all matters for the Church's good. Nothing could have been more plausible ; the bait was very attractive ; the proposal looked most innocent. Little wonder was it that Davidson's warnings went unheeded. In an evil hour the thing was done. Fourteen ministers were appointed, mostly devoted to the King's policy, although there were among them one or two " true blue " Presbyterians who gave to the commission an appearance of impartiality which it did not possess.[1] These fourteen were to advise him " in all affairs concerning the weal of the church and entertainment of peace and obedience to his Majesty within his realm ". It was a rash and dangerous step for the Church to take. The new Commission was entirely different from those appointed by former Assemblies to look after particular measures, though even in *them* Row had found " the first evident and seen wrack of our Kirk ". Those Commissions had caused James much annoyance on account of the jurisdiction they possessed—the very thing he now desired for this new one. This Commission became, in course of time, a permanent ecclesiastical council having Episcopal powers, in which the King ruled all the affairs of the Church in very much the same manner as in the Privy Council he managed the affairs of the State. According to Calderwood[2] it was " the King's led horse, and usurped the power of the General Assembly and government of the whole Kirk " and the same historian adds in bitterness of spirit that it became " a wedge taken out of the Church

---

[1] *Book of the Universal Kirk*, p. 461.
[2] Calderwood, Vol. V, p. 644.

to rend her with her own forces—the very needle which drew the episcopal thread ".

When Parliament met in December, the commissioners of Assembly, on the advice of the King, presented a petition praying that the Church as the first estate[1] of the kingdom might be admitted to have a voice in Parliament. His Majesty secured without difficulty the passing of an act which declared " that such pastors and ministers as the crown provided to the place and dignity of a bishop, abbot or other prelate, should have voice in parliament as freely as any other ecclesiastical prelate had in any former age ".[2] This was, it will be seen, a well-planned attempt to bring in Episcopacy by a side wind and there were not wanting men who saw through it and were ready to expose it. In the Synod of Fife the question was raised as to whether " it were expedient that ministers should have vote in Parliament for and in name of the Kirk ". James Melville argued against it most convincingly. Ministers, he maintained, could not be admitted to a place in Parliament without first being made bishops, and to support any such proposal would mean building up what they had been destroying all their days.[3] The aged Ferguson branded it as a court stratagem which, if suffered to succeed, would prove as fatal to the Church as the famous wooden horse had done to the Trojans. " Let the words ", he said, " of the Dardan prophetess ring in your ears. *Equo ne credite Tencri.*"[4] Davidson followed with a few words much in the same strain.

[1] Calderwood, Vol. V, pp. 668, 670.
[2] Spottiswood, Vol. III, p. 67. *Act. Parl. Scot.*, Vol. IV, p. 130.
[3] Calderwood, Vol. V, p. 680.
[4] Melville's *Diary*, p. 437.

Unveiling the ultimate design of the King and his supporters—a future bench of bishops with their primate at their head, he cried, with witty and biting irony, " Busk, busk him, buske him als bonilie as yee can, and bring him in als fairlie as yee will, we see him weill eneugh, we see the hornes of his mytre."[1]

The Commissioners, in spite of all protests, pursued their purpose and an Assembly was held in March 1598, at Dundee again, to consider the whole matter. The first two days passed in nothing except ministers continually visiting the King and receiving instructions as to their votes. At the roll call the King challenged the name of Andrew Melville and declared that since he was no longer Rector of St. Andrews University[2] he had no right to be present. Melville maintained that, being still a doctor in the Church, " he had received a commission from it and would not betray it ". " There are none here," said the King, " that seek to betray it." Davidson intervened by reminding his Majesty that his office was simply to oversee the proceedings, not to overbear them. " Sir," he said, " yee are to remember that yee sit not heere as *Imperator*, but as a Christian ; *ades ut intersis non ut praesis*." At these words the King started to his feet, but, after a moment's reflection, evidently seeing and admitting the distinction, he resumed his seat in silence. Davidson seeking to conciliate him a little said, " Sir, we are affrayed to speake except yee be equall and indifferent. Therefore we crave that libertie which is due to this

[1] Calderwood, Vol. V, p. 681. Melville's *Diary*, p. 437.
[2] He had been deprived of the Rectorship by the King through the new Commission of 1597.

Assemblie."[1] The King made no reply but would not permit business to proceed till Melville withdrew. Mr. Andrew then made a brief statement of his views on matters to be brought before the Assembly and thereafter retired. The following day, when the King learned that ministers were consulting him at his lodgings, he commanded him and his colleague Jonston to leave the town under pain of rebellion. The Assembly having resumed, John Knox, nephew of the great Reformer, complained of the treatment meted out to Melville, whose learning the court obviously feared. Davidson joined in the complaint. " Would ye have nothing but pleas here ? " asked the King. " No Sir," replied Davidson, " but that ye would permit them to be present." " I will not hear one word of that," said his Majesty twice or thrice. " Then," replied Mr. John, " we must crave help of him that will hear us."[2]

The King's favourite measure of conferring the right to sit in Parliament on a certain number of ministers, he now introduced in a long and studied harangue from the throne. He adroitly aimed at convincing his hearers that what he sought was not " to bring in Papistical or Anglican bishops " but simply to advance the Church's interests by giving some of the wisest and ablest of the ministers—who should be appointed by the Assembly—a representative place in Parliament. The matter of adequate provision for the ministry was astutely used ; better also would it be for the churchmen to have a say in their own affairs and " not to stand always at the door like

[1] Calderwood, Vol. V, p. 683.
[2] Ibid., p. 684.

poor suppliants utterly despised and disregarded ". Thus the King's ostensible purpose was to vindicate the Church from poverty and contempt but in reality it was to convert them into tools for the overthrow of their own order.

There was, in the Assembly, a band of honest ministers who knew James too well to be taken in by his fair speeches and who would neither be bribed nor browbeaten by the Royal Dictator, while others, who ought to have known better, had been won over to his side by his kingcraft.[1] A vigorous debate took place. Some of the ablest ministers—Bruce, Aird, James Melville and John Carmichael as well as Davidson denounced the project in the strongest language as unscriptural, unconstitutional and dangerous. Thomas Buchanan, Robert Pont and George Gladestains took the opposite view. In the course of his argument, Gladestains held that, since all the subjects were divided " *in tres ordines* " for the sake of the common weal the Kirk must necessarily be *one* estate. Davidson simply disposed of that statement, saying, " We hold not our living of Kings or States." Gladestains having pleaded the power which the priests had among the Romans, " *in rogandis et ferendis legibus* ", Davidson replied that in Rome the priests were consulted but had no vote in making laws, " *praesentibus sacerdotibus, et divina exponentibus, sed non suffragia habentibus* ". " Where have ye that ? " asked the King. " In Titus Livius," said Davidson. " Oh ! are you going then from the

[1] Among these were Rollock, the Principal of Edinburgh University, Pont, minister of St. Cuthbert's, and David Lindsay, minister of Leith, who had been the honoured friend and coadjutor of Knox. Later in his life he became Bishop of Ross. Calderwood, Vol. V, p. 697.

Scriptures to Titus Livius," exclaimed his Majesty.
" Nay," replied Mr. John, " but for Roman terms
which Mr. George alledged, I have brought a simile
out of the Roman practice, to express my minde."[1]
Davidson, it is clear, with his fine knowledge of the
classics and his skill in debate, had the best of it,
although as M'Crie says, there were flatterers present
who applauded the King's wretched witticism " and
they were encouraged to laugh at the old man who
pursued his argument with equal disregard to the
puerilities of James and the rudeness of his minions ".[2]
At length the roll was called and the vote taken,
when it was found that the royal proposal had been
carried by a majority of ten, as being " expedient for
the weal of the Church ". According to Calderwood[3]
the North[4] was solidly in favour of it, " the sincerer
sort " glorified God in opposing it, while a third lot
" were mistaikin both in reasoning and voting ".
To the credit of the ministers, be it said that it was
largely with the help of the elders that the King
gained the day. The victory was a very narrow one,
indeed surprisingly so when it is remembered that
James had had recourse to all his usual arts to produce
success and " men were won by threats and persuasions beforehand ".[5]

There were several important points, however,
that remained to be settled—what the number of the
Kirk's Parliamentary voters was to be, how they were

---

[1] Calderwood, Vol. V, p. 695.
[2] *Life of Melville*, Vol. II, p. 46.
[3] Calderwood, Vol. V, p. 695.
[4] Calderwood describes the northern ministers as a sad subservient rabble,
led by Mr. Gilbert Bodie, " a drunken Orkney ass "—all being for the body
with small regard to the spirit. See also Melville's *Diary*, p. 440.
[5] Calderwood, Vol. V, p. 695.

to be elected and by what name they were to be called. Davidson counselled the Assembly not to decide these weighty matters suddenly,[1] but to consider the example of the Romans who *in rogandis et ferendis legibus*, gave *trinundinum spatium* to examine them, but no attention was paid to his words. Rollock, whose advice was sought, said that lordship could not be denied them that were to sit in Parliament nor allowance of rent to maintain their dignity. " See ye not, brethrein ", exclaimed Mr. Davidson, " how bonilie yonder bishop beginneth to creepe out! *Novus palliatus episcopus* "—an old friend with a new cloak,—" at which words ", says the historian, " the King and a great number burst furth in laughter, so light accompt made they of the mater." Caring nothing about such derision Davidson proceeded to ask " have we not done muche to it, that so long have striven against this corruption, to bring furth suche a birth now? " Rollock then sought to extenuate the matter but the dissatisfied Davidson appealed to Robert Pont to say what difference there was between the bishopric now proposed and the kind condemned by former acts of Assembly. " We shall shew that afterward," said Pont, "when we come to that point." " It will never be shewed," replied Davidson, "saving that this last hath suche a consent and approbatioun." He was then desired by some to present a protestation which he had in readiness, although it appears to have been a kind of last resort. Having declined to vote, he now protested in his own name and in the name of all who would adhere to his protest, that they dissented from all the proceedings in that and

[1] Calderwood, Vol. V, p. 697.

the two former Assemblies, as not having the privilege of free Assemblies, " which heere ", he said, " I present in writt, that it may be insert in the bookes of the Assemblie ".[1] The King raised an objection on the grounds that Davidson had voted and reasoned on former occasions, to which Mr. John replied, " Never, Sir, but without prejudice of my protestatioun made and to be made, which words I used sindrie tymes before I spake." That was quite true, for at an earlier session, James had tried to counter him on a technical point, questioning his qualification to take part in the discussion. " Have ye a commissioun," the King had asked. " Yes," said Davidson, " from my Maister." " That is witche-like spoken," observed James, " are yee a commissioner or messinger from Christ ? " " Yes," Davidson boldly answered, " and that ye sall finde, by the grace of God." The King, we are told, "shrunke" at that reply. Davidson went on to complain of the restrictions placed on the ministers' freedom ; it was because of these restrictions that he protested against the Assembly's proceedings. James was extremely annoyed and declared that Davidson spake " anabaptisicall-like " and was too friendly with Mr. Penry, the Puritan from England. Davidson, however, denied that he was an Anabaptist and said that he did not agree with Penry, as some of his friends could testify who remembered the occasions on which the Puritan and he had engaged in high dispute on the nature and extent of the liberty possessed by the individual member in the Assemblies of the Church. The significance of the King's reference to Penry is

[1] Calderwood, Vol. V, p. 698.

his acquaintance with the outstanding features of the Puritan's views on Church polity, and his belief that these had affected the attitude of the ministers to his episcopalian proposals. " He had heard that Penry claimed free fellowship in Christ to be superior to, and therefore free from, interference from all secular organizations."[1] His Majesty called that *Anabaptism*,—the common, loosely-used epithet for extreme reforming views. Davidson, with a Presbyterian's respect for the law and for civic institutions, would not have gone nearly so far.

When the Assembly of 1598 came to deal with some of the weightiest matters, many members, as Davidson had predicted, had departed. He had the utmost difficulty in obtaining permission to speak, the King being, as Calderwood[2] puts it " more than Moderator " and doubtless the protestation was rankling in the royal mind. Mr. John at length received a hearing. He compared the Kirk to a sick wife and the ministers to physicians. The malady was a great schism which could be cured only by the removal of its cause. That cause he considered to be the wrongful dismissal of the Assembly's Commissioners from Edinburgh by public proclamation in November 1596. The King, interrupting him, said that he was not speaking the truth, as it was the sermons in the pulpits which had led to the discharge. To that Davidson was not permitted to reply. At the request of the Moderator he handed in his protestation which the King took up, read, showed to the Moderator and then put in his pocket.

[1] Pierce, *Life of John Penry*, pp. 302, 303.
[2] Calderwood, Vol. V, p. 698.

The protestation[1] was in courteous if very frank terms. It deplored the great corruption, confusion and disorder in the Assembly and the great inconveniences to the Kirk which had come through the discharge of the commissioners and through the Assemblies at Perth and Dundee " wherein that freedom due unto a free assemblie is utterlie denied unto us ". Davidson declared his adherence to a former protestation of his, that he and such other brethren in the ministry as agreed with him, would continue to use their wonted freedom in the ministry " according to the Word of God and good lawes and pratick of this realme, notwithstanding anie law or act made or to be made, in the contrare ". Finally, as already indicated, he protested in his own name and on behalf of brethren of similar mind, that they dissented from all the proceedings in that and the two former Assemblies as not having the privilege of free Assemblies permitted unto them.

The Assembly next proceeded to discuss the number and quality of the voters in Parliament and were designed to go on to the caveats and other matters, but the King and Commissioners finding the brethren disposed to relent a little, resolved to delay for a time. They contented themselves with agreeing that the number of ministers to represent the Church should be fifty-one, according to the ancient number of the bishops, abbots and priors " in the time of the papistical Kirk ", the election to belong partly to the King and partly to the Church.[2]

[1] Calderwood, Vol. V, p. 699.
[2] The specific terms of election were remitted for the consideration of presbyteries and synods, with the doctors of the universities.

Meanwhile Davidson left the town, and in the afternoon at the last session the King asked who would stand to the protestation he had given in. We are told that " the brethren thought good to keepe silence ".[1] Thomas Buchanan, ever Mr. John's wilful opponent, would have had him censured and condemned for it ; the Assembly refused to register it.[2] Nevertheless it is obvious that the hearts of many brethren were with him although unfortunately they lacked his courage and so feared the King. He had scarcely crossed the river from Dundee when three or four score overtook him and subscribed his copy. However, on reaching St. Andrews, they deemed it expedient to cut off the names and burn them in the fire.

Certain instructive articles for preventing abuses and corruptions in the Kirk were drawn up to be presented to this Assembly. Calderwood[3] found them among Davidson's papers and in his handwriting, but it is doubtful if he was the author of them. Wodrow[4] regards them as " very like Mr. Davidson's style ". Certainly they deal with matters dear to his heart, such as liberty due to all commissioners of Assembly " freelie to speeke, propone and vote " in the presence of any ; the need for ministers " edifeing God's people by life and doctrine " ; personal behaviour of ministers being such as to offer a good example to their flocks. Possibly the most important of the articles was the one on doctrine, in which the

[1] Calderwood, Vol. V, p. 701.
[2] *Book of the Universal Kirk*, p. 476.
[3] Calderwood, Vol. V, p. 702-5.
[4] Wodrow MS., p. 34.

Assembly was petitioned to make an Act against a " curious kinde of preaching, yea, rather a certain unprofitable and profane κενοφωνια without the right cutting of the word, which of a long tyme has been unprofitablie used by manie, and, by their exemple, beginneth now to be more excessivelie used of moe to the great hinderance of true edificatioun wherethrough the people . . . under a shadow of religioun are interteaned in atheisme without all true knowledge and feeling." Instead of this new style, preaching should, as of old, stand " rather in the evidence of the Spirit ", that the faith of the flocks be " not in the wisdom of men but in the power of God ".[1]

Bishop Spottiswood declares that this Assembly closed " with the great content of all ". From his history it is impossible to learn that the King did anything which was not most laudable, far less that he encountered any formidable opposition. His narrative, however, is not according to fact. From the registers and from Calderwood's manuscripts[2] it is clear that no Assembly had ever been so divided not only on the question of the ministers' vote in Parliament but on the act regarding the powers of the Kirk's commissioners, the burying of grievances, and the procedure with the Popish lords. The Bishop, always ready to vent his spleen on the bold Reformer, adds that " Mr. John Davidson only, a man given to contention, finding that things went not to his mind, especially in the planting of Edinburgh, to the ministry of which he was always aspiring ",[3] did protest that

[1] Calderwood, Vol. V, p. 704.
[2] Wodrow MS., p. 34.
[3] Spottiswood, Vol. III, p. 71.

this was not a free Assembly. That is simply a tissue of falsehoods. To begin with, Davidson was not a man of contention, unless opposition to prelacy and the corruptions of the Church is to be so regarded. Then, the " planting " of Edinburgh was no ground of his protestation and indeed was a matter of very minor importance in that Assembly, and one with which Davidson had already dealt as seemed right to him.[1] He never aspired to the ministry of Edinburgh, although, as we saw, he was for a time at St. Giles, and when he found that his free manner in the pulpit offended some, he expressed his willingness to leave, but was not allowed. It is adding insult to injury for Spottiswood to say further that he fled away as his custom was when he made any trouble and " lurked a while, till his peace was made again ".[2] Whether that was a reference to Davidson's flight into England in 1574 when prosecuted by Morton, we cannot say. If it was, Dr. M'Crie in a footnote to his life of Melville makes an effective comment— " it is very easy for a time-serving priest, who, by his tame compliances, can always secure himself from falling into danger, to talk thus of a man from whose rebuik he more than once shrunk, and to accuse him of cowardice merely because he fled from the lawless rage of a despot ".[3] It is not true that Davidson either fled or concealed himself at this time. He went home to his charge and maintained his ground, as we shall see, when prosecuted illegally by the Court.[4]

[1] Wodrow MS., p. 34.
[2] Spottiswood, Vol. III, p. 71.
[3] *Life of Melville*, Vol. II, p. 47.
[4] Wodrow MS., p. 34.

There is reason to believe that, after King James left the Dundee Assembly of 1598, his wrath against Davidson for his protestation declaring it unlawful, increased rather than diminished. One Mr. George Nicolson in a letter to Lord Burghley from Edinburgh, dated March 29th, wrote :—" The King hath, since his return from Dundee, thought more and more hard of Mr. John Davidson's protestation.[1] The royal displeasure led to proceedings against Davidson in his own Presbytery. James directed Mr. William Melville and Mr. David Magill, two Lords of the Sessions, with commission to the Presbytery of Haddington, to complain of Mr. Davidson's " misbehaviour " in the Assembly, as his protestation was termed.[2] Davidson being absent was summoned to a special meeting and he compeared at the risk of his life, for he was very ill. " So far was he from lurking ", adds Wodrow.[3] He expressed himself to the Presbytery as very much surprised that he should thus be dealt with for a protestation which was, in itself, quite lawful and with which the King had found no fault in the Assembly. He desired that his brethren would desist from such proceedings, not that he had any fear for his cause but that he was concerned for the King's weal. With great assurance and simplicity, he said :—" The Earl of Morton was observed never to thrive after he persecuted me, and ere that matter was ended he would have given ten thousand pounds he had not entered in it,"[4] and it cannot be denied that there was a deal of truth

---

[1] *State Papers, Scotland, Queen Elizabeth*, Vol. lxii., No. 13.
[2] *Records of Presbytery of Haddington.*
[3] Wodrow MS., p. 34.
[4] Calderwood, Vol. V, p. 710.

in his words. Following some discussion a deputation
was appointed to accompany Mr. John to Edinburgh,
consult with the brethren there, and with them wait
upon the King. When they came into the royal
presence, his Majesty conversed with Mr. James
Carmichael and Mr. James Gibson but would not
allow Mr. Davidson to speak. Allowing himself
to get into a great rage, he called Davidson " a starke
fool, a heretick, an Anabaptist, a traitour to him, to
the commoun weale, to Christ and his Kirk ". As
nothing came of that visit, the process was renewed
at next Presbytery meeting, but it was attested to
that court that Mr. Davidson was " stayit be ane
heavie fever ". A few days later " the presbyterie
w^t consent of his Mat^{ies} commissioner continewit all
farder dealing in this matter till ye said Mr. Johne
at the pleaso^r of God suld be restorit to his health ".[1]
Finally the commissioners of the Assembly sent a
pursuivant to the Presbytery for an extract of the
proceedings against Davidson but the Presbytery
declined to give it, as the matter had not been disposed
of. Some of the brethren were sent to confer with
Mr. David Magill anent it, but after some time the
matter was allowed to drop.

The publication of his *Basilicon Doron*[2] about this
time, afforded proof, if such had been needed, of the
King's settled purpose to introduce Episcopacy into
the Scottish Church. Many considerations, however,
had to be faced up and disposed of before the decision

[1] Records of the Presbytery of Haddington. M'Crie, *Life of Melville*,
Vol. II, p. 47n.

[2] In that book he declared that a large part of the King's office was the
ruling of the Kirk ; that parity among ministers did not agree with a monarchy ;
that Puritans were pests in Scotland and bishops must be set up.

reached at Dundee could be put into effect. Certain conclusions had been come to by commissioners from the Synods, meeting at Falkland, and the matter had been fully discussed at a conference of ministers in Holyrood House, under the King's direction. Sanction was now sought from the Assembly which met at Montrose in 1600. According to James Melville,[1] although many good brethren offered a stout opposition, yet authority, dissimulation and craft carried the matter away. It was agreed with regard to the ministers who were to vote in Parliament, that each one should be chosen by the King from six recommended by the Church, and that, on provision being made for churches, colleges and schools the remainder of any Episcopal benefices might be given by his Majesty to the ministers who had been raised to parliamentary honours. Several restrictions were then enacted to prevent them from abusing their powers, among which were the following :—They were to propose nothing in Parliament in the name of the Church without her express warrant and direction, nor consent to the passing of any act prejudicial to her interests under pain of deposition from their office ; at each Assembly they were to give an account of the manner in which they had executed their commission. Further they were to attend to their pastoral work in their congregations ; they were to have no more power in the church courts than other ministers ; they were to remain subject to the censures of the ecclesiastical courts and, in the event of their deposition from the ministry, their seat in parliament and their benefice were *ipso facto* to become

[1] Melville's *Diary*, p. 540.

vacant.[1] Every year their commission was to be reconsidered and would be renewed only on receipt of a satisfactory account of their stewardship. The name given them was to be "commissioners" and not "bishops". "Thus", says Calderwood, "the Trojan horse—the Episcopacy—was brought in, busked and covered with caveats, that the danger and deformity might not be seen ; which was, notwithstanding, seen of many and opposed unto. But force and falsehood prevailed."[2] Row's verdict is, "Thus the King obtained his grand purpose in getting the ministers to be the third estate in Parliament, to vote in place of bishops, abbots and priors, as in the tyme of Poperie : it was a prettie devyse to put men in an unlawfull and corrupt office, and then sett down a number of caveats (lyke Samson's half-burnt coards) to binde him to honestie and to hold him from corruption."[3] The net result of all the King's manoeuvring, however, was singularly small. As Gardiner says, "the whole of the labours and intrigues of the last three years had been thrown away and James had done nothing more than he might have done immediately upon the passing of the Act of Parliament in 1597".[4] Vacant sees, however, were promptly filled. Three of the commissioners, in a convention of Synods were nominated to Caithness, Ross and Aberdeen ; and the new bishops sat and voted in Parliament a month later.

The whole subject of the Church's Parliamentary Commissioners was now allowed to slumber for a year

[1] *Book of the Universal Kirk*, 1600. Calderwood, Vol. VI, pp. 1-20.
[2] Calderwood, Vol. VI, p. 80.
[3] Row's *History*, p. 203.
[4] Gardiner. Quoted by Mathieson, *Politics and Religion*, Vol. I, p. 280.

or two, although it was by no means forgotten. Mr. Michael Cranston, preaching at the Synod of Lothian in 1601, recalled the troubles and labours of some prominent ministers in that connection. He referred specially to John Davidson, their neighbour, "whom God yitt ever approved". Davidson himself took a prominent part in the Synod. Causing to be read Chapter xiii. of Deuteronomy and the acts of parliament against idolaters, Jesuits, and seminary priests, he complained of the remissness of the Assembly's Commissioners, and said that if they persisted in flattering the King and defacing good brethren, they ought to bear the blame of the schism which was likely to happen.[1] Directing himself to Mr. David Lindsay, who had been placed in the chair at the Perth Assembly by the influence of the Court, he said, "assure yourself, I love neither your bishopping nor your mounting to be a counsellor. For all this is come of your corrupt course, in making yourself moderator at St. Johnstoun, or at least in accepting the moderatorship against all good order." He desired the brethren to be plain from their pulpits touching the present dangers of Popery and Prelacy, and not "to wink any longer". Mr. David hung down his head and answered Mr. John not a word.

The year 1601 was comparatively uneventful as far as ecclesiastical affairs were concerned. Possibly the most important happening was the Assembly at Burntisland, although it did little beyond deploring that the country was running into "papistrie" or atheism. It was, however, a momentous Assembly for John Davidson. He does not seem to have been

[1] Calderwood, Vol. VI, p. 104.

present at Montrose in 1600 and in his enforced absence from Burntisland he sent to the Assembly a letter,[1] setting forth his views and giving his brethren a warning ; which letter increased the wrath of the King against him and later caused him much suffering. As if he would awake his brethren fallen asleep, he began with a strong cry—" How long sall we feare or favour flesh and blood, and follow the counsell and command thereof? Sould our meetings be in the name of man ? Are we not yitt to take up ourselves and to acknowledge and leave our former errours and feebleness in the work of the Lord ? " All this had reference to the subject of free Assemblies, his defence of which had been so objectionable to his Majesty. He now went on to deal with the abuses of the time and he asked, " Is it tyme for us now, when so manie of our worthie brethrein are thrust out of their callings without all order of just proceeding against them and Jesuits, atheists and papists are suffered, countenanced and advanced to great rowmes in the realm, for the bringing in of idolatrie and captivitie more Babylonicall, with a high hand, and that in our cheafe citie—Is it tyme for us, I say, of the Ministry, to be inveigled and blindfold with pretence of preferment of some small number of our brethrein to have a voice in parliament and have titles of prelacy ? Sall we with Samsone sleep still on Dalilah's knee, till she say ' The Philistins be upon thee, Samsone ' ? "

If the letter had ended there, it would have been bad enough, as James was already terribly incensed at Davidson for his opposition to the ministers having

[1] Calderwood, Vol. VI, pp. 110-12.

a vote in parliament. Mr. John, however, went much further and scorned the recent doings of the King. " But Bonnytoun[1] is executed, an infamous theefe in the highest degree ! What is that to the caus of religion whereof no question was moved ? Is there no papist nor favourer of papists in Scotland but Bonnytoun ? But the King and Kirk being sound in religion what can the adversareis doe ? Being sound, the danger were the lesse, but there is nothing either in Church or King according to our callings." He urged the Assembly to join together as one man to purge the land of idolatry, leaving over all other matters to a later date. Without such zeal for the Lord and his cause, no blessing could be expected from the hands of God. In a postscript to the letter, he wished his brethren to be wary of determining anything touching the planting of Edinburgh in respect of any promises against Papists, and to remember that *Melius et optabilius est bellum pace impia, et a Deo distrahente.*

The King, having read the letter, held it to be treasonable, but the Assembly " allowed " it.[2] Spottiswood has some curious reflections upon it which are somewhat difficult to understand. He says that some laughed at it while others (whom he calls " the wiser sort ") were offended by it and would have had the writer censured there and then.[3] These " wise " men were probably the commissioners of Assembly or the bishops and such as were eager to become

---

[1] The Laird of Bonytoun was one of the Romanists who caused trouble to the early Reformed Church in Scotland. He was executed and is said to have died " an obstinat papist". Calderwood, Vol. V, p. 314 ; Vol. VI, p. 104.

[2] Calderwood, Vol. VI, p. 112.

[3] Spottiswood, Vol. III, p. 98.

prelates. He adds that the King interceded, but Calderwood[1] affirms that the King called it treason and willed them to leave the punishment to him. That is the more probable story. The King could hardly be said to " interceed " when he proceeded to imprison Davidson and used, as we shall see, the utmost rigour that he could exercise against him.

One is surprised at the King's vehemence over that letter, for Davidson had said and written things concerning the King quite as strong, if not stronger, on former occasions. Perhaps he was irritated at a subject being brought up again which he had regarded as disposed of, or perhaps he desired to enforce the silence of others who were known to be still opposed to it. As Wodrow[2] remarks " this was a season when it was thought proper to give an instance of what was to be expected by such who would stand by our Reformation Rights. And Mr. Davidson was a very fit person to begin with."

It is not within the limits of our subject to trace any farther the struggle of the Kirk against the King's drive for prelacy. Suffice it to say that, despite the vigorous opposition of men like Andrew Melville, John Davidson and others, his Majesty had triumphed, at least for the time being. The Assembly of 1602 agreed that ministers should be appointed to all the prelacies[3] and so the State had defeated the Church and had been able also to dictate its own terms of peace. James had secured an Episcopacy which, however, was not satisfactory either to Episcopalians or Presbyterians. The prelates had no part in the

[1] Calderwood, Vol. VI, p. 112.
[2] Wodrow MS., p. 36.
[3] Calderwood, Vol. VI, p. 179.

government of the Church and the presbyteries were still operative. Yet, as Davidson had foreseen, the King, having succeeded in getting the Church to accept bishops, used them to deprive it of its internal freedom. With his apophthegm, " No bishop, no King", ever in his mind, James became—especially after the union of 1603—more and more unsympathetic to the Scottish Church, and, under the baneful influence of some of his English counsellors he tried to coerce the stalwart Presbyterians into becoming Episcopalians. It was the resentment of the Scots against such an exercise of royal prerogatives in ecclesiastical affairs, that eventually defeated his efforts and indeed led to the final overthrow of the Stewart Kings. It is worthy of note that thus a prophecy of Davidson was fulfilled for he had said in the presence of the King at Edinburgh, " Sir, there is an ordinary proverb, No Bishop, No King, but God hath enjoined me to tell your Majesty that if that corrupt office be forced upon us the days shall come when there shall neither be bishop nor King in your Majesty's dominions."[1]

[1] Woodrow MS., p. 41.

CHAPTER IX

LATER PUBLICATIONS

(A) POEM ON TWO WORTHY CHRISTIANS

IT may seem remarkable that all Davidson's poetical efforts were made before he entered upon his ministry, but it has to be remembered that he never claimed to be a poet in the ordinary sense of the word. His effusions were the outcome of strong feeling on themes which stirred his youthful mind—a wrong done to the Kirk, the death of Knox, who was the greatest inspiration of his life, the loss of a noble couple who had befriended him in difficult days. During his ministerial career he was too much a man of affairs to be concerned about poetry and in this he differed from a contemporary like Hume or a predecessor like Sir David Lindsay. His lot was cast largely amid the Church's battles, and the arena of ecclesiastical controversy does not usually provide either a setting or an atmosphere for the cultivation of the muse. Seldom is the ecclesiastic also a poet.

Thus it was that the poem we have now to consider was written in the year 1574 when its author was still a teacher at St. Andrews and when his only literary effort of public interest was his " Dialogue " against the Regent Morton, printed in the previous year. For the long period of twenty-one years the copy lay among Davidson's papers till a chance reading of it to some friends led to an urgent appeal for its publication. It is much inferior to his other poems and is of interest, not for any literary merit, but for the information it contains concerning the two people whom it commemorates and also for some facts relating to the history of the times. Its full title is " A Memorial of the Life and Death of Two Worthye Christians, Robert Campbel of the Kyneancleugh, and his wife Elizabeth Campbell. In English Meter. Edinburgh: Printed by Robert Waldegrave, printer to the King's Maiestie 1595. Cum privilegio Regali."

Robert Campbell was a member of the house of Loudoun and it has been conjectured that he was a grandson of Sir George Campbell of Loudoun, founder of that family, who was living in 1489. The date of his birth is unknown[1] but he died on April 22nd, 1574, and we have seen that, at his death, he was employed in protecting Davidson from the wrath of Morton. His wife survived him only two months, passing away in the June following. As his only son had predeceased him, his only daughter, Elizabeth, succeeded to the estate, which it is believed was in possession of the family till 1786 when it was sold to Claud Alexander of Ballochmyle.[2]

Davidson dedicated his memorial poem to Elizabeth Campbell, his " deare sister in Christ " in a beautiful letter breathing the finest courtesy and sincere affection. He informed her of how long he had kept the manuscript beside him and how its publication was now due to the desire of friends who believed that it would mean " the stirring up of the

[1] It was probably about 1530 as may be inferred from Davidson's reference to his age, at time of his death.
[2] Robertson, *Ayrshire Families*, Vol. III, pp. 94-8.

zeale of God's people amongst us which now beginneth almost to be quenched in all estates none excepted ". When we remember that this was in 1595 we see that Davidson had a real prescience of what was about to happen to the Church of Scotland—that stormy period in which he played so prominent a part. He quoted Knox whose words were proving true, " That as the Gospel entred among us, and was received with fervencie and heat : so he feared it should decay and lose the former bewtie through coldness and loth-somnesse, howbeit it should not utterly be overthrown in [Scotland] til the comming of the Lord Jesus to iudgment, in spite of Sathan and malice of al his slaves." He also cited George Wishart as having prophesied the victory of the truth in Scotland and yet as having warned the people that if they became unthankful for the great light and liberty of the Gospel terrible plagues would follow.

Davidson had long been unwilling, he said, to print the poem because of the simple form in which it was written. Yet he had regarded that form as suitable for the moving of the people to emulate the excellent Christians whom he had commemorated. Now he yielded to his friends' request in the hope that its publication would tend to profit, committing the issue to God Who sometimes benefits His Church by base means according to His good pleasure. He was also encouraged by a saying of Gregory Nazianzen concerning Basil the Great to the effect that " it is a thing of most dutifull affection to commend the memory of holy persones that are departed, especially of such as have been of most excellent virtues, whether it be by friends or strangers ". Evidently Elizabeth

Campbell was not without some shadow upon her life, for Davidson, in expressing the hope that she might profit from a perusal of the poem and be confirmed by the worthy example of her Parents in Christianity, prayed that the Lord would strengthen her to bear " your crosse, your master's loving badge, given you no doubt for your profite ". He concluded with this sentence of Basil. " Take heede to your selfe that ye may take heed to God " and signed himself " Your assured Friend in Christ, J.D."

It will be well at this stage, to make mention of the interesting historical allusions found in an early part of this long poem. The lines containing them are quoted in full by M'Crie in a note to his *Life of Melville*,[1] dealing with " Ante-Reformation in Scotland ", and they indicate how far, even in those early days, the influence of the Scriptures was beginning to be felt. After making mention of some zealous people who had, even then, procured by some means or other, copies of the New Testament in the vulgar tongue, he adds that some particulars respecting pre-Reformation witnesses are to be found in Davidson's " rare " poem on the two worthy Christians.

Davidson, in those lines refers somewhat loosely to a very interesting story which had been told to James V concerning his Majesty's father in a work by " a cunning Scottish Clark, called Alisius ".[2] The story[3] was to the effect that John Campbell,

---

[1] Vol. I, p. 419.

[2] Alexander Alane or Alesius was born in Edinburgh in 1500. He became a distinguished *alumnus* of St. Andrews University. The " work " referred to was " Alexandri Alesii Scotti Responsio ad Cochlei columnias," 1534.

[3] It is translated in *The Annals of the English Bible* by Rev. Christopher Anderson. Vol. II, pp. 400-1, and by Dr. D. Hay Fleming, *Reformation in Scotland*, pp. 27-8.

Laird of Cesnok (of which house Kinzeancleugh's wife was descended[1]) was in the habit of having the priest in his household read regularly to him and his family the New Testament in their vernacular language. Being of a kindly disposition, and to show his impartiality he permitted a number of monks as well as others to dwell in his hospitable abode. These monks, however, took unfair advantage of his kindness, violated the laws of hospitality and preferred a charge of heresy against him before the Bishop. In great danger of his own and his wife's life,[2] Campbell appealed to King James IV who determined to hear the case himself on both sides. When the trial came on, the husband was so modest and shy that he could scarcely make his defence, whereupon the King commanded the wife to plead. This she did so effectively and convincingly, quoting the Scriptures and ably refuting all the charges, that his Majesty not only acquitted the worthy couple but came down and caressed the lady, extolling her diligence in Christian doctrine. Then he reproved the monks and threatened them with severe punishment if they ever troubled these honourable persons again, while to the Laird he presented certain villages in token of his goodwill.

In his reference to this story Davidson appears to confound father and son, for he says that the incident happened " eighty years sensyne and mare ". As

[1] The poem says " Of surname they were Campbells baith."
and　　　　　　　" Scho of a gude and godly stock
　　　　　　　　　Came of the old house of Cesnok."

[2] Davidson has preserved an ancient tradition to the effect that this Laird of Cesnock mentioned by Alesius was being led to the scaffold in Edinburgh when the King set him free, and further—
　　　　　　　" Some sayes death was aswel prepard,
　　　　　　　　For Priest and Lady as the Lard."

he was writing in 1574 and evidently did not alter this when he printed the poem in 1595, that would date it round about 1494, in which year an earlier member of the same family, *George* Campbell of Cesnok was, with several other Lollards of distinction, prosecuted before the Archbishop of Glasgow for certain "new opinions" and reprimanded.[1] The incident related above must have taken place at a later date but not after 1513, in which year James IV died. Calderwood[2] made the same mistake in connecting the incidents related by Alesius and Davidson with the prosecution of 1494, and he apparently thought that Knox was in error in giving *George* as Campbell's Christian name. Knox, however, has the support of the record evidence; and unless Alesius wrote *John* in error, the occasions must have been different. This view is strengthened by Knox's emphasizing the part played by Reid of Barskimming, and ignoring Campbell's wife who according to Alesius behaved so nobly. Davidson says,

> This story I could not passe by
> Being so well worth memory :
> Whereby most clearlie we may see
> How that the Papists loudly lie :
> Who our religion so oft cald
> A faith but of fiftie yeere ald :

He then indicates even greater evidence to prove that for "mair than thrice fiftie" years the Protestant faith had been known in Scotland—

[1] George Campbell was Laird of Cesnock in 1490-1 ; he was dead before October 30th, 1509. John Campbell was his son and heir. Register of the Great Seal 1424-1513, Nos. 2315, 2836 ; 1513-46, No. 218 (Dr. Hay Fleming, *Reformation in Scotland*, p. 27).

[2] Calderwood, Vol. I, p. 54.

As by the storie ye may knaw
Of Resby burnt before Paul Craw
The thousand yeare four hundrethe five
In Perth while Husse[1] was yet alive.

It will here be seen that the author makes reference to some of the best known pre-Reformation heroes. James Resby[2] has been described as an English Presbyter of the Wiclif school. He was accused as a heretic and burned at Perth for declaring that the Pope was not *de facto* the vicar of Christ and that no one is Pope or Christ's vicar unless he is holy. Davidson is mistaken in the date of Resby's martyrdoms which took place not in 1405 but in 1407.[3] Paul Craw or Crawar was a native of Bohemia, said to have been sent to Scotland by the heretics of Prague with the purpose of " infecting the realm ". He seems to have been well versed in the Scriptures and other sacred literature, and he maintained and defended the doctrines of the Pragites and of the followers of Wiclif with wonderful courage. He was burned for his faith at St. Andrews in 1433.[4]

The good man whose splendid qualities are extolled in this poem was a stout champion of the Reformed faith in Scotland and a close and much esteemed friend of John Knox. He was one of the three brethren who sat in turn by the Reformer's death-bed, and it was to him, the nearest and dearest of them, Knox committed the care of his wife and children when the end drew near. " I rely on your

[1] John Huss, reformer and martyr, born at Husinec about 1369. He was put to death at the stake, July 6th, 1415.
[2] Spottiswood says that he was " de schola Wicliffi ".
[3] Hay Fleming, *The Reformation in Scotland*, p. 14.
[4] Spottiswood and others are wrong in making the date 1432. Hay Fleming, *The Reformation in Scotland*, pp. 17-18.

becoming to them ", he said, " as a husband and a father in my room."[1] We have already seen how angry he was over the Assembly's vacillating behaviour with regard to Davidson in 1574,[2] how he befriended the young man, taking him to his home, protecting him and showing him the utmost kindness and consideration. Another outstanding example of his kind-heartedness, with which was combined true Protestant zeal, is referred to briefly in the memorial lines but is more fully related in a prefatory notice to the poem in Maidment's edition of Davidson's *Poetical Remains*. The story is taken from the *Analecta*[3] of Robert Wodrow and is to the following effect. Robert Campbell who was on friendly terms with the Regent Moray informed his Grace on the morning before the battle of Langside that he was well persuaded that the Queen's party would be defeated. The matter had given him grave concern, knowing as he did that the whole Reformation depended upon it and that victory to the Queen would mean Popery again for Scotland. He had arrived at his happy assurance, he said, not from probabilities or outward appearances, which were none too promising, but from deep concern in prayer for divine interposition. He was convinced that God had heard the prayers of all earnest Protestants deeply concerned about their religion. Under this expectation of victory he begged a favour from the Regent. The estates of the Queen's adherents would be forefaulted after the battle and given to the victors, and in that case he desired that there might be given to him the

[1] M'Crie, *Life of Knox*, p. 345.
[2] See Chapter II.
[3] Vol. V, pp. 67, 68. MS. in National Library of Scotland.

estate of the Sheriff of Ayr a young friend of his own, though on the contrary side. His Grace, expressing the hope that he might be right in his prediction, granted him the request on that understanding. When Kinzeancleugh had received the promise, he intimated his intention of returning the estate to its owner who, he said, was but a youth " bred in ignorance and drawn away by ill company ". He hoped to win to the Regent and the Reformation, by soft measures, this man who was really of good temper and excellent disposition and who might yet prove serviceable to the Protestant cause in the West. " All which came directly to pass," adds Wodrow. " The battle was gained—many were forefaulted, and the Sheriff of Ayr's estates given to Kinzeancleugh, and he gave it back, and brought him to be a firm and useful Protestant."

It is good that the virtues of a man like Robert Campbell have not been left unrecorded and unsung, for surely he was one of the greatest laymen of the early Reformed Church in Scotland. "Like the heroes of primeval times ", it has been said, " such as Wallace and Bruce, not to speak of Hector and Achilles, he has had his deeds embalmed in rhyme, which if not lofty, is at least laudatory."[1] Since poets in all times, like Homer and Seneca, Virgil and Ovid and many others, have celebrated men of " vertuous deid ", and have taken great pains to praise others for vain and earthly things that bring small or no true comfort, Davidson feels himself constrained to deal with a higher theme.

[1] Edgar, *Old Church Life in Scotland*, p. 272.

Why should we not with all our might
Write in thir daies of so great light
Of faithful godly men and wise.
Who for the truth durst interprise :
To hazard at the Lord's command,
All that they had, both life and land.

Such a work, we are informed, ought to be undertaken
not to flatter the flesh but to give God the glory. It
is hoped, too, that posterity may note from what has
been written, that their fathers delighted in the ways
of light and not in the blindness and idolatry of
Papistry. The true religion will be vindicated in
face of all the lies of Romish chroniclers by noble
living on the part of those who profess the truth of
Christ. The virtues of the good Regent, of John
Knox " that valyant Conqueror " and of many more,
the author says he will pass over, since these have been
celebrated by other writers. He hastens to extol
the goodness of Kinzeancleugh and his faithful wife.

Sic twa I knowe not where to finde
In all Scotland left them behinde :
Of sa great faith and charitie.
With mutuall love and amitie :
That I wat an mair heavenly life
Was never betweene man and wife.

Although there is no attempt at anything like
arrangement in the poem, it may be said that there
are three main divisions of the subject. These may
be set forth thus—(1) The singular zeal and activity
of Campbell in the early days of the Reformation.
(2) The constant sympathy and unselfish assistance
of his wife in all his doings. (3) His personal piety,
beauty of character and domestic felicity. We shall
look at these in turn.

(1) In the days when it often meant obloquy and sacrifice to stand on the side of the reformed religion, Robert Campbell was a great encourager of the preachers, whom he generously entertained and whose every need he sought to supply. Everywhere he was eager to have the Mass overthrown and the Gospel proclaimed.

> Sa privatelie in his lodgeing
> He had baith prayers and preaching :
> To tell his friends he na whit dred,
> How they had lang bene blindlins led :
> By shaveling Papists, Monks and Friers,
> And be the Paipe these many yeares :
> When some Barrones, neere hand him by,
> And Noble men he did espie,
> Of auld who had the truth profest
> To them he quicklie him addrest :
> And in exhorting was not slak,
> What consolation they would tak,
> How orderlie they might suppresse
> In their owne bounds that Idole messe :
> In place thereof some preaching plant,
> To quhilk some noble men did grant.

It will here be seen that he was instrumental in getting men to preach the Gospel throughout the country. These found it necessary to declare before the Queen and Council that what they aimed at was no alteration in affairs of State but simply the reformation of religion, " that Papistrie being supprest, Christ might be preached East and West ". In all the upheaval of the Reformation days, Campbell showed boundless enthusiasm while preserving Christian consideration toward his enemies. His journeys near and far in the interests of the cause were incessant, and Davidson

has not failed to do justice to such disinterested zeal
and energy :—

> Then Robert like a busie Bie,
> Did ride the post in all Countrie :
> Baith North and Sowth, baith East and West
> To all that the gude cause profest :
> Through Angus, Fyfe, and Lawthaine,
> Late journies had he many ane :
> By night he would passe forth of Kyle,
> And slip in shortly to Argyle :
> Syne to Stratherne and to all parts,
> Where he knew godly zealous harts,
> Exhorting them for to be stoute,
> And of the matter have no doubt :
> For although, said he, we be few,
> Having our God we are anew.

Campbell spared no expense and took no end of
trouble " for the libertie of Christ's Kirk and the
Gospell ".   None did more than he to bring the godly
together in a strong band for the resistance of error.
He was ever ready to risk even his life for the good
Cause and both in Congregation and General
Assembly his counsel was greatly valued.   He was
famed for his sincerity and earnestness, particularly
as he was absolutely free from anything in the nature
of self-interest.   That was in striking contrast to the
majority of the nobles who held firmly to the tiends
which really belonged to the Church.   Those of
Ochiltree which were in the possession of Kinzeancleugh, he handed over most willingly, thus providing
an example for others, which, however, they were in
no hurry to follow.

(2) The lady comes in for a large share of Davidson's praise.   In reading the lines concerning her,
one is reminded of the description of the virtuous

woman in the Book of Proverbs. She was, quite evidently, no ordinary person. Toward the close of the poem her private virtues are praised—her godliness and honesty, her knowledge of the Scriptures and her delightful way of speaking about them to others, her love for the society of none but godly people, and her wisdom and providence in the affairs of her own household. Kinzeancleugh was fortunate in having a wife so utterly at one with him in all his enterprises. She encouraged him in his frequent expeditions in the interest of religion, never complained of his long absences from home and, unlike the wives of some others, never grudged the expenses he incurred. " In describing the ungracious reception which the husband of one of these thrifty dames received at his home-coming, the poet informs us of the arrival in Scotland of a singular female colony, whose race, it is hoped, is now extinct among us ; although, perhaps, some acute and keen-set antiquary may be able still to track them, and stoically fearless of a ' rebegeaster ',[1] to point out some descendants of these Norwegian Amazons."[2]

> that balefull band
> That Sathan hes sent heir away,
> With the black fleete of Norroway :
> Of Whome ane with her Tygers tong
> Had able met him with a rong :
> And reaked him a rebegeastor
> Calling him many warlds weastor.

Campbell's wife was of a very different type. So far from murmuring she gave a glad consent to whatever

---

[1] Apparently a severe stroke with a rung ; probably a cant term— *Jamieson's Scottish Dictionary.*
[2] M'Crie, *Life of Melville,* Vol. II, p. 494.

her husband deemed right, rejoicing that he had the zeal to take so great a part in the interests of Christ's Kirk.

(3) It was to the honour of Robert Campbell that he was best loved where he was best known. Davidson gives us a pleasing picture of the man at home on his estate. He was most liberal and kind to all in need, continually offering to many, a safe lodging and ample food. Nor did he forget their souls, for nightly after supper, he called them to the hall to be examined " of Lord's Prayer and Beleefe and ten Commandments ", and every Sabbath his servants had to give similar reckoning " of chiefe heades of Religion ". It was such sincerity and earnestness proceeding from true faith, which impressed John Knox, with whom he became so familiar and whose trusty friend he remained, often through much adversity, to the very end.

Though a great champion of the Reformation whose courage did not fail even in time of war, Campbell was, nevertheless, the most peaceable of men. He possessed a singular gift for settling the disputes of his neighbours and advising both rich and poor in their affairs ; and so wise was his judgment and so obvious his uprightness that even Papists were to be found among those who sought his aid. His kindness of heart came out specially in his treatment of his tenants. He never pressed them for payment of rent but was prepared to take it whenever they felt able. None were ever asked to remove, except for downright wrongdoing and contempt of God's truth. And so the folks on the estate lived most happily, all striving to please a master who was so deeply interested in their welfare.

Like his zeal for the cause of religion, this consideration for his dependants and tenants was shared by Campbell's godly wife. Their home was ideal in its wedded love and Christian piety. Davidson could write of that from personal experience, for in the time of his suffering in 1574, on retiring with Kinzeancleugh to the West, there " he saw suche a gude example of pietie and holie exercise, in his familie, that he thought all his lyfe-time before but a profane passing of the time ".[1]

Davidson relates at some length and with much moralizing the circumstances of Campbell's death. The young Sheriff of Ayr had requested his honoured kinsman to ride with him to Rusco, the seat of the Laird of Lochinvar, to advise upon some business. Davidson was included in the company. On the morning after their arrival—Easter-day—Campbell became very ill, and, despite all the attentions of his friends and those of his wife hastily summoned from her home, he passed away some days later. Although Davidson tells how at the sick man's request he read to him " the whole Psalmes twise ouer in prose " and records some of his last sayings, he does not appear to have been with his friend and benefactor at the end, his own affairs having necessitated an even earlier separation.[2] Kinzeancleugh had seen " God's just Judgements " approaching fast to his country and he had also a vision of heavenly bliss, so he was not sorry, —though according to Davidson not more than forty-three years of age—to follow his friend John Knox into the unseen. His body was borne in a litter

[1] Calderwood, Vol. III, p. 312.
[2] Ibid., p. 313.

14

to Mauchline and buried (where his wife was also laid, less than two months later, as has already been stated) amid universal lamentation.

> As was not seene in Kyle before,
> This hundreth yeares and many more.

(B) Davidson's Catechism

Growing distress over the ignorance of so many of their people in the rudiments of religion, and also the pressing necessity of finding suitable instruction for the young, led the Reformers to set forth the truths which they desired to teach, in catechisms which form a most illuminating study. They saw that where commentaries and more elaborate works failed, their end would be served by the simple method of question and answer. Truth would thus come in even at lowly doors and the intellect would be quickened as well as the heart touched and the conscience awakened.

The earliest and best-known of these catechisms were those by Luther and Calvin and also the Palatine or Heidelberg Catechism, an English translation of which appeared at Edinburgh in 1591 and which claimed on the title-page to be " now authorized by the King's Maiestie for the Use of Scotland ".[1] In the sixteenth century catechisms multiplied quickly, however, as the Reformers were keen upon instructing their people, convinced that therein lay both their duty and their safety. Calvin's work seems to have been the inspiration and basis of most of these.

[1] Dunlop, *Collection of Confessions*, Vol. II, p. 273.

The first Catechism in the language of the people, issued by the Reformed Church of Scotland, was produced by John Craig[1] in 1581. It was prepared simply for his own congregation at Aberdeen, but it soon became very popular throughout the country. Ten years later a smaller publication[2] by the same author for use before communion received the approval of the General Assembly.[3]

It was not till the closing years of his ministry at Prestonpans, amid growing infirmity and enforced absence from the public affairs of the Church, that John Davidson added one more to the Catechisms of the Reformation, those precious works of which it has been justly said—" Our Scottish catechisms, though grey with the antiquity of three centuries, are not yet out of date. They still read well, both as to style and substance ; it would be hard to amend them or to substitute something better in their place. Like some of our old church bells, they have retained for centuries their sweetness and amplitude of tone unimpaired."[4]

It is not improbable that Davidson had attempted something in the nature of a catechism some years earlier. In the *Life of Archbishop Whitgift*[5] there is a short account of a " quarrel " which evidently originated with Martin Marprelat[6] over a small Catechism of two sheets of paper, " made by one Davidson, an obscure person " and printed by

---

[1] Bonar, *Catechisms of the Scottish Reformation*, p. 177.
[2] Dunlop, *Collection of Confessions*, Vol. II, p. 363.
[3] *Book of the Universal Kirk*, p. 356.
[4] Bonar, *Catechisms of the Reformation*, Preface, p. viii.
[5] Strype, *Life of Archbishop Whitgift*, p. 306.
[6] Martin Marprelat was the comprehensive name under which were published a series of vigorous pamphlets by a few Elizabethan Puritans against official Episcopacy.

Waldegrave in 1587. It seems that when that work was brought to the Archbishop to be licensed for the press, its examination was entrusted to his chaplain, a certain Dr. Wood. That gentleman objected to Salvation being attributed, as the Author had it, to the Word *preached* and so would not have it printed. His reason, he said, was to have the work of Man's Salvation ascribed to the Word *Read* (that is, as well as preached). The paper is then briefly dismissed with this comment—"Some Party Pamphlet belike it was, like to that busy and unlearned Scot, then termed to be the Author thereof."

Wodrow[1] confesses that he does not know what to make of this passage of Strype. The information which he himself has provided concerning Davidson, he regards as a proof that the Reformer was neither so obscure nor so unlearned as some English writers would have us believe. This Catechism, he is convinced, was quite another thing from the Catechism which Davidson printed fifteen years later, and he conjectures that it was possibly a short work drawn up by him when in England for the use of some religious family where he had been kindly entertained. After his return to Scotland in 1585, it may have been printed, probably without his knowledge. Wodrow further remarks that, if it was fact that the Bishop's chaplain blotted out the word "*preached*", meaning that the word preached was not a means of salvation, it was contrary to many passages in the New Testament. If his meaning was not to deny that power to preaching but to take in the word " *read* " it would have been much better for the Doctor to have added

[1] Addition to MS. Vol. X. Glasgow University.

" *and read* "—an emendation to which neither Mr.
Davidson nor any Puritan would have had the slightest
objection.

Davidson's Catechism is his chief publication in
prose and it appeared in 1602. Its full title is " Some
Helpes for Young Schollers in Christianity, as they
are in use and taught, partly at the Examination
before the Communion ; and partly in the ordinarie
Catechisme every Sabbath-day in the New Kirk
of Salt-Preston.—Edinburgh, Printed by Robert
Waldegrave, Printer to the King's Maiesty. 1602.
Cum Privilegio Regio."

The opening paragraph is a short address to the
reader who is forewarned of repetitions seemingly
" tedious and superfluous " to be met with in the work.
The author pleads as his justification for these, that
he is dealing with rude beginners, and repetition is
needful for those who are young in knowledge or
rather ignorant.

There follows a brief dedication to his people,
simple and beautiful, in these words—" To his loving
flock of Salt-Prestoun who by the preaching of the
Gospel, beleeve and turne to the Lorde. John
Davidson, wisheth increase of Faith and Repentance,
with constancie therein, to the end and in the end.
Amen." He then refers to the doctrine he had
preached since his settlement in their midst and he
recalls, as we saw in a former chapter, the themes
on which he had discoursed when he first appeared
before them on November 16th, 1595. After out-
lining what was the burden of his message and the
points in his teaching, he concludes thus—" For the
better keeping in memorie whereof, I have thought

good to put them in writ in divers formes, and set them to printing for your use as ye see, that nothing bee wanting that maye further the sounde grounding of you, according to your meane capacitie, in the true Christian religion, so farre as in me lyeth. Wherefore it rests, that yee bee not slouthful in exercising your selves and your families in reading, learning and practising heerof."

Several very apt passages of Scripture follow. Davidson had a singular facility in supporting all that he had to say with suitable portions of God's Word. It is interesting to note that in his Catechism he uses the translation of the " Bishop's Bible " and not the Geneva version which the Scottish ministers generally made use of at that time.[1]

The Catechism proper, as its title indicates, is divided into two parts. The first, which is by far the longer, was meant specially for those in preparation for Communion. It is described as " The Forme of familiar instruction and examination of rude[2] people, entring to be disciples in the schoole of Christ." Reference is made by Davidson to a short service of Prayer and exhortation which the minister had with intending communicants. This must have taken place previous to another service at which they would be formally admitted—like the brief service of admission of " Young Communicants " to full communion so common in the Scottish Churches to-day. The demands which Davidson made of those young people,

[1] Bonar, *Catechisms of the Reformation*, p. 326n. Evidently he quoted from memory as there are slight deviations. " Strong drink " is an evident *erratum* for " strong meat ".

[2] *rude :* dull, ignorant (Latin=rudis) ; not generally used in this sense by Scottish writers.

echo those of the Book of Discipline—that they must be able " to say the Lord's Prayer, the Articles of the Belief and declare the sum of the Law ".[1]

The essence of all doctrine he states thus simply— " that all wha wald have rest to their saules and life eternall, must only come to Christ Jesus, the sonne of God and to none other." The state of man and the way of salvation is set down under four points— (1) Our miserable estate by nature and the cause thereof. (2) Our redemption and the cause thereof. (3) Our assurance of this redemption and salvation, with the cause and means thereof. (4) Our duty resulting from our being saved or assured of salvation. Each section begins with a careful and full statement on the particular doctrine, by way of introduction to the series of questions and answers on the same. Thus, (1) " As concerning our condition by nature we are children of disobedience, that is altogether given to rebellion against God and his Word and so are plaine rebelles to God," etc. (2) " Our help and safety is only from the Lord our God who hath made both the heaven and the earth : who said, I am the Lord and beside mee there is no Saviour. For our salvation commeth not of nature but of grace," etc. (3) " Meanes is there nane that properly joyneth us with Christ, but only Faith, whilk is ane hearty receiving of Christ crucified and risen againe : our alane and sufficient Saviour," etc. (4) Being in Christ we must be newe creatures, not in substance, but in qualities and disposition of our mindes, and change of the actions of our lives . . . we must deny ungodliness and warldly lustes and must live

[1] Knox, *Works*, Vol. II, p. 240.

soberly and righteously and godly in this present warld," etc.[1]

The second part of this Catechism covers the same ground as the first but only by question and answer, and it is in much shorter form. It was used week by week at the ordinary services of the Church. In a brief introduction Davidson shows, that by taking a portion every Sabbath, the principles of religion were gone through in the course of a month. He also explains his method. After the reading of an appropriate Scripture lesson, two children would stand up, one asking the questions and the other supplying the answers. Then the minister would ask a few questions either of man or child on some principal things " after sik easie manner as I thinke his capacity is able to understand : whairof (praised be God) baith I, and the party answering, many times receaves comfort, and the Kirk edification."

Davidson made it clear that his Catechism was not intended to be anything more than a guide for the edification of his own people.[2] It seems, however, that when the Provincial Assembly of Lothian gave it their approbation,[3] it was destined for a much greater usefulness. Both the author and the work deserved a wider constituency. For John Davidson was a typical representative of the Evangelical

[1] Davidson's divisions bear close resemblance to the plan and arrangement of the Heidelberg Catechism which has three parts, (1) the sin and misery of man, (2) man's redemption in Christ, (3) thankfulness of the redeemed, or the Christian life.

[2] See *Catechism*, Bonar, p. 347.

[3] " The Provincial Assembly of Lowthiane and Tweddale, having red and considered the forme of Examination, and Catechisme, written by our brother, Maister John Davidson, approves the same, and agrees that it sall bee imprented. Extract furth of the books of the provinciall assemblie of Lowthiane and Tweddale by mee Richarde Thomesone, clerk thereto. At Edinburgh the 7 of November 1599." (Quoted by Bonar, p. 348.)

Protestant divines of our Scottish Reformation epoch and perhaps the best monument that remains to tell of the faith that was in him is just his Catechism. This little work had such an abiding influence that the memory of it was still fresh a full century after the writer's death. Both he and it held such a place in the esteem of the divines of the post-Reformation era that in Thomas Boston's notes[1] on The Marrow of Modern Divinity the Catechism is quoted no fewer than eleven times. Now, there were few documents that exercised a more definite influence on the thinking of the Evangelical School during the eighteenth century and particularly in the Secession Churches than those notes of Thomas Boston's. Thus indirectly or mediately Davidson's influence continued to tell on the life of his most devout countrymen for full two hundred years.

What specially served along this line to preserve his influence was his statement of the doctrine of Faith—the central and most important part of his Catechism. The definition which he gave of this saving grace was presented in alternate forms—" a hearty assurance of forgiveness or a hearty receiving of Christ ". The variation of these forms is significant ; they are not strictly equivalent. His first statement is in full keeping with the unabated assurance doctrine that was common to the first Reformers.[2] The variant definition is in keeping with the modified and more carefully stated Reformed doctrine, as that

---

[1] The General Assembly condemned The Marrow, but as Rev. Dr. Colquhoun of Leith used to say, they did not condemn Boston's Notes on The Marrow !

[2] e.g. in Calvin's *Institutes* and his Geneva *Catechism* ; also in the Heidelberg Catechism (Q. 21), faith is described as necessarily implying or comprehending assurance.

is set forth in the Westminster Confession of Faith which expressly discriminates between the faith which receives Christ and the assurance of personal salvation.[1]   In both he takes the ground of the Church of Scotland that " regeneratioun is wrocht be the power of the Holie Gost working in the hartes of the elect of God ".[2]   Faith and the assurance of it do not proceed from natural powers with us but in His inspiration.   The writer of a pamphlet on the Marrow Controversy,[3] who refers to Davidson as " the once burning and shining light of this Church ", after stating the two definitions of faith as set forth in the Catechism adds :—" Yet, in a former part of the same Catechism, he gives us to understand what sort of assurance and persuasion it was he meant, as follows : ' And certain it is ', says he, ' that both the Inlightning of the Mind to acknowledge the Truth of the Promise of Salvation to us in Christ ; and the sealing up of the certainty thereof in our Hearts and Minds (of the whilk Twa Parts, as it were, Faith consists) are the works and effects of the Spirit of God.' "

The casuistical divines of the first post-Reformation age were faced with difficulties in connection with the definition of Faith that was currently accepted among them.   They were also involved in controversial difficulties in connection with the controversy with Rome which was then the live issue for the Reformed Churches.   These two classes of difficulties told in the direction of compelling a more carefully guarded

[1] *Westminster Confession of Faith,* Chapter XVIII.
[2] *Old or First Confession of Faith,* Art. 3.12.
[3] Queries Agreed unto by the Commission of General Assembly and put to Ministers who gave a representation and petition against the 5th and 8th Acts of Assembly, 1720, together with their answers.

statement as to what the faith of the Gospel is. The Reformed ministers, as pastors, met with cases of sincere Christians, who might be even the most serious people of their charge, who were in great distress as to their assurance of grace and salvation, because they could not claim to have the abiding persuasion that Christ was indeed theirs—in keeping with the accepted Protestant teaching which made assurance of this, part and parcel of saving faith. They felt in dealing with such cases that their definition went too far and was proving a stumbling block to many of their most worthy hearers. These were sometimes on the brink of despair because their conscience told them that they did not have this confident persuasion at all times that Christ was their Saviour indeed.

The difficulties that thus emerged in the practical life of the Churches conspired with the difficulties from the side of the Roman controversy to bring about an adjustment of the accepted definition of the grace of faith. The Church of Rome did not deny assurance to the Reformers but they maintained that it could not be enjoyed with a divine certainty of faith, apart from the testimony of the Church or a special heavenly revelation. Bellarmine puts the question at issue between the two parties in this way : " Whether anyone without a special revelation ought to be or can be certain with the certitude of a divine faith in which a false element can by no means be found, that his sins are forgiven."[1] In opposition to the Romanist view, the Reformers affirmed their possession of assurance of forgiveness with a divine certainty, as the normal attainment

---

[1] Cunningham, *Reformers and Theology of Reformation*, p. 144.

of all true believers. This assurance they regarded as an essential of justifying faith and it was constantly repeated by them in their teaching though not embodied in the most important Confessions. Later on, many theologians felt that they had been driven by the controversy into a rather extreme position. It was even going beyond the warrant of Scripture to pronounce saving faith as essentially including a conviction that the believer's own sins are forgiven.[1] A more guarded statement on the subject is to be found in Davidson's alternate definition—" Or after this manner : it is the hearty receiving of Christ offered in the preaching of the Word and sacraments by the working of the Holy Spirit, for the remission of sins, whereby he becomes one with us and we are with him, he our head and we his members." This alternative, as has been indicated, is not a strict equivalent of the first statement but it lends itself to the carefully guarded statement of the Westminster divines—" This infallible assurance doth not so belong to the essence of faith, but that a true believer may wait long and conflict with many difficulties, before he be partaker of it."[2] If Davidson gives his alternative of set purpose as a definition that was not strictly equivalent to his first one, he is working along the same line as William Perkins the Elizabethan divine,

[1] This is borne out by the following passage from Principal Cunningham's book, " God requires us to believe nothing that is not true before we believe it and which may not be propounded to us to be believed accompanied at the same time with satisfactory evidence of its truth ; and, if so, the belief that our sins are forgiven and that we have been brought into a state of grace, must be posterior in order of nature, if not of time, to the act of faith by which the change is effected and cannot therefore prove a necessary constituent element of the act itself, cannot be its essence or belong to its essence." p. 119.

[2] *Westminster Confession*, Chapter XVIII. Section 3. It also affirms that true believers may have their assurance shaken, but none the less it holds forth the privilege and the duty of being thus assured.

who from Cambridge wielded such influence among
the doctrinal Puritans of the Church of England.
For Perkins in his Catechism explains the grace of
Faith to be " a wonderful grace of God by which a
man doth apprehend and apply Christ and all His
benefits unto himself ". This is in full keeping with
the more mature seventeenth century definition.
But in the same Catechism he says also, " This
applying is done by Assurance when a man is verily
persuaded by the Holy Spirit of God's favour towards
himself particularly and of the forgiveness of his own
sins." Another of the same school, John Rogers of
Dedham, has a similar description of faith. His
words are, " Faith is a particular persuasion of my
heart that Christ is mine and that I shall have life
and salvation by His means ; that whatever Christ
did for the redemption of mankind, He did it for me."[1]
It is easy to see how Boston in his exposition and
defence of the Marrow doctrine, should appeal to
statements of this kind, and in keeping with the teaching of his school, should affirm that this persuasion
is a persuasion of the truth that in the Gospel Christ
is freely given to me to be received. The assurance
that he and his fellows taught as essential to saving
faith is not the assurance that I have believed but the
assurance that Christ is given me in the Gospel. The
assurance of personal salvation comes only when there
is the confident persuasion that I the sinner have
received the Christ who is thus so freely offered and
to whom I am so welcome.

The second statement that Davidson makes is
quite accurate as an exhibition of what was, from the

[1] *Treatise of Faith*, p. 23.

first, regarded by the Reformers as a leading element entering into the faith of the Gospel. It was one, however, which did not introduce an assurance of personal salvation as a thing that enters into the essence of saving faith. Taking this line it fitted in with the later definition which we find in the Westminster Confession, already quoted.[1] With the acceptance of this position there was a marked tendency in the seventeenth century and onward, in the Calvinistic churches to lay less stress than in the previous century on the assurance of salvation which found such a place in the earlier teaching of the Reformed Churches. Accordingly men fought shy of the earlier definitions, and in the proceedings taken against the Marrow Men, their defence of the statements of the Marrow in regard to the assurance of Faith was made a ground of accusation against their soundness in the Faith. Davidson's language as expressive of the sentiments of the Reforming age proved useful to Boston and his fellows in making good their case that their doctrine was fully supported by the language of the older worthies of the Scottish Reformed Church.

To the Catechism there are appended two short simple prayers to be used before and after meals. The author states that these forms of prayer and thanksgiving are only for " thankful persons to God for His benefits, and not for profane abusers and gracelesse devourers thereof " who the more wealth they have by God's gift the more forgetful of Him they are, and who are apt to think the praising of God, especially at table, " but Monkish hypocrisie,

[1] Chapter XVIII. Section 3. *Larger Catechism*, p. 81.

a Popish ceremonie, or lost time ". The forms are
not obligatory on anyone so long as some kind of
thanksgiving at meals is reverently offered to God,
not merely by children or servants, but by the whole
household, " for the chiefest is unworthie ynough to
praise God's halie Maiestie ".

Then follow the ten commandments and excellent
Scottish versions of metrical Psalms cxxx. and cxvii.
with a final ascription of praise.

That this work of Davidson's met with great
commendation can be gathered from the testimonies
of two " learned men " in a note to the author, which
are printed in its various editions. (1) " I thank God
for your precious pearle little in quantitie but infinite
in waight. I allow and approves the perspicuitie,
ordour, and substantious comprising of so great
mysteries in little bounds." (2) " There is not an
idle word heir." To these eulogies the author adds
the following modest words of his own. " If anything
be wrang heir, it is of weaknesse, and not of wilfulnes :
and therefore is humbly submitted to the loving and
advised correction of the godlie learned, by God's
Worde."

In the year 1708 Davidson's Catechism was
reprinted by Mr. William Jameson, Professor of
History at the University of Glasgow. This edition
is of special interest and value because of its introduction or preface, which is entitled " A Discourse ;
Giving an Account of the Occasion of this Impression
&c." The title page says that it also contains " several
things useful for determining of the Episcopal Controversy ". After paying tribute to Davidson as a
man of great piety and singular enduements, and

indicating how the Catechism was first compiled for " babes and rude novices " in the author's own parish, Jameson proceeds to narrate why the present reprinting of the work had become a pressing necessity. A signal injury at once to Truth and to the memory of the author had been done by an Episcopal minister, Mr. Robert Calder, in his *Vindication* of a sermon he had preached on January 30th, 1703. He alleged therein that Davidson, toward the close of his life, recanted from his Presbyterianism and embraced Episcopacy. " Mr. Davidson," he declared, " in a Catechism, dedicated to his own Parish, the Panns, has a small tractate at the end of that Catechism which he calls *The Burthen of a Loaded Conscience*, in which he confesses and bewails the several failings and follies of his youth, manhood and ministry ; and gives many good instructions to all the readers of his book, as to religion and Loyalty ; And as to Epis-copacy he has these very words, *Be obedient to Arch-bishops and Bishops, and stand not out against them as I have wickedly done.*"

Professor Jameson replies in most effective terms to this indictment which is so ludicrous in the light of Davidson's consistently uncompromising attitude to prelacy. To begin with, he is convinced that the whole thing is a manifest forgery and he is confirmed in that view by Calder's excuses and subterfuge, when asked repeatedly to produce the book with the recan-tation in it. " There is," he says, " no such thing as he alleges, no such Tractate, either at the end or anywhere else." There must be, he feels sure, in the breast of every honest and reasonable man, at least a strong justified suspicion, if not a firm persuasion,

that never one jot of what Calder attributes to Davidson came from that good man's pen. Calder must
have known the pretended quotation to be " mere
forgery to the syllable ".

A further argument against the possibility of such
a recantation is found in Davidson's record of service
to the Church. No one examining that, says Jameson,
could credit such a story. He was among the first
who " spied the Hierarchie Bishops creeping into our
Church under the name of Ecclesiastical Voters in
Parliament, and with all Christian vigour and forti-
tude endeavoured still to block up their passage."
Besides there were his Protestations in the presence of
the King, at Edinburgh in 1596 and at Dundee in
1598, and also his letters to the Dundee Assembly
of 1597 and that at Burntisland in 1601. These he
would never acknowledge to have been in error even
when, in later years, he could have obtained his
release from confinement to his own parish.

Again, Jameson employs a negative but, as he
calls it, an irrefragable proof, namely the silence of
all the prelatical authors on the subject. Quite
convincingly he argues that Spottiswood, for example,
could not have been ignorant of such a public recantation of so famous an adversary of prelacy. If he
had known of it, " would he have failed to set it down
at full length and erect his trophies upon it ? " From
all we know of the Bishop's predilections and of his
attitude to Davidson we can well believe that he would
have gloated over such a piece of information had it
been in his possession and well founded. Jameson
is inclined to think that even if Calder had seen such
a tractate as he spoke of, he must have been imposed

on by some late spurious piece of writing wherewith its author had designed to cheat mankind. Wodrow[1] regards this view as a very charitable conjecture and considers Calder as being quite unworthy of it, and this seems the wiser verdict. The Episcopalian cannot be excused in any way from palming upon the world, so foolishly and maliciously, a story which he was not able to substantiate, and from citing a tractate which evidently did not exist and which certainly he was unable to produce.

In an addition to his prefixed discourse, Professor Jameson refers in glowing terms to the esteem in which Mr. John Davidson had been held by Scottish Presbyterians generally and by his own people at Saltpreston particularly. He finds a fresh argument for his abiding Presbyterianism in the way in which his memory was revered, as manifested in writings, discourses and other directions. The more zealous the Presbyterians were, the greater was the warmth of their affection to his memory—" highly honouring him as a choice servant of Christ and a chief champion and sufferer for Presbytery." In view of all that, the Professor asks a very pertinent question. Would it have been likely that these people would have so honoured him long after his death and passed on his name from father to son with affection and reverence, if he had told to the world that it was a wicked thing to stand against Archbishops and Bishops? The thing is incredible. Truly, " no man of judgment will believe it, no man of honour affirm it ". It is, however, in keeping with the ordinary practice of the defenders of prelacy in Scotland at that time.

[1] Wodrow MS., p. 44.

It is interesting to note that Wodrow[1] supplies
another line of reply to Calder. It may be described as
of a double nature and concerns another work evidently
written by Davidson although never printed. Perhaps
it was part of his *History*, referred to by himself in a
letter to the King in 1603. Row,[2] who calls Davidson
" one of the constant opposers of Prelacy " says that
a little before his death he penned a treatise, *De
Hostibus Ecclesiae Christi* wherein he affirmed that the
erecting of Bishops in the Kirk of Scotland was the most
subtle and prevalent means to destroy and overthrow
religion that ever could have been devised, which
they who lived to see its effects would readily grant.
Spottiswood,[3] in a sermon at a visitation of Kinghorn
in 1622, the Presbytery of St. Andrews being present,
made mention of the same work, whose author, he
declared, was the maddest man he ever knew. He
said that in it Davidson brought in the King last as
the greatest enemy of all, and that he presented the
book to the King, who, after he had read it, cut it in
pieces and burned it. The latter part of this story
would need a better authority than that of the Bishop,
yet his reference to Davidson in such terms so long
after the Reformer's death is another proof, if such were
required, that the story of his recantation is utterly
unfounded.

---

[1] Wodrow MS., p. 44.
[2] *History of the Kirk of Scotland*, p. 421.
[3] Calderwood, Vol. VII, p. 502.

CHAPTER X

LAST DAYS

THE closing years of Davidson's life were clouded and troubled. Enfeebled health hindered him from taking his full share of the Church's work and rendered him depressed in spirit. The apparent success of prelacy, and the carelessness of some of the ministers contributed to his despondency. As the sixteenth century drew to its close, he felt that it was passing in increasing gloom. Writing to a brother minister[1] from his manse at Prestonpans he bemoaned " the horrible crymes and breaches of the walls of our Jerusalem that daylie rusheth to the ground so fast ". In the short years granted to him in the new century, his voice was seldom heard in the courts of the Church, from which he was hindered, first by infirmity and latterly by royal restraint. Despite his weakness, he was able, as we saw, to address occasional letters to the Assembly, one of which in 1601 led to disastrous consequences to himself. The King had really never forgiven him for his protestation of 1598, and this letter to the Burntisland Assembly seems to have been, as far as James was concerned, the proverbial last straw. He summoned the offender before the Privy Council, to whom he gave instructions to have him warded in the Castle of Edinburgh " in anie cace whatsoever ". Davidson compeared, acknowledged the letter, and after writing to the King[2] at the desire

[1] Walter Balcanquhall. Calderwood, Vol. VI, p. 97.
[2] This letter is simply referred to by Calderwood. We know nothing of its contents. Vol. VI, p. 125.

of some of his brethren, entered the Castle on May 26th, 1601. That epistle was delivered to his Majesty on the following day by Patrick Galloway, John Hall and Peter Hewat, who brought back a warrant to transport him from the Castle to his own house, there to await further trial.[1]

To a man like Davidson it must have been very irksome to be confined within the limits of his manse and adjacent yard. So four days later, encouraged by his " moyeners "[2] who alleged that the King desired it, he wrote to his Majesty at some length.[3] The substance of the letter is as follows :—Beginning with an expression of his sincere affection for the King, to whom he would not wilfully occasion anger or grief, he hoped that his Majesty would acknowledge him to be, according to his rank and mean gifts, a faithful subject and a true servant of God, notwithstanding the misconstructions which had been placed upon his speeches and actions through misreports. No doubt, partly his plainness and partly " conscience in his calling to condemn sin in all persons " had moved his Majesty now and then " to have his manner of dealing in some jealousie ". Coming to the subject of the letter to the Burntisland Assembly he explained that its purpose was to move the brethren to discharge their ecclesiastical office to the uttermost, by repressing and removing idolatry which was now raising its head so insolently in the land. Referring to his speeches in the Synod of Lothian for confirmation of this, he pointed out that his object really was to secure for the King the Assembly's assistance in so

[1] Calderwood, Vol. VI, p. 126.
[2] A moyener is one who employs his interest for another.
[3] Calderwood, Vol. VI, pp. 126-9.

important a matter. Not that he meant the rooting out of idolaters by way of blood but rather by the execution of good laws made for the purpose, that they might depart from the country, and so trouble to Kirk and common weal would be avoided. He had not subscribed the letter, less the baseness of the writer might bring prejudice to the cause in hand. He urged the King to fulfil his promise to the Assembly and go forward in his administration of justice, concluding with the hope that his Majesty would send by the bearer of the letter—his wife—a loving reply with a writ restoring him to his wonted liberty.

The King was not pleased with Davidson's explanation, which it may be admitted, did not deal with everything in the offensive letter. Yet since he wished to avoid slander as well as the ill-will of those who favoured the preacher, his Majesty granted him permission to exercise his ministry within the bounds of his own parish but not beyond it.[1]

Great efforts were made by Davidson's brethren to secure his remission from the King, but without success. On April 28th, 1602 the Presbytery of Haddington passed the following resolution :— " Forasmekell as Mr. Johne Davidsone has remaned in ward within his owne paroche this long time, it was ordained that his case sh^d be remembered to the Provincial assembly that some suit and dealing be made to his Ma^{jtie} for his relief."[2] Nothing seems to have come of that and a few months later a similar fate befell another attempt of Davidson to obtain his freedom. He had been informed that the King, " at

[1] Calderwood, Vol. VI, p. 129.
[2] Records of the Presbytery of Haddington.

the commissioner's request,"[1] had agreed to grant him release if he made application for it. Accordingly Mr. John addressed a letter to his Majesty who was then at St. Johnston.[2] It was unlike his former one, very brief and to the point. He had, he wrote, obeyed the King's will for a year now, in submission and reverence, even to the impairing of his health, and he now craved to be restored to his " wonted liberty of a free subject ". Appearances, he added, pointed to his not enjoying it for long, and soon God would call him to " a farre better freedome ". One would have thought that such a pathetic appeal would have moved James to magnanimity, as it quickly would have a better and a kinder man. The unrelenting monarch, however, did not find in it any confession of a fault, and he made it plain to Mr. John Hall, a friend of Davidson's who interceded on his behalf, that that only was the price of clemency. " I am gentle and courteous," he said, " but not a lipper "—whatever he meant by that. That he remained inflexible is illustrated by the following incident which took place somewhat later and is related both by Wodrow and Calderwood.[3] The General Assembly of 1602 had under consideration an Act against encroachments on the Sabbath, particularly by the going of the salt pans. Two of the ministers, John Knox and David Black, the King being present, moved that Mr. Davidson might be sent for to give his advice on a matter with which he was so well acquainted. The proposal was met with an angry outburst from James who said " No, he sall not come

---

[1] It is not stated who this official was.
[2] Calderwood, Vol. VI, p. 152.
[3] Wodrow MS., p. 37.   Calderwood, Vol. VI, p. 184.

here. If I knew there were six of his judgement in the Assembly, I should not byde in it, more than in Sodom or Gommorha. If he teache not upon the fyft of August,[1] he sall not teache in Scotland. If he were not ane old man, he sould be hanged."

Davidson was doomed to disappointment, although at times his hopes were raised. In March 1603, the King ascended to the throne of England and on the news reaching Edinburgh, its ministers and those of the surrounding district went down to the Palace to offer their congratulations. At the same time, some of them made mention of Davidson and found that James did not seem so adverse to his release. Thereupon the Presbytery of Edinburgh suggested to their brother that he should send to his Majesty a message of congratulation and an assurance of personal affection.[2] He replied to his brethren in grateful terms, promising to do as they advised, and asking their further guidance.[3] He would pray that God would preserve the King in soul and body, and give him true success " in getting prerogative of the honour of the union of these two kingdoms, never yitt united after suche sport from the beginning ." A characteristic touch was added by his requesting the ministers to remind his Majesty of certain texts of Scripture which he deemed suitable to a King in such a situation !

On April 1st Davidson penned his last letter to James.[4] Besides offering felicitations on the English

[1] August 5th was ordained by James VI to be observed as a day of solemn thanksgiving for his miraculous deliverance from what was known as " The Gowrie Conspiracy ". The Church of Scotland agreed to keep the day. *Book of the Universal Kirk, Assembly, 1602*, p. 526. Calderwood, Vol. VI, p. 185.
[2] Calderwood, Vol. VI, p. 210.
[3] Ibid., p. 211.
[4] Ibid., pp. 212-14.

accession and setting forth with frankness some suitable Scriptural advice, he dealt at some length with the King's inquiry about a History of Scotland which he was reported to have written. He said that a dozen years before, he had contemplated writing on the antiquity of the Scottish Church and its martyrs, and it had been his intention to entitle the work CATALOGUS MARTYRUM SCOTIAE.[1] The appearance, however, of Camden's *Britannia* with which he found himself in disagreement, revealed to him the necessity of more careful research ; and so, except for gathering a few facts where he could, and as long as he had health and liberty, he had really abandoned the project for about ten years. Doubtless his searching of antiquities had given rise to the rumour that he was writing such a History, but he assured the King that nothing of the kind would ever have been undertaken without his seeking the royal approval and permission. After promising fervent prayer for the " happie directioun and safe protectioun " of his Majesty in his great work, and expressing earnest desire for his spiritual welfare, he craved permission to kiss his hand when he passed through the parish of Prestonpans on his way to his new home in England.

No mention is made in this letter of the subject of his release, but Davidson evidently had new hope that at last it would be granted. He sent the epistle by the hand of Richard Thomson, the Presbytery Clerk, to whom he entrusted a form of warrant to be held in readiness for the royal signature, should the King relent. This we learn from a letter of Davidson's

[1] Calderwood, Vol. VIII, p. 146.

to Thomson, found among the Wodrow Manuscripts in the National Library of Scotland.[1] It is
addressed to " Brother Richard " and asks him to
consult with discreet and godly men on the matter,
and if he finds them approving, to prepare a fair
copy of the warrant.

The letter was delivered to James by his servitor,
Alexander Dickson, who informed Davidson in a short
note that the King was willing to receive him to his
presence, release him from restraint and restore him
to favour, provided he acknowledged that he had
failed his Majesty and humbly craved pardon. Dickson advised him to do that, adding a postscript which,
according to Calderwood,[2] was dictated by the King
himself to the effect that, in any apology he might
make, Davidson must mention specially his offences,
namely, his protestation against an Assembly at
Edinburgh and his letter to the Kirk concerning
another. Thus we see that James had not relented
of his wrath, and besides it is probable that he may
have been pressed by the bishops to insist on Davidson's resiling from the faithful testimony he had given
against their corrupt courses. The terms, at any
rate, were such as Davidson could not accept without
hypocrisy since he did not feel that he was at fault
either in anything that he had done or written.

So the hopes of the honest little man were again
dashed. It adds to the general contempt one has
for James that at the time when he had realised his
heart's desire he allowed such an opportunity for the

[1] Wodrow MSS., Folio XLII, 44. The letter and also the form of warrant
have been printed in Davidson's *Poetical Remains*. Maidment, Edinburgh,
1829. We have set them down in the Appendix G.
[2] Calderwood, Vol. VI, p. 215.

exercise of clemency to pass. Probably it was due to fear that any renewed intercourse of Davidson with his brethren would endanger the interests of the bishops. When he passed southward, the Provincial Synod of Haddington left their business to greet him and they instructed a deputation to wait upon him for answer to some articles, one of which was, " for libertie to the warded and distressed brethrein of the ministrie in Scotland ". In reply he mentioned what had been done in the case of several of them and then added, " As for Mr. Johne Davidsone, he looked he should have offered himself to him as he came through Prestoun but he came not."[1] Another account has it, that to those who pleaded for Davidson's release and restoration he angrily replied, " I may be gracious, but I will be also righteous, and until he suitably confesses his fault, he may lie and rot there."[2] To the Laird of Ormiston he returned a very different answer. His hands, he said, were bound, as he was under promise to the Commissioners of Assembly not to release him.[3] It is therefore evident that Matthew Crawford in his manuscript hint of Davidson, quoted by Wodrow,[4] is wrong in the account he gives of the issue of this unhappy business. He relates that the King, having great reverence for Mr. Davidson's zeal and piety, when going up to England in 1603, stopped at Salt Preston, called for Mr. Davidson, conferred kindly with him and sought his blessing and the assistance of his prayers. That is what ought to have happened ;

[1] Calderwood, Vol. VI, p. 222.
[2] Rogers, *Three Scottish Reformers*, p. 48.
[3] Calderwood, Vol. VI, p. 222.
[4] Wodrow MS., p. 39.

it is what we wish had happened ; but it is, never-theless, highly improbable. It is not at all likely that James would seek the blessing of a man against whom he had conceived a violent hatred and whose repeated requests for release he had treated with contempt. Besides we may take the silence of Davidson himself as evidence that no such visit was made. In what is called " The Book of buriall of Saltpreston " there is an entry in the minister's handwriting as follows :—" Thursday ye 24th (March). Queen Elizabeth departed at Windsor." " 1603. Apr. 5th. The K. ryding by to England."[1] It is incredible that Davidson would have been content to leave the record in that way, without adding the more important item of a royal visit to himself. On his Majesty's triumphal journey south, the jails were opened and the prisoners, with the exception of murderers and those guilty of treason and Romish disloyalty, were set at liberty. " And yitt ", as Calderwood adds, " Mr. Andrew Melville and Mr. Davidsone could not gett the favour that malefactors gott ! "[2]

That good and great man, now sick and infirm, was thus left to continue the suffering of confinement in his own parish, where for a little more than another year he laboured faithfully and zealously in his Master's work, in preaching and other ministerial duties, and in constant adherence to the Reformation of the Scottish Church in doctrine, worship and discipline. He died in 1604, some time between August 16th, when a minute of Session appears in what is thought to be his handwriting, and September 5th

[1] Rogers, *Three Scottish Reformers*, p. 48n.
[2] Calderwood, Vol. VI, p. 223.

following when the Presbytery granted supply for his vacant pulpit. Four individuals, we are told, " having comissione of the haill parish of Saltprestoun bot especially of ye laird of Prestoune, compeirit lamenting ye death of or father Mr. Jon Davidsone yr last pastor."[1]

Of Davidson's private and domestic relations there is nothing to record. He had a wife concerning whom we have nothing but the merest unimportant references ;[2] what her name was or what part she played in her husband's varied and eventful career, we do not know. From his bequeathing all his patrimony, which from the extent of his charities must have been considerable, to the Church at Prestonpans, we infer that he had no family.[3] There are no particulars of his Will. The register for the period happens to be awanting but in the " Index of Testaments "[4] there is a minute to the effect that it was confirmed on August 28th, 1607.

Davidson's private papers came into the hands of John Johnston, Professor of Divinity at St. Andrews —a colleague of Andrew Melville. Johnston died on October 20th, 1611, and an " eik " to his will dated August 5th of the same year, contains this clause—" Item, I leave the trunk that lyes under the bwirde, with Mr. John Davidsone's paperis thairin, to Mr. Robert Wallace and Mr. Alexr Hoome in Prestonpans." The " trunk " unfortunately has disappeared and the papers were never allowed

---

[1] Records of the Presbytery of Haddington, September 5th, 1604.
[2] Calderwood, Vol. VI, p. 129. Page 230.
[3] Row states that he had no children. *History of the Kirk of Scotland*, p. 420.
[4] In H.M. Register House, Edinburgh.

to see the light of day. At Johnston's death, the Privy Council gave orders to the Rector of the University and Provost and Bailies of St. Andrews to "cause his coffers to be closed ",[1] as it was understood " that he had sundrie paperis writtis and books, pairtly written be himselfe and pairtlie be utheris—qlk contenis sum purpose and mater whairin his Ma[tie] may have very iust caus of offens, gif the same be sufferit to come to licht."[2]

[1] *Register of Privy Council of Scotland*, Vol. IX, p. 640.
[2] Quoted by M'Crie in *Life of Melville*, Vol. II, p. 111n., from Collection of Letters in the possession of the Earl of Haddington.

CHAPTER XI

CHARACTER AND INFLUENCE

OF Davidson's personal appearance we have no hint, except that he was small of stature. The family to which he belonged is wrapped in obscurity. In the story of his career there are revealed none of those intimate relations by which a man's character and habitual mood can best be appraised. His health does not appear to have been good, especially in his later years, when his distress was aggravated by the persecution which he suffered. Thus Davidson enjoyed none of the advantages which have meant so much to some public men—ancient lineage, commanding presence or powerful physique. He was, nevertheless, a man of singular natural endowments, including a large share of that peculiar sagacity which the character of his times was well fitted to uphold and sharpen. The mental picture of him which we form for ourselves is that of a small, serious, courageous man, determined to see through whatever he took in hand.

It is most regrettable that there is no record of his early spiritual pilgrimage. We have no account of how he became so whole-hearted a Christian and so splendid an upholder of the Reformation. That he owed much to David Ferguson, the minister of his youth, and to Knox we are aware, but we have no information concerning his conversion or such influences as make a most moving page in the life of his contemporary, Robert Bruce.

Intellectually Davidson was far above most of the ministers of the early Reformed Church. Learning in those days was not on a very high level, though a few had foreign education,[1] and it was not till 1575 that the Assembly resolved for the first time that Latin was a necessary qualification for the ministry.[2] Archibald Douglas would not adventure himself in the Greek Testament when examined with a view to the charge of Glasgow. Davidson, however, while by no means a scholar like Andrew Melville and probably much inferior even to Patrick Simson, possessed a knowledge of the Classics as well as of the Scriptures, revealed in his writings and speeches, to which few of his contemporaries could lay claim. He deplored the prevailing ignorance of so many of the clergy in his day[3] and did all in his power to promote earnest and devoted study among them. His own sound knowledge combined with a fiery eloquence, made him one of the most forceful and impressive preachers of his generation. He was a devoted evangelist, a faithful soul-winner and a sound Calvinistic theologian. With power born of his knowledge, and zeal inspired by the Holy Spirit, he placed himself unreservedly at the disposal of the Church. By reason of his outstanding gifts his words carried great weight with his brethren over whom he exercised a wonderful influence.

[1] Lang, *History of Scotland*, Vol. II, p. 252.

[2] *Book of the Universal Kirk*, p. 146. Cunningham says that probably not ten ministers in the Assembly at this period could read the New Testament in the original tongue—p. 354. In those days it was a proverb "Graecum est, non legitur," Row, p. 422.

[3] John Davidson's younger contemporaries obtained a very high level of learning under Andrew Melville's prescriptions in Glasgow and St. Andrews.

There was no more zealous upholder and defender of the Reformed Church than John Davidson. His absolute sincerity, purity of motive and heaven-born courage characterized all his dealings both with it and with the King. In his uncompromising attitude to all the evils of the time as well as to the machinations of the Court, he stands out in contrast to men like Rollock and Pont who were usually inclined to a policy of yielding, and to Galloway and Lindsay, whose personal convictions were never particularly strong. From Knox he had learned the duty of opposing the despotism of kings and of maintaining the independence of the Church. He was a stout supporter of Andrew Melville whose views he shared, and he was at least his equal in zeal and devotion and in unwearied service to the Church and the Kingdom of God. There was no better skilled debater on religious and ecclesiastical subjects in the Church of Scotland. Sometimes, it is true, he bore down on his opponents with terrific vehemence, and on all occasions he expressed himself " with the unrestrained earnestness of a forcible conviction ". He was always contending earnestly for the faith, even if occasionally he lacked patience and longsuffering with those differing from him. His adversaries, however, were often even more vehement, refuting themselves by their own excess. By his parishioners and the more devoted of his brethren he was held in the highest esteem and affection, although it must be admitted that in the Church courts he forfeited a good deal of influence by his obstinacy and bitter invective. He was decidedly blunt and lacked the suavity which is essential in a really typical ecclesiastic. His speeches

16

sometimes seem to pass the limits of generous controversy; but one has, in judging, to remember the characteristics of the age in which he lived, and the judgment he had formed of these. " The men of the sixteenth century staked life and fortune in the expression of their convictions ; and in controversy carried on under such conditions, words were real battles and not mere broadsides of ink."[1] It would be a mistake to attempt to idealize one who thus so often manifested the defects of his virtues. Stubborn and sometimes even vindictive, Davidson would resolutely pursue the object of his heart with an acerbity which did not help his aims. More quickly and easily would he have gained his end, if only he had been less ready to expose his feelings and more careful to restrain his ardour. Besides, he would certainly have escaped many of the troubles with which his life was beset. We must, however, be slow to condemn. The ministers of the early Reformed Church lived in constant dread of an enemy they could not see and, not without reason, they were suspicious that they could not even count upon the support of their king. It was the custom, too, to bring all matters of public interest to the pulpit, for they considered that it was their calling to apply the principles of the Kingdom of God to every side of human life. The functions which they thus exercised have now to a large extent been relegated to the public press. Their concern was with things social and political as well as religious, and their power, through excommunication and in other ways, was as great as that of the civil magistrate to-day.

[1] Hume Brown, *Life of George Buchanan*, p. 360.

Liberty had been purchased at a great price and there was always the fear that it might be filched away again. Vigilance and outspokenness were born of past suffering, and thus Davidson's career was rendered memorable by his vehement assertions first against Morton, and later against the King, as well as by his pungent criticisms of the Church itself.

It says much for his standing and influence in the Church, that Davidson was so frequently appointed to interview James, for not in any way could he be regarded as a courtier. The style of approach to the royal presence was, of course, very different in the sixteenth century from what it came to be later. Davidson addressed the King with an amazing frankness which left no doubt as to his meaning ; he was quite as uncompromising as Knox and Ferguson, and as uncourtly as Melville and Bruce. For plainness and faithful personal dealing, his words surpass even the most famous of Melville's speeches. Both in the pulpit and in private he was ready to speak out his mind without fear. Yet none was more loyal to his Majesty, for whom he cherished a real affection and whose well-being was his constant concern. It softens his apparently hard utterances to remember that. He cared for his King but the key to his life is the supreme care which he had for the Church and truth, and for his Master. For him, as for his great contemporaries Melville, Bruce and Welsh, there was " another King, one Jesus " Who had always to take precedence of King James the Sixth.

The ministers of the Scottish Church in the sixteenth century do not seem to have been troubled with much in the way of intellectual doubt. Few evidently found the road to truth very hard, or were perplexed with grave misgivings. An exceptional soul like Bruce might fight his way through the mists of doubt to the clear light of faith, but for the most part assurance and confidence were the marks of the age, as they were the characteristics of the reforming movement. Davidson was no exception. He was as sure of himself as he was of the cause he had espoused—sure of himself and it, because sure of the God whom he served and whose law was, for him, the basis of all human action. Presbyterianism as the divinely appointed system of church government found in him a loyal and consistent supporter; and because he was so confident of that, he was prepared to defend it with all his power.

Davidson's influence in Church and Nation seems, however, to have been due more to his personal piety than to any other of his great qualities. If a man is to be judged by his peers, then he passes the test exceedingly well and their good opinions have been echoed by many modern writers. Fleming in *The Fulfilling of the Scriptures* says he was " eminently zealous and faithful for his Master in a time of the Church's defection ", and quotes Didoclavius (i.e. Calderwood) as calling him " *Cato, et Constans, Cato sui temporis* " in his preface to the *Altare Damascenum*. M'Crie sums up his qualities in this verdict—" Davidson was a man of sincere and warm piety and of no inconsiderable portion of learning, united with a large share of that blunt and fearless honesty which characterized the first Reformers." Boyd of Trochrig in his *Philotheca* terms him " a whip of false priestrule and a very keen promoter of a purer teaching, an absolutely apostolic chap, and after Wishart and Knox, not lacking in prophetic grace as everyone knew to whom he was well known." He adds that Davidson often made honourable mention to him of his father, Archbishop Boyd, with whom he had lived on most intimate terms, and in the name of that friendship he used to show paternal affection to himself.[1] Wodrow adds as a postscript to what he has written concerning this eminent minister, the following words :—" I shall add Mr. Kirkstoun's character of Mr. Davidson which is very just and well-founded, ' Mr. John Davidson was excellently learned, eminently pious, and endued with the spirit of prophecy. He was the salt of the Church of Scotland both in the pulpit and judicatories, both for zeal and constancy, and died a sufferer under King James, notwithstanding all the respect he professed for him.' " We require no further witness to prove that in the pages of Scotland's history there has been no man more highly regarded by that school which carried on the succession of the Reformers. The intention of his soul was to bring all life into line with Christ's purposes, and his loyalty to the Master and His Cause was so unquestionably great that he could not refrain from speaking out, wherever and whenever he saw error, ecclesiastical or moral.

It will be noticed that in some of the tributes to Davidson just quoted there is a reference to his possessing the gift of prophecy. Such a gift has, at different times, been attributed to great and good men by

---

[1] Roberti Bodii a Trochoregia Philotheca : Wodrow's *Life of Archbishop Boyd*, pp. 3, 4, MSS., Vol. IV. University of Glasgow.

enthusiastic admirers and followers, and in the early days of the Reformation many attributed it to John Knox and other ministers. Andrew Lang simply dismisses the subject with the sneer that their " subliminal premonitions " gave them part of their power with the people. Burnet is even less complimentary, remarking thus on Davidson and Bruce who were supposed to have inherited the gift from Knox :— " Some of the things that they foretold came to pass ; but my father, who knew them both, told me of many of their predictions that he himself heard them throw out, which had no effect ; but all these were forgot, and if some more probable guessings which they delivered as prophecies were accomplished, these were much magnified."[1] Against these views we must set others, as in Davidson's case the question of prophetic utterances cannot be so lightly dismissed. Wodrow sets up a strong defence of it on the grounds that men of singular piety, especially in the more extraordinary periods of the Church, have been favoured with singular communications of the Lord's mind and notices of things to come ; " and in a way perfectly consistent with the full revelation in the Word, the only rule of faith and practice ; to which these persons highly favoured of the Lord have still showed the greatest regard." He is aware of a great unwillingness on the part of many to credit such prophecies and he holds that they ought to be well vouched for. He himself, he says, is not given to an easy credulity in such matters and he tests them in the same way as he tests all facts concerning the Reformation and following years. He has " the

[1] Gilbert Burnet, *History of His Own Time*, Vol. I, p. 31.

repeated and good testimonies of credible witnesses, under no bias, having full opportunity to be informed, and many of them living in time of these facts ". Regarding Davidson's case and the facts he relates concerning him, he cites as his supports Scot of Coupar, Row, Livingston, Fleming and " an interrupted account yet remaining in the parish where Mr. Davidson died ".[1]

The judgment of M'Crie on a subject like this ought also to be borne in mind. " The Reformers ", he writes, " were men of singular piety ; they were exposed to uncommon opposition and had uncommon services to perform ; they were endued with extraordinary gifts and why may we not suppose that they were occasionally favoured with extraordinary premonitions, with respect to certain events which concerned themselves, other individuals or the Church in general ? But whatever intimations of this kind they received, they never proposed them as a rule of action to themselves or others, nor rested the authority of their mission upon these, nor appealed to them as constituting any part of the evidence of those doctrines which they preached to the world."[2] All that is true of Davidson. Although Row describes him as " a verie prophet of God " and Wodrow dwells at length on his gifts in that direction, yet he never presumed on the possession of them. The warnings by which he frequently enforced his counsels, and the threats he made were so often realized, that they led to belief in his preternatural powers. Many interesting stories have thus been related concerning

[1] Wodrow MS., pp. 39-40.
[2] *Life of Knox*, p. 368.

the minister of Prestonpans, one or two of the most
striking of which may be set down here.[1]

It has been already observed more than once
that Spottiswood in his history invariably refers to
Davidson in terms of disrespect and even contempt.
The following anecdote, related by John Livingston,[2]
may explain to some extent the Bishop's antipathy to
that eminent minister. When Davidson was
Moderator of the Synod of Lothian, two young
ministers, Mr. John Spottiswood of Calder, and
Mr. James Law of Kirkliston, were brought before the
brethren to be censured for playing at football on the
Lord's Day. He urged that they might be deposed
but the Synod would not go so far as that. When
they were called in, Davidson said, " Come in, ye
pretty football men, the Synod hath ordained you
only to be rebuked " ; and, turning to the Synod,
he said, " And now, brethren, let me tell you what
reward you shall get for your lenity. These two men
shall trample on your necks and the necks of the
ministry in Scotland." It is well known what an
accomplishment this prediction had, as both, after
becoming bishops, " did much mischief ".

Being at dinner on one occasion with Robert
Bruce, who was then in great favour with the King,
Davidson uttered the following words in giving
thanks after meat :—" Lord, thy servant here is now
a great favourite of the court and in much respect ;
but he shall be within a little as much persecuted as
he is now in favour, and go down the streets, when
many who have him this day in esteem will not give

---

[1] The others which have been recorded, will be found in the Appendix H.
[2] Livingston's *Select Biographies*, Vol. I, p. 296.

him a salutation " ; this was very manifest soon afterwards. At another time when he and Bruce dined with an Edinburgh magistrate who was very friendly to the godly ministers, he gave utterance to words like these :—" Lord, this good man hath respect for thy sake to thy servants, but he little knoweth that in a short time he must carry us both who are here to prison " : which words greatly troubled the magistrate, though in the course of his duties it fell to him to do exactly as Davidson had predicted.

Not very long before his death this faithful minister was visited after Communion by Mrs. Kerr, the widow of Knox,[1] and her son John. The young gentleman had lately come from France and was attired in courtly garments. Davidson did, in a solemn manner, charge him to cast off his scarlet cloak and lay aside his gilded rapier and take him to study ; " for you are the man ", says he, " who is to succeed me in the ministry at this place ". Kerr went home pondering the minister's words and later he offered himself as a student for the ministry. He did succeed John Davidson at Prestonpans where he was, for many years, a holy and faithful minister of the Gospel.[2]

Despite these and many other instances of his prophetic gifts Davidson made no claim for himself, over his brethren. He was the most modest of men, transparently honest and purely disinterested. In his manifold services to the Church he gave himself to the work of God without counting the cost.

[1] Knox's second wife, Margaret Stewart, married Andrew Kerr of Fauldonside, two years after the Reformer's death.
[2] These stories are recorded by Row p. 420 and p. 462, by Wodrow MS. pp. 40, 41, 43, and by Fleming in *The Fulfilling of the Scripture*, pp. 110-12.

Spottiswood, among his many unjust statements concerning this godly man, has asserted that he was " always aspiring " to be one of the ministers of Edinburgh. Nothing is farther from the truth ; in Wodrow's words the statement is " without any proof, void of foundation and contrary to fact ".

Although both in Scotland and England his discourses were greatly appreciated, Davidson modestly declared himself " no preacher ", and when invited by the Moderator to address the Synod of Fife when present as a visitor, he would not take precedence of the aged Ferguson who, he said, had been an " actor " in the early days of the Reformation when he himself had been but a " spectator ".[1] A short letter which he wrote in 1600 to the well-known preacher, Walter Balcanquhall, reveals a striking tenderness of heart and modesty of spirit most beautiful in the otherwise stern and uncompromising champion of the Kirk. He had heard some evil reports as to their friendship and he must needs remove any misunderstanding lest Satan should have his way and their Christian love should be shaken. Each, he says, mislikes certain things in the other, but if they do right, each will see many things to " mislyke and damne " in himself. He is persuaded of their tender regard for each other and he pleads that they please one another in what is good, that they break not unity in truth and Christian love. He protests his utter good-will and thus concludes :— " And therefore, loving brother, let us be wise in Christ. And though Satan has desired to sift us, let us be assured that Christ hath prayed for us that our

[1] Calderwood, Vol. V, p. 435.

faith fail not."[1] Such love in the strong man is very impressive.

A not uncommon fault with the Church leader is that he finds it difficult to believe that he can ever be wrong. Davidson, however, was not guilty of so grave a defect of character. He was willing to be advised to withdraw some of the extravagant speeches which the provocative behaviour of the King or the supineness of his brethren had led him to make. He could be wonderfully apologetic at times, not from any fear of consequences to himself but just because he evidently felt that he had gone a little too far.

In the foregoing chapters there has constantly been indicated the great influence of Davidson upon the Church of his day. There were few matters of importance in which he did not have a share, and his brethren were continually committing to him tasks of the utmost importance. One marvels, however, that so prominent a minister was never Moderator of the General Assembly. Although nominated with others on one or two occasions, he failed to secure the majority of votes. Despite that trifling fact, it is true that the Scottish Church has had few greater men and few who have been listened to with greater respect or to greater purpose by their brethren, even if at times excessive vehemence robbed him of some of his power. It can be affirmed with confidence that no braver or more disinterested man has ever championed the rights of Christ's Kirk and of the Kingdom of God in Scotland. If it be true that God sent Andrew Melville to keep the

[1] Calderwood, Vol. VI, pp. 96-7.

Nation and the Church loyal to their inheritance of liberty, it is equally true that God sent John Davidson to be one of that great man's most ardent supporters in the carrying on of the good work.

Davidson's life and service, however, must not be regarded as dependent upon Melville. Quite apart from that leader of men, he exercised upon the whole Church an influence all his own which did much to reanimate its waning zeal. In a degree not inferior to any of his most distinguished contemporaries he upheld those principles of freedom which at length having secured consolidation and force, expelled a dynasty and laid the foundation of constitutional government. He may, at times, have been rather too assertive and pugnacious, but only such a temperament could suffice for the age in which he lived. What Professor Mackinnon says of Melville can be said with perfect justification of Davidson— " Choleric and impulsive as he was, his stout words in defence of his convictions and in defiance of authority arbitrarily used have in them the ring of a powerful individuality, which impressed itself on his countrymen and bequeathed its inspiration to their resistance to coercive methods in Church and State."[1] In addition to that, in his public witness to the Gospel and in the pastoral work of his own parish, he proved himself a leader wise in counsel, persuasive in conference and decisive in action. His services rendered to the cause of reformed religion, often without fee or reward, and his munificent gifts for the advancement of education, entitle him to grateful remembrance.

[1] *A History of Modern Liberty*, Vol. III, p. 211.

It only remains to be said that, after a careful consideration of Davidson's many and varied activities and after seeking to appraise his service to Church and Nation, the outstanding impression which a study of his life leaves upon the mind is the moral splendour of the man himself. His was a fervent and disinterested zeal, combined with inflexible adherence to what he believed to be the cause of righteousness and God. He could have neither part nor lot with that sort of worthy people who so annoyed Voltaire because, seeing a wrong, they simply groaned over it, went home to their supper and forgot all about it. Davidson was made of sterner stuff ; what mattered to him mattered supremely. He saw his way and resolutely pursued it. Even when his health was seriously impaired he could not be induced to violate his conscience by making any unworthy compliance. Though he sometimes erred he was infinitely to be preferred to the mere compromiser who was neither hot nor cold. Like some other Reformers whose names are held in highest honour John Davidson had the courage and strength of those who believed that it was better to suffer than to sin, and that in all circumstances and at any sacrifice we ought to obey God rather than men. He is a great personality in Scottish Church history who has given us a shining example of the moral daring which is " the greatest property of the human soul and the spring of its noblest achievement ". Thus his place in the records of the Reformed Church of Scotland is one that cannot be challenged.

APPENDICES

APPENDIX A

LATIN Poem by John Davidson, regent at St. Andrews, cele-
brating the success of David Ferguson, minister of Dunfermline,
in refining his vernacular language, and prefixed to a sermon
of Ferguson's preached at Leith before the nobility and afterwards published.[1]

Graecia melifluo quantum det nestoris ori,
Aut Demostheneo debeat eloquio ;
Ipsi facundo quantum (mihi crede) parenti
Attribuat linguae turba togata suae ;
Nos tibi, Fergusi, tantum debere fatemur,
Scotanam linguam qui reparare studes.
Sermonem patriam ditas ; inculta vetustas
Horret qua longe barbariemque fugas ;
Adde etiam, neque abest facundis gratia dictis,
Respondet verbis materia apta tuis.
Quod satis ostendit nobis tua concio praesens,
Qua nihil in lucem doctius ire potest.

---

[1] M'Crie's *Life of Knox*, Note RR., p. 446.

APPENDIX B

An Apology or Defence made by Mr. John Davidson, for not entering the 17th day of June 1574, in the Tolbooth of Edinburgh to underly the law.[1]

Davidson introduces his apology in these words :—" Becaus diverse men may diverslie judge of me, that I entered not to underly the law, as they terme it, at the day appointed, I have thought good to declare the caus of my non-compearance in writt ; that als weill the godlie, who, perchance, might have beene somwhat moved with the mater, may be satisfied, as the mouths of the adversareis, who ever rejoice, and begin to sing the triumphe, at the least appearance of overthrow of the truthe, or of God's servants, may be stopped." He did not stay away, he said, through fear of any consequences to himself, for God, having put his hand to the work, granted him strength to answer any charge concerning it ; and the promise of His presence was more comfortable to him than if he had been guarded with a thousand men of war.

He gave the following reasons for " not entering " at the day appointed. (1) He desired not to tempt the Lord God by casting himself in danger without His express command. That was what he would have done, if he, a single man, had entered, without all worldly force, where were convened a number of armed men ready to convoy him anywhere, at the command of the supreme power. " He that hath the command of God for him, ought not to stay for anie danger, howbeit never so imminent or perellous." It may be said that God wills that men should be ready to give account of their faith when and wheresoever charged, but Davidson felt that that was not what his compearing would have meant, but the answering of the censures of such as were enemies of his cause and who had little or no judgment concerning the matter of which he was accused. He had already on several occasions, before Regent and council, given accounts of his book and why he wrote it. He saw nothing in the new proceedings against him save that which gave rise to grave suspicions, and so he had no assurance that he could appear, without tempting God.

[1] Calderwood, Vol. III, pp. 314-26.

(2) The second cause of his non-compearance was the avoiding of a tumult among the people, which he greatly feared. For writing the truth he had been counted a seditious person, like God's servants of old. He briefly outlined what he had done—his argument against the four kirks to one minister, which he had declared to be " evil and consequently devilish " and which could be proved by " that invincible and most strong argument, called experience ". Such a book as he had written could not be regarded as a cause of tumult since it contained nothing but truth, nor could his behaviour since writing it be called seditious. By his non-appearance he desired to remove any occasion of tumult, which the pursuit of him by the supreme magistrate and the raising of the hearts of the godly at the same, would inevitably have brought about.

(3) The third and last cause was the express command of Christ—" when they persecute you in one city, flee into another ", the practice of which commandment is found in the most dear servants of God. It might be asked of him if execution of justice could be called persecution and he would reply that pursuit of an innocent man under the form of execution of justice was a most crafty and mighty kind of persecution, because the outward appearance of justice deceived many and made the party more to be abhorred, rendering thus his persecution the more grievous. " Wherefore," he added, " it is not to be thought strange that I call the summoning of me to underly the law (as they terme it) persecuting of me, as if no wrong could be done to anie, under colour of justice ; for, as have declared, there is no meeter meane to oppresse innocent men."

The remaining portion of the " Apology " is taken up with a recital of the details of the persecution, dealt with in Chapter II.

17*

APPENDIX C

Davidson's Letter written from Argyll to Regent Morton, November 1574.[1]

Since God had seen fit by means of his troublous estate during the past year on account of his writing and speaking what was the truth, to thrust him out to bear the glorious message of his Son to an ungrateful people beginning to forsake Him and to follow their own ways, he thought it good, before making any public objection to his Grace's proceedings to first privately and earnestly desire him to call to mind how God in all ages and in all places had poured forth his terrible judgments upon all who had opposed themselves to His Church or otherwise troubled the same. God had at times, for trial of his own people, suffered the wicked to vex the Kirk, yet it had happened to them in the end, as to those who attempt to throw some very heavy stone which falls back upon them and bruises them to powder.

Persuaded that his Grace is familiar with examples of such, he stays not upon it, but proceeds to the main purpose of his letter. " The end ", he says, " wherefore I writt this is, that your Grace may be plainlie admonished, for the discharge of my conscience, to desist in time from troubling the Kirk of Christ within this realme, wherewith your Grace (I darre not flatter) hath begunne to tig (as we say) too roughlie, als weill in calling the authoritie of the same in doubt, which God hath established by his Word, as also in troubling and persecuting me, a member of his Kirk, for truthe and righteousnesse' sake." If he had not been assured that his action was just and upright, and also that he had the defence of his God in the same, he would have recanted every word at the first examination. He then exhorted his Grace to desist from meddling with the Kirk or any member of it while God mercifully called him to repentance. If the Regent obeyed, there would be mercy in store for him ; if he stubbornly and disdainfully refused, God would provide for his own, and destruction both of body and soul would follow. He had written, he said, for the discharge of his conscience, warning his Grace of the plague plainly forewarned ; and finally he commits him to the divine protection. Contrary

[1] Calderwood, Vol. III, pp. 326-7.

to all that " some soullesse flatterers " say of him to his Grace, he prays daily that God will grant him a " sight of his estate and zeale to sett out God's glorie ".

Wodrow makes the following significant comment on the above letter in his MS. hint on Davidson's life :—" This remarkable letter was remembered seven or eight years after, when the Regent was brought to an untimely end : and indeed it was remarked that his introducing Tulchan Bishops to the Church was in the issue ruining to him ; and his affairs went very much cross after this severe prosecution of this worthy man ; but I incline to be tender in connoting providences, otherwise I would almost reckon this letter among the predictions made by him."[1] In the margin of his MS. he refers to Davidson's saying in the letter that he was troubled for " writing and *speaking* of that which is the truth," and adds " This seems to import that he was a minister when regent at St. Andrews." There is, however, no foundation whatsoever for such a supposition, and Davidson himself disclaims the office of preacher at this time.[2]

[1] Wodrow MS., p. 2.
[2] Calderwood, Vol. III, p. 323.

APPENDIX D

LETTER of Mr. John Davidson to Mr. John Field.[1]

Grace mercie and peace.

I thank you beloved brother for your letter daited the 22 of
July last whiche as it wes moist acceptable unto me so wes it
comfortable to the brethren of the ministrie in these quarteris
who at that tyme wer heavilie trubled be those adversaries
whome the myghtie hand of our god hath now myghtilie beaten
down. God grant that we never forget so myghtie and mervalus
deliverance. On the morrow efter I resaved your letter I
resaved an other frome the Rotchell [La Rochelle] tending
to the same end, to wit lamenting our trublous state and
tharewithal comforting us in our god. It is no small comfort
brother (as ye and I have diverse tymes spoken in conference)
to brethren of one natione to vnderstand the state of the brethern
in other nationes and tharefere let us practise it as occasione
will serve. For my part I sall not be vnmyndfull when I may
have meit beraris.

Thair is a motione brother in the heads of some brethern
heir wherein your advyce wold do goode as we think to wit that
a generall sute be made be our general assemblie nixt (whiche
will be the 24 of Aprile nixt be Godis grace) to the Kings g[race],
and hole state that a reqweast frome thame and the hole generall
assemblie be dressed to the Quenes maiestie with hir state and
your churche, touching the reformatioun of some abuses in
your churche and especiallie that sincere men may have libertie
to preache without deposing be the tyrannie of the bishoppes.
This I thoght goode onelie to move vnto yow rudelie for the
present to the end with advyce of brethern thare, your fordar
infermatioun in this cace may direct ws forder if it shall be
thoght expedient. God grant ws the spirit of faythfulnes
wisdome for the vsing of all lawfull meanes for the advanceing
of Godis glorie and proffeit of his churche. Goode Mr. Bowes
doeth goode service heir for the wellfare of the churche of God
boyth thare and heir in that he travaleth faythfullie and most
diligentlie to keip these two countreis knit in amity and trew
freindship. For no goode man can be ignorant how muche

[1] Nat. Lib. Scot. MS., 6.1.13, fol. 83.

our concorde and unitie helpeth the goode caws of Christ whiche
is not alytill invyed be satan and his instrumentis, the Spirit
of our Lord Jesus Christ remane with yow allwayes brother
to the end and in the end. Amen. Now my hartie commendationes remembered to the brethern thare and especialie to
goode Mr. Stubbis, Mr. Sheik and to him whose commendationes
caried be me to yow made our fyrst acquentance togyther with
Mr. Brounes half brother Mr. Satfeild not forgetting my wyves
commendationes to you and your bedfellow. I tak my leve of
yow frome Edinburgh the fyrst of Januar 1582.

Your assured freind
and to my powar

Mr. Johne Davidsone.

I pray yow also salute my cousing Davidsone in Great Wood
Streit and his wyf in my name.

[Added in another hand.]

Concerning this to answer in generall termes that the brethern
shall think themselves beholdinge to them if they shal be so
cairfull.

The letter is addressed

To his loving brother in Christ Mr. feild preacher of the Word
of God deliver this in Londone.

and is endorsed in another hand Davidson to feild whether the
Synods might take order for the K : moving her majestie for
reformation. It was liked by the brethren here.

APPENDIX E

A SHORT Form of Evening and Morning Prayer, and of Graces before meat, and after meat, by Mr. John Davidson.[1]

EVENING PRAYER

We hairtlie thank thé, Hevinlie Father, for all thi goodnes this day past, beseiking thé to forgive us our sinnes for Christ Jesus thi Sonnes saik, and to bles us, and give us good rest this nycht. Continew the trew preaching of thi Word among us, and give us grace to esteme moir of it than hitherto we have done, and save us from merciles strangeris. And tak not thy peace from this land. Send us sesonabill wether, and stay this greit derth. Lord blis the Kirk, our King, Quene, and Prince, for Jesus Christ thi Sonnis saik. To quhome, with thé, O Father, and Haly Gaist, be all praise, gloire, and honour, for ever and ever. Amen.

MORNING PRAYER

We hairtlie thank thé, Hevinly Father, for all thi goodnes this nycht past, beseiking thé to forgive us our sinnis for Christ Jesus thi Sonnis saik, and blis our labouris, and guid us this day in thi trew feire. Continew the trew preaching of thi Word among us, and give us grace to esteme moir of it than hitherto we have done, and save us from merciles strangeris. And tak not thy peace from this land. Send us sessionabill wether, and stay this greit dearth. Lord blis the Kirk, our King, Quene, and Prince, for Jesus Christ thi Sonnis saik. To quhome, with thé, O Father, and Haly Gaist be all praise, gloire, and honour, for ever and ever. Amen.

THE FORME OF THE GRACES
And first
Befoir Meit

Blis us, guid Lord, and ther thi creatures, quhilk the prepairest for our norishment, through Jesus Christ our Lord. Amen.

Grace efter Meit

Blissit be yow, O Lord, for this nurishment of our bodies at this tyme, and mekle mair for the continuall nurishment of our saullis, by Christ crucifyit. To quhome, with the Father, and the Haly Spreit, be praise and glory for ever. God save the Kirk and cuntrey, King, Queine, and Prince. Amen.

[1] *The Miscellany of the Wodrow Society*, Vol. I, pp. 539-40.

APPENDIX F

VERSION of Twenty-third Psalm, said to have been written by John Davidson in 1602.[1]

> God who doth all nature hold
>> In his fold
> Is my shepherd kind and helpful,
> Is my shepherd and doth keep
>> Me, his sheep
> Still supplied with all things needful.
>
> He feeds me in fields which been
>> Fresh and green
> Mottled with springs, flowery painting
> Through which creep with murmuring crooks
>> Chrystal brooks,
> To refresh my spirit fainting.
>
> When my soul from heaven's way
>> Went astray
> With earth's vanities seduced,
> For his name's sake, kindly he
>> Wandering me,
> To his Holy fold reduced.

[1] In *Weekly Christian Teacher* for 1838, with the words following it "—Davidson A.D. 1602."

APPENDIX G

DAVIDSON's Letter to Richard Thomson, Clerk of the Presbytery of Edinburgh.[1]

Brother Richard. Heir ze have my letter to his majestie with a forme of warrand to be subscrived by him concerning ze quhilks, ze ar to advise with some discreit godlie brethren what they think of them ; and give they be approued, cawss the warrand to be written in fare wryt to be in reddiness to be subscrived by his majestie give he accept of my bill. I love not to provoke his majestie to forder rigor, and if it wer not in hope to get the turne easlie past, (whereof it appears ye ar in conceapt), I wold have expected the lords lasor without wryting one word, for I have small cawss offered by the bretheren, who disdaine to deale with me by themselves or ther letters to that effect ; the matter is not so small importance in god's sight, howsoever it seme small and light in mannis sight as they mak of it ; god prosper the matter as he seeth goode, and give zow wisdome to keip me free of the bondage of men. Amen.

Zour brother, Johne Davidsone.

WARRANT REFERRED TO IN ABOVE LETTER

Our will is, that our lovit Mr. John Davidsone, minister at Saltprestone, be presentlie releued of his warde, and have libertie frome this furth, of a fre subject to vse his lawful advis as occasione shall seme, wher he thinks gude by this our warrand, subscrivit with our haud at   the
day of   1602.

---

[1] Wodrow MSS., Vol. XLII, No. 44. Nat. Lib. Scot. Printed in Maidment's Edition of Davidson's Poems.

APPENDIX H

EXAMPLES, not previously mentioned, of the prophetic spirit that appeared in John Davidson.

My Lord Newbottle whose interest in Davidson's settlement at Prestonpans had been obtained by the Presbytery, promised to help forward the building of a church. Soon after, however, he withdrew his promise and later came even to frustrate the work. Davidson, in an interview, told him that the walls, which were then in the course of erection, would stand as a memorial against him, and that ere long God would root out him and his estate from that parish and he would not have a piece of land of the same. He also prophesied that his Lordship would die by an unknown hand. Shortly afterwards his lands were alienated and, adds Wodrow, " the way of his death is a secret, he having died in his chamber, and was the ground of a debate in one of our Scots parliaments ".[1]

There was a number of persons of the same surname in the Parish of Saltpreston who caused Davidson and the whole district much trouble and anxiety. He did everything within his power to reclaim them but without success. At length he declared publicly that in two generations the Lord, in his providence, would cast out all of that name from the parish. This accordingly came to pass and not one of them was left. It was observed later by the inhabitants that few or none of that surname were among them, though formerly it was very common.[2]

A gentleman nearly related to a prominent family in the parish, but a strong opponent of piety, did, on that account and without provocation, beat a poor honest man who lived there. In addition to other blows, he struck him on the back saying, " Take this for Mr. Davidson's sake " ; the man complained of feeling that stroke more than any other and was, on account of it, forced to keep his bed for some time. Davidson referred to this matter on the following Sabbath when he was speaking on the oppression of the godly and the enmity which wicked men showed to them. He said that it was sad that a

[1] Wodrow MSS. Fleming, *The Fulfilling of the Scripture*, Vol. II, p. 110.
[2] Wodrow MSS.

profane man should openly dare, without cause, to vent his rage against those who were seekers of God in the place. Then with great authority he added, " He who hath done this, were he the laird or the laird's brother, ere a few days pass, God shall give a stroke, that all the monarchs of the earth dare not challenge." It was publicly known how, at the end of that very week, the evil doer was struck dead with a thunderbolt as he stood before his own door.[1]

During meetings of the Synod at Dunfermline soon after the death of David Ferguson, minister there, Davidson, in giving thanks after dinner said, among other things :—" Lord ! thou hes now removed thy worthie and faithfull servant who laboured heir among this people in the gospell, etc. ; but, Lord! who shall succeid him in his ministrie, thou knowes ! Many are gaping for it, and using moyen at Court to gaine it, but it will be Jok up-a-land ; it will die in thy hand, (pointing at Mr. Andro Forrester, who at the tyme, with sundrie other ministers, wes sitting at the table with him, having dyned there,) therefor the backe shall beare the sadle-band," etc. This prophecy, though uttered in these ridiculous expressions, was in course fulfilled, for Andrew Forrester did succeed Ferguson and he fell into gross sins, for which he was deposed and his ministry there did " die in his hand " ; and being deposed and disgraced, " his backe did beare the sadle-band ". We are told that when Davidson made this prophecy, his hearers laughed at it, but when they found it fulfilled, they acknowledged him a true prophet.[2]

Davidson was one day in the company of several of his brethren when the conversation turned to the Edinburgh ministers Patrick Galloway and John Hall, who at the time were of excellent reputation and greatly commended by some. Davidson said, " These two men pretend much but are in reality back friends to the Church of Scotland," and he added, " they shall both die without anybody seeing them ", which fell out accordingly.[3]

---

[1] Fleming, *The Fulfilling of the Scripture*, Vol. II, p. 111. Fleming says that he had this story confirmed " by some worthy of credit " who had it handed down from those familiar with Davidson.

[2] Row, *History of the Kirk of Scotland*, p. 463.

[3] Wodrow MS., p. 42.

BIBLIOGRAPHY

(1) Works by John Davidson

Ane Dialog or Mutual Talking between a Clerk and ane Courteour. (Edinburgh, 1574.)

The Poetical Remains of John Davidson. (Edinburgh, 1829. Maidment.)

Some Helpes for Young Schollers in Christianity. (Edinburgh, 1602. Reprinted, Edinburgh, 1708, with preface by William Jameson.)

D. Bancroft's Rashnes in Rayling against the Church of Scotland. (Edinburgh, 1590, in Miscellany of Wodrow Society, Vol. I.)

Preface to Discoverie of the unnatural and traitorous conspiracy of Scottish Papists (in Pitcairn's Criminal Trials).

(2) Manuscripts

Wodrow. Essay to recover somewhat of the Life of Mr. John Davidson. University of Glasgow. (Transcript of above obviously edited by Wodrow with pages numbered.)

Struthers. Records of The Presbytery of Haddington, transcribed by Rev. John Struthers of Prestonpans, for years of Davidson's Prestonpans Ministry. (Presented by The Antiquarian Society of Scotland to National Library of Scotland in 1934.)
Records of the Presbytery of Edinburgh.

(3) Printed Works

Argyle. Presbytery Examined. (London, 1848.)

Balfour of Burleigh. The Rise and Development of Presbyterianism in Scotland. (Cambridge, 1911.)

Brown, Hume. History of Scotland. (Cambridge, 1902.)
Life of George Buchanan. (Edinburgh, 1890.)
John Knox. (London, 1895.)

Brown, T. Church and State in Scotland. (Edinburgh, 1891.)

Bonar. Catechisms of the Scottish Reformation. (London, 1866.)

BIBLIOGRAPHY

CALDERWOOD. History of the Kirk of Scotland. 8 volumes. (Edinburgh, 1845. Wodrow Society Edition.)

COOK. History of the Church of Scotland. (Edinburgh, 1815.)

COUPER. Scottish Revivals. (Dundee, 1918. Privately printed.)

CUNNINGHAM, JOHN. The Church History of Scotland. (Edinburgh, 1882. Second edition.)

CUNNINGHAM, WILLIAM. The Reformers and the Theology of the Reformation. (Edinburgh, 1862.)

DE FOE. Memoirs of Church of Scotland. (Perth, 1844.)

EDGAR. Old Church Life in Scotland. (Paisley, 1886.)

ELDER. Spanish Influences in Scottish History. (Glasgow, 1920.)

FERGUSSON. Alexander Hume. (Paisley, 1899.)

FIGGIS. The Divine Right of Kings. (Cambridge, 1896.)

FLEMING, HAY. Critical Reviews Relating chiefly to Scotland. (London, 1912.)
The Story of the Scottish Covenants. (Edinburgh, 1904.)
The Reformation in Scotland. (London, 1910.)

FLEMING, ROBERT. The Fulfilling of the Scripture. (Edinburgh, 1850.)

FRASER. The Kirk and the Manse. (Edinburgh, 1857.)

GOOD. Liberton in Ancient and Modern Times. (Edinburgh, 1893.)

GRUB. Ecclesiastical History of Scotland. (Edinburgh, 1861.)

GWATKIN. Church and State in England. (London, 1917.)

HENDERSON. Scottish Vernacular Literature. (London, 1898.)

HEWAT. Makers of the Scottish Church at the Reformation. (Edinburgh, 1920.)

HEWISON. The Covenanters. (Glasgow, 1913.)

HOWIE. The Scots Worthies. (Edinburgh, 1870. Edited by Wylie and Carslaw.)

HUME OF GODSCROFT. History of the House of Douglas and Angus. (Edinburgh, 1743.)

LAIDLAW. Robert Bruce's Sermons on the Sacrament. (Edinburgh and London, 1901.)

LANG. History of Scotland. (Edinburgh and London, 1902.)

LAW, GRAVES. Collected Essays and Reviews. (Edinburgh, 1904.)

LEE. History of Church of Scotland. (Edinburgh, 1860.)

MACEWEN. A History of the Church of Scotland. (London, 1918.)

MACGREGOR. Scottish Presbyterian Polity. (Edinburgh, 1926.)

MACKIE. History of Scotland. (Oxford, 1930.)

MACKINNON. A History of Modern Liberty. (London, 1908.)

MACLEAN. Aspects of Scottish Church History. (Edinburgh, 1927.)
The Counter Reformation in Scotland. (London, 1931.)

MACNICOL. Master Robert Bruce. (Edinburgh and London, 1907.)

M'CRIE. Life of Andrew Melville. (Edinburgh, 1824.)
Life of John Knox. (Edinburgh, 1839.)

M'CRIE. The Story of the Scottish Church. (Edinburgh, 1874.)

McMILLAN. The Worship of the Scottish Reformed Church. (London, 1931.)

McNEILL. Prestonpans and Vicinity. (Edinburgh, 1902.)

MATHIESON. Politics and Religion in Scotland. (Glasgow, 1902.)

MELVILLE, JAMES. Autobiography and Diary, etc. (Edinburgh, 1842. Wodrow Society Edition.)

MITCHELL. The Scottish Reformation. (Edinburgh and London, 1900.)

MOFFATT. The Presbyterian Churches. (London, 1928.)
The Bible in Scots Literature. (London.)

MORISON. Andrew Melville. (Edinburgh, 1899.)

MOYSES. Memoirs of the Affairs of Scotland. (Edinburgh, 1755.)

PEARSON. Thomas Cartwright and Elizabethan Puritanism. (Cambridge, 1925.)

PETERKIN. The Booke of the Universall Kirke. (Edinburgh, 1839.)

PIERCE. John Penry, His Life, Times and Writings. (London, 1923.)

POLLEN. The Counter Reformation in Scotland. (London, 1921.)

RALEIGH. Annals of the Church of Scotland. (Oxford, 1921.)

BIBLIOGRAPHY

ROGERS. Three Scottish Reformers. (London, 1874.)

ROW. Historie of the Kirk of Scotland. (Edinburgh, 1842. Wodrow Society Edition.)

SCHAFF. The Creeds of the Evangelical Protestant Churches. (London, 1877.)

SCOTT. Fasti Ecclesiae Scoticanae. (Edinburgh, 1866 and Edinburgh, 1815. New Edition.)

SCOT. An Apologetical Narration. (Edinburgh, 1846. Wodrow Society.)

SPOTTISWOOD. The History of the Church of Scotland. (Edinburgh, 1851. Spottiswoode Society Edition.)

TWEEDIE. Select Biographies. (Edinburgh, 1845. Wodrow Society Edition.)

TYTLER. History of Scotland. (Edinburgh, 1842.)

WALSH. The Jesuits in Great Britain. (London, 1903.)

WATT. Representative Churchmen of Twenty Centuries. (Edinburgh, 1927.)

YOUNG. Life of John Welsh. (Edinburgh, 1866.)
Cambridge Modern History. Vol. II.
Edinburgh Christian Instructor. Vol. XXII. (1823.)
Miscellany of the Wodrow Society. Vol. I. (Edinburgh, 1844.)
New Statistical Account.
Satirical Poems of the Time of the Reformation. (Scottish Text Society, 1889-93.)
Warrender Papers. (Scottish Text Society, 1931-2.)
Acts of Parliament of Scotland.
Calendar of State Papers of Scotland.
Register of the Privy Council of Scotland.
Dictionary of National Biography.

INDEX

A

Adamson, Patrick, 54, 91, 92, 95
Allen, 80
Anabaptism, 91
Angus, Earl of, 114, 116, 128, 129
Anne (of Denmark), Queen, 87, 127, 143
Armada, Spanish, 24, 25, 113
Arran, Earl of (James Stewart), 22, 55, 78

B

Balcanquhall, Walter, 84, 150, 228, 250
Bancroft, Richard, 90, 91, 92, 93, 94, 95, 96, 97, 98, 99, 101, 102, 103, 104
Bellarmine, Cardinal, 219
Black Acts, the, 23, 96
Black, David, 26, 160, 161
Blanks, the Spanish, 26, 114, 118
Book of Discipline, First, 17, 20
Book of Discipline, Second, 22
Boston, Thomas, 217
Bowes, Robert, 70, 100, 101, 114
Boyd, Archbishop, 57
Boyd, Lord, 47
Boyd, Robert, of Trochrig, 244
Brown, Charles J., 166
Brown, P. Hume, 167
Browne, Robert, 77, 92, 97, 103
Brownism, 92
Bruce, Robert, 32, 143, 149, 153, 154, 155, 177, 239, 243, 248
Buchanan, George, 31, 78, 93
Buchanan, Thomas, 121, 158, 177, 183
Burghley, Lord, 100, 101, 102, 103, 186
Burnet, Gilbert, 246

C

Calder, Robert, 224, 227
Calderwood, David, 87, 110, 113, 118, 156, 158, 165, 173, 178, 181, 183, 189, 193, 244
Calvin, John, 210
Calvinism, 12
Campbell, Elizabeth, 196, 197, 198, 207
Campbell, Robert, 46, 196, 199, 202, 203, 204, 205, 206, 207, 208, 209
Carmichael, James, 85, 187
Carmichael, John, 177
Charke, William, 53
Charles I, King, 103
Charles IX, King, 126
Cockburne, Barbara, 137
Convention of Leith, 18, 20, 21
Craig, John, 211
Cranston, Michael, 190
Craw, Paul, 201
Crawford, Matthew, 235
Creighton, William, 114
Cunningham, John, 15
Cyprian, 113

D

David I, King, 54
Davidson, John, birth, 30 ; education 31 ; first poem, 36-9 ; poem on Knox's death, 40 ; second literary venture, 40-51 ; ministry at Liberton, 54-79 ; in exile, 78, 80 ; in London, Oxford and Cambridge, 83, 84 ; return to Scotland, 85 ; settled in Canongate, 88 ; controversy with Bancroft, 93-105 ; in conflict with James VI, 107, 108, 109, 111, 112, 113 ; and the "Spanish Blanks", 116-29 ; settlement at Prestonpans, 130 ; ministry at Prestonpans, 132-46 ; on deputations to the king, 143, 145, 146 ; and the revival of 1596, 147-66 ; opposes the king's policies, 170-194 ; his poem on *Two Worthy Christians*, 196-210 ; his *Catechism*, 210-23 ; alleged recantation of his views, 223-27 ; ill-health, 228 ; warded in Edinburgh Castle, 228 ; confined to his parish, 230 ; efforts to secure his liberty, 231 ; last letter to the king, 232 ; death of, 236 ; estimate of character and influence, 236-53

INDEX

INDEX

Melville, James, 31, 32, 33, 51, 81, 82, 83, 85, 149, 159, 160, 161, 164, 165, 169, 174, 177, 188
Melville, William, 186
Meynville, 71
Mitchell, A. F., 33
Moffatt, James, 39
Montgomery, Robert, 19, 57, 58, 59, 60, 61, 62, 63, 64
Moray, Earl of (Regent), 202, 203, 204
Moray, Earl of (the " Bonnie "), 111
Morton, Earl of (Regent), 13, 19, 20, 40, 41, 42, 43, 44, 46, 47, 48, 49, 50, 51, 83, 195, 196, 243
Murray, Sir Patrick, 169

N

Newbattle, Lord, 114
Newbottle, Lord, 135, 138
Nicolson, James, 153
Norton, John, 92

P

Penry, John, 89, 180
Perkins, William, 220, 221
Philip II, King, 11, 12, 114
Pont, Robert, 58, 149, 177, 179, 241

R

Reformation, the, 11, 12, 13, 34, 35, 55, 67, 110, 132, 202, 203, 211, 239
Resby, James, 201
Rollock, Robert, 149, 153, 179, 241
Row, John, 15, 76, 189, 227, 247

Rutherford, John, 43, 45
Ruthven, Lord, 55
Ruthven, Raid of, 23, 69, 72, 75, 77

S

Simson, Patrick, 149, 153, 161, 240
Spottiswood, John, 57, 87, 88, 184, 225, 227, 248

T

Thirlstane, Lord (Sir John Maitland), 24, 102, 103
Thomson, Richard, 233
Tomson, Laurence, 53

U

Udall, John, 89

V

Voltaire, 253

W

Waldegrave, Robert, 89, 116, 196, 212, 213
Wallace, Robert, 237
Walsingham, Sir Francis, 53
Welsh, John, 243
Whitgift, John, 90
Wiclif, John, 201
William of Orange (" the Silent "), 12
Wishart, George, 29, 197, 245
Wishart, Sir John, 36, 37, 38
Wodrow, Robert, 51, 55, 64, 70, 72, 81, 85, 127, 183, 193, 212, 245, 247, 250